SOUTHERN LAW JOURN

I0036783

EDITOR-IN-CHIEF

Diana M. Brown
Sam Houston State University

ASSOCIATE EDITOR

Laura L. Sullivan
Sam Houston State University

SENIOR ADVISORY EDITOR

Henry Lowenstein
Coastal Carolina University

REVIEWERS

Susan R. Dana
Black Hills State University

Jennifer Barger Johnson
University of Central Oklahoma

Susan Park
Boise State University

Michelle Evans
Texas State University – San Marcos

Brian Elzweig
University of West Florida

Marcia Staff
University of North Texas

Lee Usnick
University of Houston – Downtown

Tricia A. Wald
Southwestern Oklahoma State
University

ONLINE JOURNAL EDITOR AND WEB MASTER

Ray Teske
University of Texas – San Antonio

The *Southern Law Journal* is an
official publication of the
Southern Academy of Legal Studies in Business
ISSN: 1056-2184
ISBN: 978-1-955581-21-9
Listed in *Ulrich's International Periodical Directory* and *Cabell's Directory*
Available at www.southernlawjournal.com and through
EBSCO, an electronic university database

Published by Parson's Porch Books (www.parsonsporch.com).

From the Editor's Desk . . .

With this issue, I begin my tenure as Editor-in-Chief of the *Southern Law Journal*. It is a great honor for me to assume the mantle of Editor-in-Chief of the *Southern Law Journal,* succeeding Dan Ostas, who did such an outstanding job for so many years. The new *SLJ* team seeks to live up to Dan's dedication in advancing the *SLJ* as a high quality, peer-reviewed law journal. I appreciate the opportunity to serve.

I am grateful to Laura Sullivan, who has been instrumental in the transition. Laura worked tirelessly as Executive Director of the Southern Academy of Legal Studies in Business (SALSB) to ensure that SALSB's 2020 Conference was one of the few completed in-person before the pandemic began. A number of excellent papers were presented at the conference, and those revised versions, examined by our reviewers and editors, appear in this issue. I am grateful for the research contributions of our business law colleagues in the region and elsewhere, and editing this volume has been a labor of love.

With the change in *SLJ* leadership, I am pleased to have the assistance of new editors and reviewers. Henry Lowenstein of Coastal Carolina University is serving as Senior Advisory Editor. And we continue to be indebted to Ray Teske, University of Texas-San Antonio as Online Journal Editor and Web Master.

Thank you in advance for helping the *SLJ* team continue to advance the quality, exposure, and prominence of the *SLJ* for many decades to come.

The *SLJ* **Style Sheet** may be found at our website: www.southernlawjounal.com. If you plan to submit, please follow the *SLJ* Style Sheet closely. Contributors should visit our website for recently revised *SLJ* **Submission Policies.**

Questions and submissions should be directed to SLJSubmission@comcast.net.

Kind regards,
Diana Brown,
Editor-in-Chief
Southern Law Journal

REPOSITORY LIBRARIES FOR THE SOUTHERN LAW JOURNAL
(BACK ISSUES)

Abilene Christian University .... Brown Library
Amberton University .... Library Resources Center
Angelo State University .... Porter Henderson Library
Arkansas State University of Jonesboro .... Dean B. Ellis Library
Arkansas Tech University .... Pendergraft Library and Technology Center
Arlington Baptist College .... Earl K. Oldham Library
Austin College .... George T. and Gladys H. Abell Library Center
Baylor Law School .... Baylor Law Library
Baylor University .... Baylor Collections of Political Materials
Baylor University .... University Libraries
Cameron University .... Cameron University Library
Concordia University Austin .... Founders Library
Dallas Baptist University .... Vance Memorial Library
East Central University .... Linscheid Library
East Texas Baptist University .... Jarrett Library
Grambling State University .... A.C. Lewis Memorial Library
Harding University .... Brackett Library
Hardin-Simmons University .... Hardin-Simmons University Library
Henderson State University, Arkadelphia .... Huie Library
Hendrix College .... Olin C. Bailey Library
Howard Payne University .... Walker Memorial Library
Lamar University Beaumont .... Mary and John Gray Library
Langston University .... G. Lamar Harrison Library
Louisiana College .... Richard W. Norton Memorial Library
Louisiana State University in Shreveport .... Noel Memorial Library
Louisiana State University Law School .... Prescott Memorial Library
Louisiana Tech University .... Paul M. Herbert Law Center
Loyola University New Orleans Law Library .... The Law Library
Loyola University New Orleans .... J. Edgar and Louise S. Monroe Library
Lyon College .... Mabee-Simpson Library
McMurry University .... Jay-Rollins Library
McNeese State University Library .... Frazar Memorial Library
Midwestern State University .... Moffett Library
Nicholls State University .... Ellender Memorial Library
North Central Texas .... North Central Texas College Library
Northeastern Oklahoma State University .... John Vaughan Library
Northwestern State University .... Watson Memorial Library
Northwood University .... Hach Library
Ohio Northern University College of Law .... Taggart Law Library
Oklahoma City University .... Gold Star Library
Oklahoma Panhandle State University .... Marvin E. McKee Library
Oklahoma State University–Stillwater .... Edmond Low Library
Ouachita Baptist University, Arkadelphia .... Riley-Hickingbotham Library
Rice University .... Fondren Library
Rogers State University .... Stratton Taylor Library
Sam Houston State University .... Newton Gresham Library
Schreiner University .... William Logan Library
South Texas College of Law .... The Fred Parks Law Library
Southeastern Louisiana University .... Linus A. Sims Memorial Library
Southeastern Oklahoma State University .... Henry G. Bennett Memorial Library
Southern Arkansas University, Magnolia .... Magale Library
Southern Methodist University .... Bridwell Library
Southern Methodist University .... Underwood Law Library
Southern University Law Center .... Southern University Law Center Library
Southwestern Christian College .... Doris Johnson Library
Southwestern Oklahoma State University .... Al Harris Library
Southwestern University .... A. Frank Smith, Jr., Library Center
St. Mary's University–San Antonio .... Law Library
Stephen F. Austin State University .... Ralph W. Steen Library

SALSB EXECUTIVE COMMITTEE
(2021 – 2022)

THE BATTLE OVER FIDUCIARY RESPONSIBILITY OF PENSION FUND MANAGERS: THE TRUMP ADMINISTRATION TAKES ON THE ESG MOVEMENT

FRANK J. CAVALIERE[*]
RICARDO COLON[**]
TONI MULVANEY[***]
MARLEEN SWERDLOW[****]

ABSTRACT

The ESG Movement is one of the most potent forces affecting the investment world today. ESG stands for "environmental/social/gover-nance" and it is the latest iteration of the long-established Corporate Social Responsibility (CSR) movement. ESG has been embraced by managers of some of the world's largest pension plan administration companies, such as BlackRock. The goal of the Movement is to pressure boards of directors and top management of companies where pension plan managers own significant shares of stock into doing what these pension plan managers consider to be "the right thing", even if the actions they promote result in less profitability for those companies, at least in the short run. Stockholders are not generally considered to owe fiduciary duties to the

---

[*] J.D., University Professor of Business Law, Lamar University, Beaumont, Texas.
[**] LL.M., J.D., Associate Professor of Accounting, Lamar University, Beaumont, Texas.
[***] J.D., Associate Dean for Undergraduate Studies and Administration, Professor of Business Law, Lamar University, Beaumont, Texas.
[****] J.D., Professor of Business Law, Lamar University, Beaumont, Texas.

companies in which they own stock. Pension plan managers, however, are fiduciaries of the beneficiaries of their respective pension plans. How does being a fiduciary harmonize to being a promoter of ESG when following the tenets of that Movement can result in less profitability for the plans they manage? The Trump Administration has expressed doubt over the legality of ESG-motivated actions as they relate to federally-regulated qualified pension plans subject to the Employee Retirement Income Security Act of 1974 (ERISA). According to an Administration Executive Order, the fiduciary duty of a pension plan manager subject to ERISA is to "maximize" profits for the plan beneficiaries. This paper will discuss the origins and precepts of the ESG Movement, the fiduciary responsibilities of pension plan trustees, the concerns of ESG proponents that making profits at the expense of the planet and the health of the global population is counter-productive, and arguments about whether ERISA mandates fiduciaries to maximize profits.

I. INTRODUCTION

The Environmental, Social and Governance (ESG) movement is one of the most important forces impacting investment strategies today. Some of the largest U.S. mutual fund administrators and pension plan managers are proponents of the Movement. In 2019, ESG funds attracted over $20 billion in funding from investors.[1] The rise of the ESG Movement may have implications for pension plan managers who have fiduciary duties to participants and beneficiaries of the pension plans they administer. Is the responsibility of these pension managers to maximize the benefits of their participants and beneficiaries or should they

---

[1] Greg Iacurci, *Money Moving into Environmental Funds Shatters Previous Record*, CNBC, Jan. 14, 2020, https://www.cnbc.com/2020/01/14/esg-funds-see-record-inflows-in-2019.html

consider ESG factors when making investment decisions? Recently, the administration of Donald J. Trump issued guidance expressing concerns about the use of ESG factors for making investment decisions, particularly with respect to pension plans regulated by the Employee Retirement Income Security Act (ERISA) of 1974.[2]

This paper analyzes the origins and precepts of the ESG Movement as it evolved from the concept of enlightened self-interest and corporate social responsibility. It discusses the tenets of the ESG Movement and analyzes the fiduciary responsibilities of pension plan managers. In light of a recent Executive Order and Field Advisory Bulletin from the Department of Labor, this paper analyzes arguments for and against consideration of ESG considerations in investment decisions made by pension plan managers. Finally, the paper concludes that fiduciary responsibilities of plan managers allow them to consider ESG considerations in determining an investment strategy that maximizes the risk-adjusted return to plan participants and beneficiaries. However, the consideration of ESG issues, in isolation, does not seem to be supported by the Modern Prudent Investor Rule, the "prudent man" standard of care, or the most recent administrative guidance issued on ERISA plans by the Department of Labor.

II. ENLIGHTENED SELF-INTEREST

The concept of self-interest is essential to understanding the capitalist economic system. According to the father of capitalism, Adam Smith, "[i]t is not from the benevolence of the butcher, the brewer, or the baker that we expect our dinner, but from their regard to their own

---

[2] Exec. Order No. 13868, 84 Fed. Reg. 15495 (Apr. 15, 2019); Field Assistance Bulletin No. 2018-01 (Apr. 23, 2018).

interest."[3] Less well-known is his earlier work, *The Theory of Moral Sentiments*, wherein he expressed a more philosophical approach, premised on the need of people to live in sympathy with one another:

> Without this sacred regard for general rules, no-one's conduct can be much depended on. It is what constitutes the most essential difference between a man of principle and honour and a worthless fellow. The man of principle keeps steadily and resolutely to his maxims on all occasions, preserving through the whole of his life one even tenor of conduct. The worthless fellow acts variously and accidentally, depending on whether mood, inclination, or self-interest happens to be uppermost. Indeed, men are subject to such variations of mood that without this respect for general rules a man who in all his cool hours was delicately sensitive to the propriety of conduct might often be led to act absurdly on the most trivial occasions, ones in which it was hardly possible to think of any serious motive he could have for behaving in this manner.[4]

Implicit in Smith's contention, and an article of faith among many critics of business is that it is more important to take the "long-run" view of business success, rather than a "short-run" perspective. According to Archie Carroll, one

---

[3] Smith, Adam, "An Inquiry into the Nature and Causes of the Wealth of Nations" (The Wealth of Nations) (1776) Book 1, Chapter 2, "Of the Principle which gives occasion to the Division of Labour", http://geolib.com/smith.adam/won1-02.html

[4] ADAM SMITH, THE THEORY OF MORAL SENTIMENTS 85 (1759), http://www.earlymoderntexts.com/assets/pdfs/smith1759.pdf

of the leading advocates for businesses acting in socially responsible ways, "[t]he long-range self-interest view, sometimes referred to as 'enlightened self-interest' holds that if business is to have a healthy climate in which to operate in the future, it must take actions now to ensure its long-term viability."[5]

III. THE SOCIAL RESPONSIBILITY OF BUSINESS

Social responsibility is often studied in the context of principles sometimes referred to as the "managerial ideology of business." Managerial ideology is defined as "a stream of discourse that promulgates, however unwittingly, a set of assumptions about the nature of … corporations, employees, managers, and the means by which the latter can direct the other two."[6] One of the key elements of managerial ideology has long been the idea known as "corporate social responsibility" CSR and the debate that it presents between optimum profits and maximum profits, which can be summarized as follows:

> Executives who accept the idea of enlightened self-interest today must be willing to accept optimum profits rather than maximum profits. In most annual reports, a CEO tells the company's stockholders that every measure is being taken to ensure maximum profits. In the planning session with managers, however, the same CEO may accept optimum profits, which is a satisfactory level of profits considering external pressures, such as government

[5] ARCHIE B. CARROLL, BUSINESS & SOCIETY 40 (2015).
[6] Stephen R. Barley & Gideon Kunda, *Design and Devotion: Surges of Rational and Normative Ideologies of Control in Managerial Discourse*, 37 ADMIN. SCI. QUARTERLY 363, 363 (1992).

regulation. Executives who make social responsibility decisions based on long-run goals are trading maximum short-run profits the most that could be made this quarter for optimum profits what they are willing to make this quarter in light of other developments.[7]

Today, the concept of corporate social responsibility is intimately associated with the stakeholder concept. The stakeholder concept involves the idea that a business manager must respect the legitimate expectations of a large and ever-expanding array of people, organizations, entities,[8] and even the natural environment itself.[9] According to professors Edward Freeman and Heather Elms, businesses that want to be successful in the twenty-first century cannot follow a pure profit maximization motive, which is blamed for contributing to the collapse of many companies and corporate scandals –Enron, Wells Fargo, Lehman Brothers, General Motors – all of which have cost U.S. citizens and taxpayers trillions of dollars.[10] Instead, Freeman and Elms

---

[7] JOHN H. JACKSON, ROGER L. MILLER & SHAWN G. MILLER, BUSINESS AND SOCIETY TODAY 159 (1997).

[8] ARCHIE B. CARROLL, BUSINESS & SOCIETY 66 (2015) "In short, a stakeholder may be thought of as 'any individual or group who can affect or is affected by the actions, decisions, policies, practices, or goals of the organization'").

[9] ARCHIE B. CARROLL, BUSINESS & SOCIETY 67 (2015). "When the concept of sustainability first became popular, however, the natural environment was given priority, but the natural environment has often been neglected. In keeping with sustainability, the natural environment, nonhuman species, and future generations would be considered among business's important stakeholders." *Id.*

[10] Edward Freeman & Heather Elms, *The Social Responsibility of Business is to Create Value for Stakeholders*, MIT SLOAN (Jan. 4, 2018), https://sloanreview.mit.edu/article/the-social-responsibility-of-business-is-to-create-value-for-stakeholders/ *Contra* Milton Friedman,

argue that "the social responsibility of business is to create value for its stakeholders."[11] They summarize their theory as follows:

> The stakeholder approach sets forth a new conceptualization of business, in which business is understood as a set of relationships and management's job is to help shape these relationships. Business is about how customers, suppliers, employees, financiers, communities, and managers interact to create value, and there is no single formula for balancing or prioritizing stakeholders. Creating that balance is part of what management is all about, and it will be different for different companies at different times.[12]

Adopting social responsibility principles, Larry Fink, the Chief Executive Officer of BlackRock, the world's largest pension plan management company, has stated that "[c]ompanies must benefit all of their stakeholders, including shareholders, employees, customers and the communities in which they operate."[13] Similarly, the Business Roundtable, an association of chief executive officers of America's leading corporations, has released a new Statement on the Purpose of the Corporation. In the new Statement, the executives acknowledge a fundamental

---

The Social Responsibility of Business is to Increase its Profits, N.Y. TIMES, Sept. 13, 1960, http://umich.edu/~thecore/doc/Friedman.pdf
[11] *Id.*
[12] *Id.*
[13] Liz Moyer, *BlackRock Says it's Time to Take Action on Guns, May Use Voting Power to Influence*, CNBC, Mar. 2, 2018, https://www.cnbc.com/2018/03/02/blackrock-says-its-time-to-take-action-on-guns-may-use-voting-power-to-influence.html

commitment to all stakeholders and agree to undertake the following actions:

[Deliver] value to our customers. We will further the tradition of American companies leading the way in meeting or exceeding customer expectations.

[Invest] in our employees. This starts with compensating them fairly and providing important benefits. It also includes supporting them through training and education that help develop new skills for a rapidly changing world. We foster diversity and inclusion, dignity and respect.

[Deal] fairly and ethically with our suppliers. We are dedicated to serving as good partners to the other companies, large and small, that help us meet our missions.

[Support] the communities in which we work. We respect the people in our communities and protect the environment by embracing sustainable practices across our businesses.

Generat[e] long-term value for shareholders, who provide the capital that allows companies to invest, grow and innovate. We are committed to transparency and effective engagement with shareholders. Each of our stakeholders is essential. We commit to **deliver value to all of them**, for the future success of our companies, our communities and our country.[14]

The 2019 Statement supersedes previous statements by Business Roundtable which were based on shareholder primacy—"that corporations exist principally to serve shareholders"—creating a new framework that better reflects the way corporations can and should operate in the twenty-first century.[15]

IV. THE ESG MOVEMENT

By harnessing the economic power of mutual fund and pension plan administrators, the ESG movement seeks to get corporations to act more responsibly. ESG stands for environmental, social, and governance, and it has been called an offshoot of the CSR, or corporate social responsibility movement, which was directed at the officers and boards of directors of corporations to encourage them to act more in the interests of society.[16] Like CSR, ESG is a fluid concept or theory, and the "issues" with which it is concerned change over time.

ESG is based on the adage "money talks."[17] It represents an organized, investment-centric, top-down approach to measure firm performance in three very

---

[14] Press Release, Business Roundtable, Business Roundtable Redefines the Purpose of a Corporation to Promote 'An Economy that Serves All Americans' (Aug. 19, 2019) (emphasis added), https://www.businessroundtable.org/business-roundtable-redefines-the-purpose-of-a-corporation-to-promote-an-economy-that-serves-all-americans

[15] *Id.*

[16] Frank Cavaliere, *The UN Global Compact and Principles for Responsible Investing,* 65 THE PRACTICAL LAWYER, no. 4, 2019, at 8.

[17] Frank Cavaliere, Frank Badua & Ricardo Colon, *Should Accounting for Sustainability be Mandatory?,* Today's CPA, May-June 2020, at 35 [hereinafter *Accounting for Sustainability*].

different endeavors, namely: environmental sustainability, social equity, and corporate governance.[18] Environmental criteria may include a company's energy use, waste, pollution, natural resource conservation, treatment of animals, and risk management.[19] Social criteria look at the company's business relationships.[20] Governance criteria can refer to transparent accounting, stockholder voting opportunities, use of political contributions, avoiding conflicts of interest, and not engaging in illegal practices.[21] The metrics used to document and report a company's performance in these three areas differ significantly from one another, and from traditional accounting measures that focus on financial performance.[22]

The SEC has not adopted specific disclosure requirements with respect to ESG. Today, ESG reporting relies on the concept of materiality. Issues about sustainability that are material to a company's financial condition or results of operations must be disclosed.[23] Additionally, ESG disclosures are required whenever they are necessary to prevent other financial statement disclosures from being materially incomplete or misleading and to inform investors' proxy decisions.[24] Management is

---

[18] *Id.*

[19] COLUMBIA PACIFIC WEALTH MANAGEMENT, *WHAT YOU SHOULD KNOW ABOUT ESG INVESTING*, https://www.columbiapacificwm.com/blog/insights/general/what-you-should-know-about-esg-investing/

[20] *Id.*

[21] *Id.*

[22] *Accounting for Sustainability, supra* note 17.

[23] Mary J. White, chair, securities and exchange commission, keynote address at the international corporate governance network annual conference: focusing the lens of disclosure to set the path forward on board diversity, non-gaap, and sustainability (June 27, 2016), http://www.sec.gov/news/speech/chair-white-icgn-speech.html

[24] *Id.*

responsible for identifying which ESG issues are material to a company.[25]

The landscape for ESG reporting has become more difficult to navigate as numerous companies have adopted sustainability disclosure frameworks developed by different non-governmental organizations including the Global Reporting Initiative (GRI), International Integrated Reporting Committee (IIRC), Task Force on Climate-Related Financial Disclosures (TCFD), Carbon Disclosure Project (CDP), and the Sustainability Accounting Standards Board (SASB).[26] Currently, SASB is widely accepted as a reporting framework that is aligned with the requirements of the U.S. securities laws in terms of ESG disclosures.[27] At least 308 companies use SASB for sustainability reporting.[28] SASB is comprised of seventy-seven industry-specific sets of sustainability accounting standards covering a range of industry-specific sustainability areas of interest to investors such as water management for beverage companies, data security for technology firms, and supply chain management for consumer goods manufacturers and retailers.[29]

---

[25] Congress first introduced the concept of materiality in Section 17(a)(2) of the Securities Act of 1933. Afterwards, Congress also included the concept of materiality in Section 18(a) of the Securities Act of 1934. For public company disclosures, SEC Rule 405 defines the term "material". SEC Staff Accounting Bulletin No. 99 – Materiality, sets forth standards for assessing materiality for preparers of financial statements as well as auditors.

[26] *Accounting for Sustainability*, *supra* note 17, at 38.

[27] *Id.*

[28] The complete list of companies using SASB can be found at https://www.sasb.org/company-use/sasb-reporters/

[29] Janine Guillot, Director of Capital Markets Policy and Outreach, Sustainability Accounting Standards Board, Discussion Regarding Disclosures on Sustainability and Environmental, Social and Governance Topics (December 13, 2018), http://www.sec.gov/video/webcast-archive-player.shtml?document_id=iac121318

V. BACKGROUND ON THE CONCEPT OF FIDUCIARY RESPONSIBILITY

The term "fiduciary" is often bandied about, but can differ in meaning depending on the context, and specifically whether it is premised on the historical common law or whether it has been modified by statutes. The typical situations involving this relationship include trusts, agency relationships, partnerships, and corporations. Historically, the fiduciary concept arose from the law of trusts, where the trustee has title, but not beneficial ownership, of the property delivered from one person, for the benefit of another, under the terms of a written agreement.[30] The common law standards of faithfulness imposed on trustees were rigid.[31] The trustee is required to manage the trust corpus first and foremost with the needs of beneficiaries in mind and self-dealing is strictly prohibited.[32]

Virtually all qualified pension plan assets are held in the form of trusts.[33] The trustee has a duty to manage the

---

[30] Joseph T. Walsh, *The Fiduciary Foundation of Corporate Law,* 27 JOURNAL OF CORPORATION LAW, no. 3, 2002, at 333, https://papers.ssrn.com/sol3/papers.cfm?abstract_id=338541 ("The fiduciary concept, as we know, had its origin in the law of trusts, where its literal meaning 'faithfulness' correctly described the duty or responsibility owed by one who held title, but not ownership, to property of another, who lacked legal title but could, in equity, claim the benefits of ownership. This latter individual is referred to as the beneficiary, or in earlier cases, the cestui que trust, *i.e.*, he for whom the trust was created.")

[31] *Id.*

[32] *Id.*

[33] U.S. DEPARTMENT OF LABOR EMPLOYEE BENEFITS SECURITY ADMINISTRATION, FAQS ABOUT RETIREMENT PLANS AND ERISA, https://www.dol.gov/sites/dolgov/files/ebsa/about-ebsa/our-activities/resource-center/faqs/retirement-plans-and-erisa-for-workers.pdf, at 13: "The funds must be held in trust or invested in an insurance contract. The employers' creditors cannot make a claim on retirement plan funds."

trust assets in the manner of a reasonable prudent person, in other words, not to take inordinate risks. The prudent person legal standard was established in *Harvard College v. Amory*, where the court stated "[a]ll that can be required of a trustee to invest is, that he shall conduct himself faithfully and exercise a sound discretion. He is to observe how men of prudence, discretion and intelligence manage their own affairs, not in regard to speculation, but in regard to the permanent disposition of their funds, considering the probable income, as well as the probable safety of the capital to be invested."[34]

Private pension plans are regulated by the Employee Retirement Income Security Act of 1974 (ERISA), 29 U.S.C. § 1001, et seq. Although the ERISA statute only applies to private pension funds, many public funds also follow its provisions, particularly with respect to the standards of care expected of fiduciaries.[35] ERISA adopts the prudent man standard of care and provides, in pertinent part:

> [A] fiduciary shall discharge his duties with respect to a plan solely in the interest of participants and beneficiaries and--
>
> (A) for the exclusive purpose of:
> > (i)   providing benefits to participants and their beneficiaries; and
> > (ii)   defraying reasonable expenses of administering the plan;
>
> (B) with the care, skill, prudence, and diligence under the circumstances then prevailing that a prudent man

---

[34] 9 Pick. 446, 461 (Sup. Jud. Ct. Mass. 1830).
[35] PRINCIPLES FOR RESPONSIBLE INVESTMENT & UN ENVIRONMENT PROGRAMME, FIDUCIARY DUTY IN THE 21ST CENTURY 75 (2015) [hereinafter *Fiduciary Duty*].

acting in a like capacity and familiar with such matters would use in the conduct of an enterprise of a like character and with like aims;

(C) by diversifying the investments of the plan as to minimize the risk of large losses, unless under the circumstances it is clearly prudent not to do so; and

(D) in accordance with the documents and instruments governing the plan insofar as such documents and instruments are consistent with the provisions of this subchapter and subchapter III of this chapter.[36]

State law governs public pension plans.[37] Most states follow the Uniform Prudent Investor Act of 2002 (UPIA).[38] In turn, UPIA adopts the Modern Prudent Investor Rule set forth in the Restatement (Third) of Trusts.[39] The Modern Prudent Investor Rule sets forth the duties of fiduciaries as follows:

The trustee has a duty to the beneficiaries to invest and manage the funds of the trust as a prudent investor would, in light of the purposes, terms, distribution requirements, and other circumstances of the trust.

---

[36] 29 U.S.C. § 1104(a) (2020).
[37] *Fiduciary Duty, supra* note 35, at 73
[38] *Id.*
[39] *Id.*

(a) This standard requires the exercise of reasonable care, skill, and caution, and is to be applied to investments not in isolation but in the context of the trust portfolio and as a part of an overall investment strategy, which should incorporate risk and return objectives reasonably suitable to the trust.

(b) In making and implementing investment decisions, the trustee has a duty to diversify the investments of the trust unless, under the circumstances, it is prudent not to do so.

(c) In addition, the trustee must: (1) conform to fundamental fiduciary duties of loyalty and impartiality; (2) act with prudence in deciding whether and how to delegate authority and in the selection and supervision of agents; and (3) incur only costs that are reasonable in amount and appropriate to the investment responsibilities of the trusteeship.

(d) The trustee's duties under this Section are subject to the rule of § 91, dealing primarily with contrary investment provisions of a trust or statute.[40]

The Modern Prudent Investor Rule is more flexible than the rules set forth under ERISA because it gives fiduciaries a range of diversification strategies, requiring only that investment choices be made with appropriate skill,

---

[40] RESTATEMENT (THIRD) OF TRUSTS § 90 (AM. LAW INST. 2006).

care and prudence, and for the benefit of plan participants and beneficiaries.[41]

VI. THE U.S. GOVERNMENT ENTERS THE DEBATE

On April 23, 2018 the Department of Labor issued a Field Assistance Bulletin to its agents dealing with the ESG Movement's inroads into corporate decision-making:

> Fiduciaries must not too readily treat ESG factors as economically relevant to the particular investment choices at issue when making a decision. It does not ineluctably follow from the fact that an investment promotes ESG factors, or that it arguably promotes positive general market trends or industry growth, that the investment is a prudent choice for retirement or other investors. Rather, ERISA fiduciaries must always put first the economic interests of the plan in providing retirement benefits. A fiduciary's evaluation of the economics of an investment should be focused on financial factors that have a material effect on the return and risk of an investment based on appropriate investment horizons consistent with the plan's articulated funding and investment objectives.[42]

More recently, in 2019, President Trump issued Executive Order 13868, titled "Promoting Energy Infrastructure and Economic Growth." This Executive Order extols the virtue

---

[41] *Fiduciary Duty, supra* note 35, at 74.
[42] Field Assistance Bulletin No. 2018-01 (Apr. 23, 2018), https://www.dol.gov/sites/default/files/ebsa/employers-and-advisers/guidance/field-assistance-bulletins/2018-01.pdf

and importance of the energy industry, particularly petrochemical companies, which are a huge target for environmental activists. The Purpose section of the Executive Order signals a clear departure from the Obama-era environmental approach and a shift to policies that may be more amenable to the energy sector. The ESG-related language is found in Section 5(b) of the Executive Order:

> To advance the principles of objective materiality and fiduciary duty . . . the Secretary of Labor shall, within 180 days of the date of this order, complete a review of available data filed with the Department of Labor by retirement plans subject to the Employee Retirement Income Security Act of 1974 (ERISA) in order to identify whether there are discernible trends with respect to such plans' investments in the energy sector. Within 180 days of the date of this order, the Secretary shall provide an update to the Assistant to the President for Economic Policy on any discernable trends in energy investments by such plans. The Secretary of Labor shall also, within 180 days of the date of this order, complete a review of existing Department of Labor guidance on the fiduciary responsibilities for proxy voting to determine whether any such guidance should be rescinded, replaced, or modified to ensure consistency with current law and policies that promote long-term growth and maximize return on ERISA plan assets.[43]

---

[43] Exec. Order No. 13868, 84 Fed. Reg. 15495 (Apr. 15, 2019), https://www.federalregister.gov/documents/2019/04/15/2019-07656/promoting-energy-infrastructure-and-economic-growth.

The Executive Order is silent on how the data gathered by the Department of Labor will be used. It seems reasonable to assume that the data may be used to enforce the guidance issued in 2018 on ESG plans which provides that plan fiduciaries cannot focus solely on ESG factors when making investment decisions.[44]

VII. ARGUMENTS FOR ESG'S FIDELITY TO FIDUCIARY DUTY UNDER ERISA

The primary reason to apply ESG principles to pension plans is to save the planet, because the E in ESG appears the primary motivator for the movement. Likewise, Larry Fink, the CEO of BlackRock, has stated that the "key to long-term success for companies is 'understanding the societal impact of your business' and how it will 'affect your potential for growth.'"[45] Most recently, in its 2020 letter to chief executive officers, Fink stated that "sustainability and climate-integrated portfolios can provide better risk-adjusted returns to investors."[46] Similarly, Larry Beeferman, Director of the Pensions and Capital Stewardship Project at Harvard Law School, stated "[t]he literature on [Socially Responsible Investing] is robust enough to say that there is a serious question around whether or not ESG issues are important to

---

[44] **B**etty Moy Huber, *recent executive order on energy infrastructure and economic growth – esg disclosure and proxy voting implications*, briefing: governance, apr. 2019, https://www.briefinggovernance.com/2019/04/recent-executive-order-on-energy-infrastructure-and-economic-growth-esg-disclosure-and-proxy-voting-implications/

[45] Liz Moyer, BlackRock says it's time to take action on guns, may use voting power to influence, https://www.cnbc.com/2018/03/02/blackrock-says-its-time-to-take-action-on-guns-may-use-voting-power-to-influence.html.

[46] BLACKROCK, A FUNDAMENTAL RESHAPING OF FINANCE (2020), https://www.blackrock.com/corporate/investor-relations/larry-fink-ceo-letter

investment performance" and "at a minimum, due diligence processes must include assessment of the need to take account of [ESG] issues in investment decision-making."[47] A 2018 survey by the Callan Institute, which reports trends on ESG adoption by U.S. institutional funds, found that incorporation of ESG factors into the investment decision-making process of portfolio managers almost doubled to 43% in 2018 compared to 23% in 2013, and that the most frequently stated reason for incorporating ESG concerns is to achieve an improved risk and return profile.[48]

Other arguments that favor fiduciary investing based on ESG factors are similar to the arguments used against shareholder primacy. First, ignoring ESG factors forces trustees to "focus myopically on short-term earnings reports at the expense of long-term performance."[49] Second, failure to consider ESG factors "discourages investment and innovation, harms employees, customers and communities; and causes companies to indulge in reckless, sociopathic, and socially irresponsible behavior".[50] Ultimately, disregarding ESG factors "threatens the welfare of consumers, employees, communities, and investors alike."[51]

VIII. ARGUMENTS AGAINST ESG FIDELITY TO FIDUCIARY DUTY UNDER ERISA

Recently, Max Schanzenbach of Northwestern University, and Robert Sitkoff of Harvard University, have challenged the assertion that investment management by

---

[47] *Fiduciary Duty, supra* note35, at 74.
[48] CALLAN INSTITUTE, 2018 ESG SURVEY 2 (2018), https://src.bna.com/JfS
[49] LYNN STOUT, THE SHAREHOLDER VALUE MYTH: HOW PUTTING SHAREHOLDERS FIRST HARMS INVESTORS, CORPORATIONS, AND THE PUBLIC, *Preface* (2012).
[50] *Id.*
[51] *Id.*

pension trustees is required to consider ESG implications under fiduciary law principles. Both authors reject the premise that a trustee must consider ESG factors.[52] First, as a matter of law, the Modern Prudent Investor Rule does not contain categorical rules of permissible or impermissible investments, because a trustee may invest in any type of investment so long as it is "part of an overall investment strategy having risk and return objectives reasonably suitable to the trust."[53] Second, mandating ESG investing is inappropriate because ESG factors are too fluid and their application too subjective.[54] Third, a prudent trustee could conclude that ESG factors do not give rise to a profitable trading opportunity and cannot be exploited cost-effectively for profit.[55] Fourth, an ESG investment mandate could prohibit many forms of passive investments because it would not allow trustees to invest in a broad market index funds that lack ESG investment options.[56] Passive investing is widely used, and in certain cases, represents a superior investing strategy, particularly when there is "little hope of outperforming the market."[57] Fifth, ESG factors, like any investment factor, may be over-valued in the market, and a trustee may engage an anti-ESG strategy upon concluding that firms with high ESG scores are overvalued.[58] Sixth,

---

[52] Schanzenbach, Max Matthew and Sitkoff, Robert H., *Reconciling Fiduciary Duty and Social Conscience: The Law and Economics of ESG Investing by a Trustee*, 72 STANFORD L. REV. 381 (2020); Northwestern Law & Econ Research Paper No. 18-22; Harvard Public Law Working Paper No. 19-50, https://ssrn.com/abstract=3244665 or http://dx.doi.org/10.2139/ssrn.3244665

[53] *Id.* at 50. (Citing Unif. Prudent Inv'r Act § 2(b), (e) (Unif. Law Comm'n 1994).

[54] *Id.*

[55] *Id.* at 51.

[56] *Id.* at 52.

[57] *Id.* (Citing Fifth Third Bancorp v. Dudenhoeffer, 134 S. Ct. 2459, 2471 (U.S. 2014)).

[58] *Id.* at 52.

mandating ESG investing relies on the assumption that all trusts have a long-term time horizon. In point of fact, some trusts have a short time horizon, which means that a fiduciary should favor firms with low ESG scores since investments with high ESG scores will take too long to achieve the desired return on investment.[59] Schanzenbach and Sitkoff conclude that "mandating a long-term ESG perspective for trustees or other investment fiduciaries is manifestly contrary to both law and economics."[60]

It is also troubling that influential individuals like Larry Fink, Chief Executive Officer of Blackrock, have become arbiters of which investments ought to be preferred by fiduciaries. Ultimately, trustees have a responsibility to maximize return on investment, not to "optimize profits" based on subjective standards of what is "best" for society.

IX. CONCLUSION

The growth of the ESG Movement raises important questions in terms of the fiduciary duties of pension plan trustees. The key question discussed in this paper is whether ESG factors should be a mandatory consideration for trustees of pension plans. Fiduciary responsibilities for pension fund managers have developed piecemeal through the common law, trust law, and federal and state statutory law. Fiduciary responsibilities of pension plan trustees have thus evolved to allow the consideration of ESG concerns.[61]

Against this backdrop, the administration of President Donald J. Trump has issued guidance emphasizing that ERISA fiduciaries must always put the economic interests of their pension plans first and that ESG issues should not be presumed to be economically relevant to investment choices. Ultimately, the debate seems to boil

---

[59] Id. at 53.

[60] Id.

[61] Fiduciary Duty, supra note 35, at 78-80.

down to different interpretations of fiduciary duties and responsibilities. While one interpretation sanctions considering ESG factors to determine risk and return in the context of the overall investment strategy for a portfolio, the other interpretation requires fiduciaries to maximize profits by making investment decisions considering only economic factors.

The pressure on pension fund managers to consider ESG factors and to balance those factors with the potentially conflicting fiduciary responsibilities inherent in the management of pension funds will continue given growing market awareness of the relevance of ESG issues, increasing disclosures by public companies on ESG performance, and wider societal interest in issues related to climate change and human rights.[62]

---

[62] *Id.* at 78.

FOR US, BY US, PROTECT US: AN ARGUMENT FOR BETTER INTELLECTUAL PROTECTION OF INDIGENOUS FASHION

RACHEL HAMILTON*

We are seeing healing among the stolen generations, and initiatives which are enabling Indigenous people to make their distinctive contribution to our national life.

-Malcolm Fraser

I. INTRODUCTION: THE WORLD OF INDIGENOUS FASHION

While there is no universal definition of what an idea is, one thing is clear—most people like to own what they feel they have created. This is certainly true for indigenous groups. Globally, indigenous groups are highly susceptible to having their intellectual property infringed.[1] Particularly at risk is their intellectual property related to fashion and fashion design. Indigenous intellectual property, particularly indigenous fashion intellectual property, needs protection. Marginalized communities, including many, if not most, indigenous communities, are more likely to have their intellectual property infringed.[2]

The international systems in place that help to oversee intellectual property development, primarily the World Intellectual Property Organization ("WIPO") and the

---

* J.D., University of California, Davis King Hall School of Law

[1] Peter Shand, *Scenes from the Colonial Catwalk: Cultural Appropriation, Intellectual Property Rights, and Fashion*, 3, CULTURAL ANALYSIS (2002) (explaining how indigenous intellectual property rights are infringed upon).

[2] Oscar Calvo-González, *Why are Indigenous Peoples more likely to be poor?* Jobs and Dev (2016), https://blogs.worldbank.org/opendata/why-are-indigenous-peoples-more-likely-be-poor.

World Trade Organization's ("WTO") "Agreement on Trade-Related Aspects of Intellectual Property Rights are not doing enough to protect native intellectual property when it comes to fashion. Although there are mechanisms in place that are supposed to protect indigenous intellectual property, including traditional knowledge and traditional cultural expression, among other intellectual property, these mechanisms are inadequate to protect the intellectual property of indigenous people. In other words, although international intellectual property entities are helping indigenous groups protect their intellectual property rights ("IPRs"), more work needs to be done to ensure indigenous fashion is being protected. Without more protection, indigenous fashion designs will continue to be exploited and appropriated.

In order to explore this phenomenon, this paper serves as a comparative analysis of the Maasai people of East Africa and the Navajo Nation of North America. These groups have been successful in defending their intellectual property, especially that of clothing and clothing designs. This paper will review the legal issues faced by the Maasai tribe (located throughout east Africa) to secure their international property rights. This legal fight will be juxtaposed with the issues that plague the Navajo Nation in America. Lastly, the paper will suggest potential solutions that WIPO, TRIPS and individual countries can adopt to combat the exploitation of indigenous fashion.

A. Brief History of WIPO, TRIPS, and Indigenous Intellectual Property Mechanisms

The Paris Convention for the Protection of Industrial Property was signed in Paris, France in 1883.[3] This treatise established an international agreement for the protection of industrial property in the widest sense, including patents, trademarks, industrial designs, service marks, trade names, and the repression of unfair competition.[4] It is still in force.[5] Three years after the Paris Convention, the Berne Convention met to discuss the protection of literary and artistic works.[6] From this Convention, an international agreement was created which governed copyright.[7] The copyright provisions of the Berne Convention and the trademark and patent provisions of the Paris Convention were later adopted in 1994, when the Agreement on Trade-Related Aspects of Intellectual Property Rights ("TRIPS") was signed.[8] TRIPS is "an international legal agreement between all the member nations of the World Trade Organization ("WTO")."[9] TRIPS sets the "minimum standards for the regulation by national governments of many forms of intellectual property as applied to nationals of other WTO member nations."[10]

TRIPS, although intellectual property-centered, was created by the WTO and, as such, is mostly concerned with

---

[3] WORLD INTELLECTUAL PROPERTY ORGANIZATION, PARIS CONVENTION FOR THE PROTECTION OF INDUSTRIAL PROPERTY (1883), http://www.wipo.int/treaties/en/ip/paris/.
[4] *Id.*
[5] *Id.*
[6] *Id.*
[7] WORLD TRADE ORGANIZATION, OVERVIEW: THE TRIPS AGREEMENT, https://www.wto.org/english/tratop_e/trips_e/intel2_e.htm (hereinafter *"TRIPS Agreement"*).
[8] *Id.*
[9] *Id.*
[10] *Id.*

how intellectual property effects trade.[11] However, there is an agency that is more closely related to intellectual property as it relates to general globalization rather than trade—the World Intellectual Property Organization ("WIPO"), an agency of the United Nations ("UN"). WIPO was established in 1967 to encourage creative activity and to promote the protection of intellectual property throughout the world.[12] Currently, WIPO has 191 member states and oversees 26 international treaties.[13]

All of these agencies, initiatives, and treaties have been instrumental in pushing for international cooperation in intellectual property. However, there are certainly strides that both the TRIPS agreement and WIPO need to make to ensure the intellectual property rights of all citizens, including those of indigenous people. That is not to say that there has not been progress for indigenous intellectual property rights. One way TRIPS and WIPO have advanced the cause is through protecting traditional knowledge ("TK"). TK refers to, knowledge, innovations and practices of indigenous and local communities around the world. Developed from experience gained over the centuries and adapted to the local culture and environment, TK is transmitted orally from generation to generation. It tends to be collectively owned and takes the form of stories, songs, folklore, proverbs, cultural values, beliefs, rituals, community laws, local language, and agricultural practices, including the development of plant species and animal breeds.[14]

---

[11] WORLD HEALTH ORGANIZATION, WTO AND THE TRIPS AGREEMENT,
http://www.who.int/medicines/areas/policy/wto_trips/en/.
[12] WORLD INTELLECTUAL PROPERTY ORGANIZATION,
http://www.wipo.int/about-wipo/en/.
[13] *Id.*
[14] UNITED NATIONS DECADE ON BIODIVERSITY, TRADITIONAL KNOWLEDGE, INNOVATION AND PRACTICES,
https://www.cbd.int/undb/media/factsheets/undb-factsheet-tk-en.pdf.

Also, in 2000, WIPO established the Intergovernmental Committee on Intellectual Property and Genetic Resources, Traditional Knowledge and Folklore (IGC-GRTKF).[15] This Committee, which sees TK, not as antiquated, but as "a living body of knowledge," agreed in 2009 to develop an international legal instrument that would give protection to TK, genetic resources and traditional cultural expression (TCE).[16] TCE refers to "expressions of folklore," that "may include music, dance, art, designs, names, signs and symbols, performances, ceremonies, architectural forms, handicrafts and narratives, or many other artistic or cultural expressions."[17]

TRIPS integrated facets of TK through Article (27.3)(b) which called for protection of plant varieties and patentability or non-patentability of plant and animal inventions in TRIPS.[18] This protection was further expanded by Paragraph 19 of the 2001 Doha Declaration.[19] The declaration recommended that the TRIPS Council should "also look at the relationship between the TRIPS Agreement and the UN Convention on Biological Diversity and increase the protection of TK and folklore."[20] Although Article (27.3)(b) has TK aspects knowledge of using plants can be

---

[15] WORLD INTELLECTUAL PROPERTY ORGANIZATION, *(IGC)* http://www.wipo.int/tk/en/igc/ (hereinafter "IGC").
[16] WORLD INTELLECTUAL PROPERTY ORGANIZATION, TRADITIONAL KNOWLEDGE AND INTELLECTUAL (hereinafter *TK and IP*), http://www.wipo.int/pressroom/en/briefs/tk_ip.html.
[17] WORLD INTELLECTUAL PROPERTY ORGANIZATION, TRADITIONAL CULTURAL EXPRESSIONS, http://www.wipo.int/tk/en/folklore/.
[18] TRIPS Agreement, *supra* note 7.
[19] Carlos M. Correa, *Implications of The Doha Declaration On The Trips Agreement and Public Health,* World Health Org. (2002).
[20] WORLD TRADE ORGANIZATION, ARTICLE 27.3B, TRADITIONAL KNOWLEDGE, BIODIVERSITY, https://www.wto.org/english/tratop_e/trips_e/art27_3b_e.htm.

seen in many indigenous groups[21]), this Article is primarily made to protect genetic resources and not necessarily TK.

TK and TCE are not forms of intellectual property protection themselves, but are instead, an international acknowledgement of indigenous knowledge systems. Accordingly, there is not one ideal intellectual property right that can protect the entire penumbra of TK and TCE. As the WIPO definition above suggests, TK and TCE are broad definitions, and it would be difficult to ascertain which intellectual property right would work best for both. Rather, each type of TK and TCE would have to be considered on a case by case basis, to allow for flexibility in protection. What works for one piece of TK or TCE might not work for others.

Having broad definitions and parameters for both TCE and TK should logically translate to a comprehensive protection for indigenous people. But recent legal history has shown that this is not necessarily true, especially when it comes to intellectual property rights surrounding fashion. Traditionally, at least in the United States, there is no IPR specifically related to fashion. Other regions of the world, however, do have stronger intellectual property rights than the U.S. for fashion.

---

[21] *See* David Hill, Amazon tribe saves plant lore with 'healing forests' and encyclopedia The Guardian (2017), https://www.theguardian.com/environment/andes-to-the-amazon/2017/nov/24/amazon-tribe-saves-plant-lore-with- healing-forests-and-encyclopedia.

B. *Intellectual Property in Fashion, the U.S., EU, WIPO, and TRIPS*

Fashion design denotes the creative activity related to the designing of cloth, footwear, accessories, cloth/textiles and its accessories.[22] It is a $3 trillion industry that employs millions.[23] Both developed and developing countries have varied remedies to deal with potential infringement concerning fashion. This piecemeal approach to protection also depends on the particular aspect of fashion being considered. For instance, when examining fashion and possible infringement, one must consider whether the dispositive issue is about the color,[24] sketch,[25] cut,[26] graphic design,[27] or textile design,[28] among possible other aspects. Countries, based on their own specific intellectual property rights and laws, view each of these aspects differently. One of these aspects might be copyrightable in one country, but not subject to intellectual property protection in a neighboring country. There is also variation in the type of protection available. For instance, if there is an intellectual property right dispute between a fashion designer and a store selling similar designs, some countries consider the similar designs copyright infringement, while in other countries the plaintiff would sue for patent infringement.

To understand more clearly, one only needs to look to the difference in intellectual property and fashion in

---

[22] Chron, *Definition of Fashion Designing*, https://work.chron.com/definition-fashion-designing-25262.html https://www.theguardian.com/environment/andes-to-the-amazon/2017/nov/24/amazon-tribe-saves-plant-lore-with- healing-forests-and-encyclopedia.

[23] FASHION UNITED, GLOBAL FASHION INDUSTRY STATISTICS - INTERNATIONAL APPAREL, https://fashionunited.com/global- fashion-industry-statistics.

[24] COPYRIGHT ALLIANCE, https://copyrightalliance.org/ca_faq_post/copyright-fashion-designs/ (last visited Dec 13, 2018).

America and Europe. Although comparable in culture, and being the heads of Western Civilization, these regions have very different approaches to intellectual property right in fashion. The European Union has registered and unregistered Community design rights.[29] Created specifically for fashion design and considered a strong fashion intellectual property right,[30] Community designs are industrial design rights that are recognized in the EU.[31] Industrial design rights refer to intellectual property rights that protect visual designs of non-utilitarian objects.[32] These designs include the shape or composition of the object, the pattern, the colors, or the combination of both. It must have an overall aesthetic quality to it.[33] These Community designs thus extend protection to clothing and fashion accessories.[34] Similar to Europe, the U.S. hosts a booming fashion industry

---

[25] *Id.* "Copyright protection does not extend to colors. So, if the fashion design you wish to protect is a signature color or a unique color scheme, copyright is not the avenue for you. But that doesn't mean there are no options for protecting your intellectual property. Trademark protection is sometimes available in these instances.").

[26] *Id.* ("If you create original sketches of your designs, those sketches are protected by copyright law.").

[27] *Id.* ("The way that design elements are cut and pieced together is not protected by copyright."). See also Star Athletica v. Varsity Brands, 137 S. Ct. 1002 (2017).

[28] *Id.* ("A producer of fabrics can rely on copyright to protect designs imprinted in or on fabric… if the design contains a sufficient amount of creative expression.").

[29] EUROPEAN COMMISSION, INDUSTRIAL DESIGN PROTECTION, https://ec.europa.eu/growth/industry/intellectual- property/industrial-design/protection_en (hereinafter "*EU ID*").

[30] COPYRIGHT, TRADEMARK, PATENT: YOUR GO-TO PRIMER FOR FASHION INTELLECTUAL PROPERTY LAW FASHIONISTA, https://fashionista.com/2016/12/fashion-law-patent-copyright-trademark (hereinafter "*Fashion Law*").

[31] EU ID, *supra* note 31.

[32] *Id.*

[33] *Id.*

[34] *Id.*

and with their own intellectual property rights. In the U.S., fashion can be protected through several different types of protections- some stronger than others.

Copyright

Anything that is a permanent nonfunctional piece of artistic expression is subject to copyright protection.[35] Things like jewelry can receive copyright protection because jewelry has no function and is used purely for decoration. However, generally speaking, clothing cannot be copyrighted because it is considered functional, although, if a design on a piece of clothing contains a sufficient amount of creative expression, it can potentially fall under copyright protection.[36] So although copyright could be helpful for jewelry, and even perhaps protect some designs, it is a narrowly drawn, niche protection. Also noteworthy is the fact that, even prevailing on the issue of the application of copyright does not convey absolute protection, since, even copyrighted material will eventually enter the public domain.[37] The average fashion designer would be able to protect copyrightable fashion for up to 70 years beyond their date of death.[38] However, a design copyrighted by a corporation would be protected for the shorter of 95 years from publication, or 120 years from creation.[39]

---

[35] Fashion Law, *supra* note 30.
[36] *Id.*
[37] COPYRIGHT BASICS FAQ STANFORD COPYRIGHT AND FAIR USE Center, https://fairuse.stanford.edu/overview/faqs/copyright-basics/ (last visited Dec 13, 2018).
[38] *Id.*
[39] *Id.*

1. Patents

Patents, unlike in the EU, are not helpful to most American fashion designers.[40] Under United States law, a patent is a right granted to the inventor of a process, machine, article of manufacture, or composition of matter that is new, useful, and non-obvious.[41] Patents can be used for zippers and other sorts of clasps.[42] Some high-performance fabrics like Kevlar could be protected with patents too.[43] Also, if the clothing is functional in a particular way, such as sneakers that help increase stamina, then the invention may be subject to patent protection.[44] Again, similar to copyright, this intellectual property right protects only small amount of fashion. However, the US also has design patents.[45] Design patents are for functional objects, but protect the decorative properties of functional objects.[46] A high heel with decorative heel, that by itself is not functional, but is a part of the overall functional item, could possibly be protected by design patents.[47]

Although patents may offer some protection to clothing designers, that protection comes at a high price. One of the caveats of patents and design patents is that they are expensive; initial costs to register a single patent can range from $6,000 to $10,000.[48] Also patents last only 20 years, while design patents only last 15, so not only is obtaining protection cost-prohibitive, the protection is short-term.[49]

---

[40] Fashion Law, *supra* note 30.
[41] 35 U.S.C.A. §§ 101-3
[42] *Id.*
[43] *Id.*
[44] *Id.*
[45] *Id.*
[46] *Id.*
[47] *Id.*
[48] *Id.*
[49] *Id.*

2. Trademark

Because copyright is niche and patent protection expensive and short-term, trademarks seem to be the most effective for fashion companies and designers in the U.S. Trademarks cannot be used to protect a whole piece of clothing or accessory but can protect the logo and the label.[50] Trade dress protects features of items where the "primary significance [is] to identify the source of the product rather than the product itself."[51] It cannot be used to serve any functional purpose.[52] What is very beneficial about trademark protection is that the protected label or logo will never enter into the public domain if the mark is continuously in use.[53]

According to WIPO, comparatively, none of the American protections above are as strong as the protections in the EU especially in comparison to community design protection, and thus, EU is more attractive to those in the fashion world.[54] This analysis only examines the differences between the U.S. and the EU—as mentioned above, there are certainly more variations between countries concerning fashion and intellectual property right. And if the countries cannot come to a consensus on how to protect intellectual property right for high fashion, it is foolhardy to believe they would push for uniformity for indigenous fashion.

Understandably, both WIPO and TRIPS have had to take into consideration the widely varying constructs for

---

[50] *Id.*

[51] Wal-Mart Stores, Inc. v. Samara Brothers, Inc., 529 U.S. 205 (2000).

[52] ASSOCIATION OF CORPORATE COUNSEL, THE BASICS OF PRODUCT CONFIGURATION TRADE DRESS PROTECTION https://www.acc.com/chapters/nyc/upload/ACC-Trade-Dress-Presentation.pdf (last visited Dec 13, 2018).

[53] *Id.*

[54] WORLD INTELLECTUAL PROPERTY ORGANIZATION, http://www.wipo.int/edocs/mdocs/mdocs/en/wipo_ipr_ge_15/wipo_ipr_ge_15_t2.pdf (last visited Dec. 13, 2018).

protecting fashion. WIPO, surprisingly, has not put a lot of effort into discussing intellectual property rights in fashion. The last known fashion conference that WIPO oversaw was in the winter of 2005 in Caserta, Italy, where 200 international representatives from fashion houses, national governments, and academic and consumer groups came together to discuss how companies can help to shape intellectual property right mechanisms.[55] This international symposium described copyright, industrial designs, trademarks, trade secrets and patents as "key intellectual property tools that are of great importance to the fashion industry in the knowledge- driven economy, enabling them to compete effectively in domestic and export markets in the era of increasing globalization and market integration."[56] The symposium, as this description suggests, was more concerned with how businesses and companies could ensure fashion was being globalized efficiently, rather than uniformly protected.

The symposium did not mention fashion infringement, nor did it discuss indigenous intellectual property rights in fashion at all. That is not to say that ensuring that efficient and appropriate intellectual property systems are in place is not important. However, it is interesting to note that WIPO, as an agency under the UN that is usually concerned with direct human impact and the human rights surrounding the impact of polices, puts so much emphasis on the role of businesses in this instance. This emphasis on business seems more appropriate for the WTO, rather than WIPO. Unfortunately, it seems that the best chance for the consideration of more uniform treatment of indigenous IPR lies with the IGC-GRTKF committee that meets a few times a year to discuss TK and TCE.

---

[55] Press Release, World Intellectual Property Organization, WIPO and Italian Government Host a Meeting to Highlight the Role of IP in the Fashion Industry. U.N. Press Release/2005/432 (Dec. 2, 2005).
[56] *Id.*

TRIPS, as mentioned, is an international agreement created by WTO.[57] It is mostly concerned with how intellectual property affects and is affected by trade, globalization, and international economies.[58] TRIPS specifically focuses on copyrightable and trademark material and patents and asks member nations to adhere to minimum standards, although countries have the sovereign authority to add on to these standards.[59] Similar to WIPO, the WTO and the TRIPS agreement are silent on fashion specifically. TRIPS' most prominent provisions focus on copyright and patents and speak about these intellectual property rights generally. It does provide specifics on certain types of things that the WTO thinks need or are deserving of protection, such as pharmaceutical medicines and computer code.[60] It is possible to speculate that, similar to WIPO, the WTO expects member countries to sort out their own intellectual property right regimes. However, TRIPS has always been, generally speaking, a proponent of international harmonization, so it is difficult reconcile the hands-off treatment that fashion receives. It seems that, if there was a way to strengthen fashion intellectual property right by having countries working in tandem developing a uniform system of protection, that the WTO would support such efforts.[61] For indigenous communities, the fact that the WTO and WIPO lack the framework to create IP systems to protect fashion is troubling.

---

[57] TRIPS Agreement, *supra* note 7.
[58] SEAN PAGER, TRIPs: A Link Too Far? A Proposal for Procedural Restraints on Regulatory Linkage in the WTO, 10 MARQ. INTELL. PROP. L. REV. 215 (2006) (hereinafter *"Pager, A Link"*).
[59] TRIPS Agreement, *supra* note 7.
[60] *Id.*
[61] Pager, A Link, *supra* note 58.

II. INTEGRATING TK AND TCE WITHIN WIPO AND WTO

According to WIPO, TK can benefit from protection under multiple bases—patent, trademark, geographical indication, and even trade secret or confidential information protection.[62] WIPO has suggested a myriad of possible solutions for defending TK, including both defensive protection and positive protection.[63] WIPO defines defensive protection as a "set of strategies to ensure that third parties do not gain illegitimate or unfounded intellectual property rights over TK."[64] WIPO furthers defensive protection by providing practical assistance to TK holders via a toolkit that helps these TK holders document their TK.[65] Positive Protection, while is less defined and still being explored by WIPO, is defined as protections that will prevent "unauthorized use" and the "active exploitation of TK by the originating community itself."[66] This, coupled with the IGC-GRTKF, illustrates that WIPO is trying to empower indigenous people and is dedicated to TK and TCE.

As mentioned earlier, the TRIPS agreement uses Article (27.3)(b) to discuss TK.[67] In 1992, the Convention on Biological Diversity (CBD) was signed.[68] This international treaty was designed to develop strategies to ensure the conservation of biological diversity and genetic resources.[69] Because indigenous groups are often victims of biodiversity bioprospecting where their natural resources and TK of nature are taken and exploited without

---

[62] TK and IP, *supra* note 16.
[63] *Id.*
[64] *Id.*
[65] *Id.*
[66] *Id.*
[67] TRIPS Agreement, *supra* note 9.
[68] THE CONVENTION ON BIOLOGICAL DIVERSITY, CONVENTION ON BIOLOGICAL DIVERSITY, https://www.cbd.int/convention/.
[69] *Id.*

compensation, observers hoped that the CBD and TRIPS would work to ensure the protection of intellectual property rights of indigenous groups.[70]

As Q'apaj Conde Choque, a human rights lawyer and one of WIPOs Indigenous Fellows, said, "[Indigenous people] are able to provide evidence that we suffer and are victims of implementing intellectual property regimes with a focus on economic value...We hope that we can rebalance the TRIPS agreement based on the CBD, on human rights and in particular, indigenous rights."[71] This quote suggests that TRIPS is not doing enough for indigenous groups and that perhaps CBD can help. It also highlights the fact that TRIPS is concerned with aspects of TK that are unrelated to the artistic expressions which are the focus of this paper. In other words, although TRIPS is not completely silent on TK, its focus is not artistic expression. Thus, although TRIPS could be helpful in combating biopiracy, it has not been seen as a helpful tool for fashion or other TCEs.

In sum, the WTO, and WIPO on its face, appear to take an interest in Indigenous Rights, and WIPO particularly has put forth effort into recognizing TK. TRIPS focuses more on genetic resources, rather than TK and TCE specifically. As the following cases demonstrate, both the WTO and WIPO need to do better at protecting TK, and especially TCE, if indigenous fashion is to ever have adequate, global protection.

---

[70] ETC GROUP, BIOPROSPECTING/BIOPIRACY AND INDIGENOUS PEOPLES http://www.etcgroup.org/content/bioprospectingbiopiracy-and-indigenous-peoples (last visited Dec 13, 2018). ("Biodiversity prospecting is the exploration, extraction and screening of biological diversity and indigenous knowledge for commercially valuable genetic and biochemical resources.").

[71] INTELLECTUAL PROPERTY WATCH, INDIGENOUS PEOPLES SEEK INVOLVEMENT IN WTO TO DEFEND RIGHTS, http://www.ip-watch.org/2018/06/13/video-indigenous-peoples-seek-involved-world-trade-organization-defend-rights/.

III. MAASAI TRIBE OF EAST AFRICA

The Maasai tribe have a distinct look that has been imitated throughout the fashion world.[72] The Maasai people are an African semi-nomadic tribe who mostly inhabit central and southern Kenya and northern Tanzania.[73] They are a well-known tribe due to their large population and their distinctive customs and dress.[74] Their clothing is known for its colorful block patterns and the intricate beading of their accessories.[75] The color red is heavily used, as well as black, blue, stripes and checkered textiles and cloth.[76] They have also integrated animal skins in their fashion.[77] Typical fashion includes wearing a Shúkà, sheets that are wrapped around the body, which are usually red, but can also be blue and patterned- typically in plaid.[78] They also wear kanga, which is a one piece garment and a sarong called kikoi.[79] These kikoi come in a variety colors and textiles, but are most commonly striped.[80] Maasai are also known for their beaded jewelry.[81] Traditionally, women are the ones who create the beaded jewelry and like their clothes, the jewelry is beaded in bright colors- white, blue, and red.[82] The colors

---

[72] INDEPENDENT, MAASAI PEOPLE OF EAST AFRICA FIGHTING AGAINST CULTURAL APPROPRIATION BY LUXURY FASHION LABELS, https://www.independent.co.uk/life-style/fashion/maasai-people-cultural-appropriation-luxury-fashion-retailers- louis-vuitton-east-africa-intellectual-a7553701.html ("hereinafter *Maasai People*").

[73] *Id.*

[74] *Id.*

[75] *Id.*

[76] *Id.*

[77] *Id.*

[78] THE MAASAI TRIBE, EAST AFRICA, http://www.siyabona.com/maasai-tribe-east-africa.html.

[79] Massai People, *supra* note 72.

[80] *Id.*

[81] *Id.*

[82] PHILLIP BRIGGS, *Northern Tanzania with Kilimanjaro and Zanzibar* 216 (2006).

have varying meanings and are not just adornments or accessories. Rather, the colors help to illustrate the identity and societal position of the wearer.[83]

The cultural identity of the Maasai people is long-lasting due to their clothing and protection of their culture.[84] The Maasai use dress as cultural expression and it is engrained in their cultural identity.[85] Maasai clothing, a significant part of their cultural identity, has been copied by a variety of fashion designers and stores.[86] It is estimated that over 1,000 companies, including Calvin Klein, Louis Vuitton, and Ralph Lauren have Maasai- inspired looks. Experts estimate that the Maasai people should be collecting $10 million annually in licensing fees.[87]

One instance is especially striking. In recent times, the Maasai are known for wearing sandals that are durable and affordable, and have been recycled from car tires.[88] These sandals, known as Akala, were recreated by the a company named Maasai Barefoot Technology (MBT), and sold throughout the United Kingdom.[89] Pictures of the Maasai wearing the shoes were heavily promoted in their advertisements for the sandals.[90] The sandal was also touted as a shoe created by the Maasai people.[91] The shoes were sold for between $240 and $310.[92] The Maasai were not

---

[83] Massai People, *supra* note 72.
[84] *Id.*
[85] *Id.*
[86] *Id.*
[87] INDEPENDENT, https://www.independent.co.uk/arts-entertainment/indigenous-advocates-call-on-un-to-make-cultural-appropriation- illegal-a7791851.html (last visited Dec. 13, 2018).
[88] FINANCIAL TIMES, https://www.ft.com/content/999ad344-fcff-11e7-9b32-d7d59aace167.
[89] *Id.*
[90] *Id.*
[91] *Id.*
[92] BLOOMBERG BUSINESSWEEK, https://www.bloomberg.com/news/articles/2013-10-24/africas-maasai-tribe-seek-royalties-for-commercial-use-of- their-name.

compensated and eventually, MBT, a British company wholly unrelated to the Maasai, removed all mention of the Maasai from their website.[93] Not only did the company not compensate the Maasai for the show design, but MBT also appropriated the tribe's name.[94] These examples are just two of the myriad of examples of fashion designers appropriating the Maasai's creations without giving credit or paying royalties.[95] These constant imitations led some members of the Maasai to create the Maasai Intellectual Property Institute (MIPI).[96] Founded in 2008, this organization is registered in Tanzania and incorporated in Kenya, and was made to educate members of the tribe about intellectual property related to their TK and TCE and to seek compensation from companies which infringe on the Maasai people's intellectual property right.[97]

Since its founding, two million Maasai have registered their works with MIPI.[98] Working with Light Years IP, a Washington D.C. intellectual property organization which lobbies for funds from the U.S. government for various projects, has helped the MIPI go into villages to teach tribesmen and women the best way to control their own identities and laws and regulations concerning intellectual property.[99] MIPI has educated the Maasai tribe and created bylaws that would result in their work being considered eligible for trademark protection in Western courts.[100] This is especially helpful since, as previously discussed, there are a lot of variations in what can

---

[93] QUARTZ, https://qz.com/896520/the-maasai-want- their-brand-back/ (hereinafter "*The Maasai*").
[94] *Id.*
[95] *Id.*
[96] NAIROBI NEWS, https://nairobinews.nation.co.ke/news/maasai-ngo-communitys-brand/.
[97] *Id.*
[98] *Id.*
[99] The Maasai, *supra* note 93.
[100] *Id.*

cause infringement- be it the cut, the overall design, or some other particular facet of fashion intellectual property right. It is unreasonable to expect marginalized communities to understand the nuances of international intellectual property law, and education enables tribes to make smarter, well-informed decisions. This collaboration has been successful and has led to companies paying royalties for use of community traditional and cultural property. As Stephan Faris wrote in Bloomberg:

> About eighty companies have engaged in the royalty seeking process, this being confirmation that use of Maasai community property deserves recognition and requisite permissions. In one instance, the company Land Rover remunerated the community after MIPI engagement on their use of their Maasai identity expressed through community stereotypic images depicted as part of the commercial product, leading to an agreement based on the advertisement.[101]

Maasai people achieved this success through MIPI and grassroots organization, with little help from WIPO. That is not to say WIPO was unaware of or unable to provide assistance to the Maasai. In 2006, WIPO visited the Maasai tribe and held a number of presentations on TK and TCE, raising awareness and setting up initiatives that could lead to compensation.[102] This meeting also helped to create the Creative Heritage Project, an initiative that helps indigenous

---

[101] BLOOMBERG BUSINESSWEEK,
https://www.bloomberg.com/news/articles/2013-10-24/africas-maasai-tribe-seek-royalties-for-commercial-use-of- their-name.
[102] WORLD INTELLECTUAL PROPERTY ORGANIZATION,
http://www.wipo.int/meetings/en/doc_details.jsp?doc_id=189825.

groups digitize their TK and TCE.[103] Although this was doubtlessly helpful, credit for the success of MIPI belongs to the Maasai people who worked on their own to find answers.[104] Although the point of WIPO is to help indigenous groups empower themselves, the WIPO were not as hands-on in this circumstance as they could have been. WIPO is an organization of the UN; they have the authority to provide lawyers and could have worked as a liaison between the Maasai and these corporations who were essentially stealing from them.

MIPI have helped to monetize Maasai culture for the benefit of Maasai designers and artists.[105] By using trademark protection, the Maasai TK and TCE have solid, recorded ownership. Although WIPO has been helpful and does want indigenous groups to have protection, WIPO lacks enforcement authority, and, at most, can work only as an educator or mediator. The Maasai advocated for themselves and it is largely still up to indigenous tribes to fend for themselves.

IV. NAVAJO NATION OF THE UNITED STATES OF AMERICA

In 2012, the Navajo Nation, a Native American tribe located throughout Arizona, Utah, and New Mexico, sued Urban Outfitters Inc., an American incorporated clothing company, over federal and state trademark infringement as well as for violations of the Indian Arts and Crafts Act of 1990.[106] The Indian Arts and Crafts Act is a federal act that

---

[103] Id.

[104] Id.

[105] The Maasai, *supra* note 93.

[106] Navajo Nation v. Urban Outfitters, Inc., 918 F. Supp. 2d 1245 (D.N.M. 2013). The Indian Arts and Crafts Act of 1990, Public Law 101-644, 104 Stat. 4662 is essentially a truth-in-marketing law that includes civil and criminal sanctions. For a first time violation of the Act, an individual can face civil or criminal penalties up to a $250,000 fine or a 5-year prison term, or both. If a business violates the Act, it

prohibits the selling of arts and crafts in a way that suggests that they are made by American Indians if they are, in fact, not.[107] In the Navajo Nation, the Attorney General initiates all litigation in which the Navajo Nation is an interested party.[108] Although this is a tribal issue, tribes cannot sue a non-Indian party in tribal courts, and thus, the Navajo Nation sued in federal court in New Mexico.[109] The Navajo Nation is a sovereign nation and has the ability to register trademarks under their own name.[110] In this case specifically, the registrant of the Navajo Nation's fashion trademark is Dine Development Corporation, a wholly-owned tribal enterprise of the Navajo Nation.

Some of the products involved in this suit include "Navajo Hipster Panty" and "Navajo Flask."[111] The Navajo Nation views these products as culturally insensitive and cultural appropriation. The Navajo Nation asked Urban Outfitters twice to stop infringement before filing suit.[112] According to former Navajo Nation Attorney General Harrison Tsosie, besides contesting the unauthorized use of "Navajo," the Nation "sent nearly fifty protest letters

---

can face civil penalties or can be prosecuted and fined up to $1,000,000.

[107] 18 U.S.C. § 1159

[108] THE NAVAJO NATION / DEPARTMENT OF JUSTICE, NATURAL RESOURCES UNIT, http://nndoj.org/.

[109] THE ATLANTIC (2015), https://www.theatlantic.com/politics/archive/2015/12/who-can-tribal-courts-try/419037/.

[110] Trademark Registration Search, UNITED STATES PATENT AND TRADEMARK OFFICE htttps://tmsearch.uspto.gov/bin/showfield?f=doc&state=4806:vkzz6d.3.3, (follow search query hyperlink and search using the word Navajo under ALL).

[111] JEZEBEL, https://jezebel.com/5889702/navajo-nation-sues-urban-outfitters-over-the-navajo-hipster-panty.

[112] Id.

afterward."[113] It seems that the Nation's only recourse was indeed a lawsuit.

Their briefs argue that Urban Outfitters products are hurting the Navajo brand, which they say "stands for quality, Navajo-made jewelry, clothing, and accessories — not imported Urban Outfitters tat."[114] They also allege that "[l]abeling items as 'Navajo' resulted in direct competition with items marketed and sold by the tribe through its tribal enterprises, in addition to deceiving and causing confusion by consumers."[115] The Navajo Nation was seeking injunctive relief, which would have stopped Urban Outfitters from manufacturing, selling, and marketing any products which included the name Navajo, or any Navajo-themed products.[116] They also sought damages for all infringing products sold going back to 2008.[117]

The Navajo Nation sought disgorgement of all profits from infringing products.[118] They also sought damages of $1,000 per day per item, or "three times the profit generated by marketing and retail of products using the name."[119] Urban Outfitters disputed the claims and argued that the Navajo Tribe "slept on their rights" and thus should not have waited so long to file suit.[120] They also argued that the statute of limitations had expired.[121] Urban Outfitters Inc. also denied their products infringement any

---

[113] THE FASHION LAW, http://www.thefashionlaw.com/home/what-to-know-about-the-ongoing-navajo-nation-urban-outfitters-legal-dispute (hereinafter "*Fashion Law, Navajo*").

[114] *Id.*

[115] FARMINGTON DAILY TIMES, https://www.daily-times.com/story/news/local/navajo-nation/2016/11/17/navajo-nation-urban-outfitters-reach- settlement/94029162/.

[116] *Id.*

[117] *Id.*

[118] *Id.*

[119] Fashion Law, Navajo, *supra* note 113.

[120] *Id.*

[121] *Id.*

trademark, alleging that "Navajo" is a generic term for style or design. The defendant corporation asked the Judge to cancel the tribe's federal trademark registrations for the word "Navajo."[122]

Navajo Nation and Urban Outfitters Inc. settled in 2015 and the terms of the settlement, including any monetary relief, remains confidential. The Navajo Nation, in light of the settlement, dismissed all claims with prejudice.[123] The only publicly available information concerning the settlement is that "the parties entered into a supply and license agreement and plan to collaborate on authentic American Indian jewelry...."[124] Although the suit seemed to have ended amicably, with a collaboration agreement in place, the litigation took more than four years and doubtlessly cost hundreds of thousands of dollars in legal fees.[125]

This result differs markedly from the actions of the Maasai people, who relied on grassroots efforts to the MIPI in order to pursue non-litigious remedies.[126] The difference in the makeup of Navajo and Maasai communities could account for their different approaches. The Navajo Nation became a federally recognized tribe in 1922.[127] Additionally, the Unites States has had trademark laws on the books since the 1881, and the Navajo Nation has been using trademarks since 1941.[128] The Maasai, on the other hand, are a nomadic people and thus, mobilizing their people and educating would seem difficult to do. The Navajo Nation spans

---

[122] *Id.*

[123] *Id.*

[124] FARMINGTON DAILY TIMES, https://www.daily-times.com/story/news/local/navajo-nation/2016/11/17/navajo-nation-urban-outfitters-reach-settlement/94029162/.

[125] *Id.*

[126] The Maasai, *supra* note 94.

[127] HISTORY, http://www.navajo-nsn.gov/history.htm.

[128] News Release, The Navajo Nation and Urban Outfitters, Inc. Announce a Settlement Agreement (Nov. 17, 2016).

multiple states, but the Maasai people span multiple countries.

In this specific case, another difference between the Maasai and the Navajo is that the Navajo had one specific corporate infringer, unlike the Maasai who were aware that many different companies had appropriated their intellectual property. Coordinating such complex litigation against hundreds of very profitable, sophisticated companies might not have been financially feasible for the Maasai. The Navajo Nation was also able to rely on domestic legislation in the form of the Indian Arts and Crafts Act of 1990. It is difficult to say if there are other reasons for the disparate methods used by the Maasai and the Navajo to settle their disputes. In neither case, however, did the WIPO or WTO help either party settle their disputes.

As mentioned above, WIPO was on the periphery when it came to providing assistance to the Maasai people—TRIPS has no irrelevant articles. In case of the Navajo Nation, when their case against Urban Outfitters was ongoing, over 180 indigenous groups around the world came together to speak to WIPO about rampant cultural appropriation.[129] Since 2001, members of these groups have been in a committee calling for the WIPO to impose sanctions on companies who wrongfully appropriate indigenous fashion.[130] This committee is looking for the UN to "obligate states to create effective criminal and civil enforcement procedures to recognize and prevent the non-consensual taking and illegitimate possession, sale and export of TCEs."[131] These groups want the UN to make the appropriation of TK and TCE illegal.[132] At this meeting, the

---

[129] INDEPENDENT, https://www.independent.co.uk/arts-entertainment/indigenous-advocates-call-on-un-to-make-cultural-appropriation- illegal-a7791851.html.
[130] *Id.*
[131] *Id.*
[132] *Id.*

Navajo Nation lawsuit was a major talking point, yet no action was taken to help the tribe and WIPO to this day has never imposed sanctions or levied any other type of enforcement against appropriating companies.[133]

Indigenous groups want WIPO to do more. As it stands, there are no enforcement mechanisms in place. Empowerment is important but having the ability to punish is even more so. If WIPO is limited to providing advice, and even that cannot be legal in nature, then they really cannot do much to help indigenous people. This is underscored by the fact that indigenous groups, for almost two decades, have asked for sanctions and it was not until 2017 that their collective voices were heard. And even then, nothing has come of it. International law has not changed and there has been no extension of indigenous protections. While TRIPS has been unhelpful, WIPO has been even more so, because they have not met the needs of vulnerable groups who have asked for help. These indigenous groups, many vulnerable and lacking the funds and resources and the organization to mobilize, will continue to be taken advantage of if they do not receive help from a governing body. Although grassroots efforts were a success for the Maasai and the Navajo Nation had the ability to rely on the U.S. justice system to stop infringement, these instances are the exception and not the rule.

If WIPO wants to be more effective, then it will have to start creating policy, not mere advisory practices. If TRIPS want to be helpful, they will have to dedicate more provisions that directly protect not only TK, but also specifically TCE. Be it through *sui generis* or other defined forms of intellectual property right, all facets of TK and TCE should be protected and the WTO should take overt steps to ensure that TRIPS recognize it as well.[134] Moreover, WIPO

---

[133] *Id.*

[134] *Sui generis* is Latin for "of its own kind," and is used to describe a form of legal protection that exists outside typical legal protections—

and WTO should consult with indigenous groups about WIPO's definition of TK and TCE to ensure it encapsulates how indigenous people understand their own indigenous knowledge. TK and TCE protections would be most effective if developed with the input of those it means to protect. Until then, both WIPO and TRIPS will be ineffective and indigenous groups will have to rely on other resources and solutions to stop infringement. Some of these possible solutions are detailed below.

V. POTENTIAL SOLUTIONS TO INFRINGEMENT OF TK AND TCE WITH RESPECT TO FASHION

The following solutions are not specific to TK and TCE surrounding indigenous fashion and should be broad enough to include numerous other facets of TK and TCE.

A. *Countries*

One option for self-help available to sovereign states is the ability to legislate. Laws similar to those existing in the U.S. and New Zealand are useful in preventing, or at least punishing, infringement. American tribes benefit from the U.S. legislation in place to protect indigenous products, including the Indian Arts and Crafts Act of 1990.[135] This Act, however, is not considered an intellectual property right although it functions to protect intellectual property. The Act, instead, is a truth-in-advertising law which prohibits misrepresentations in advertising of American Indian or

---

that is, something that is unique or different. In intellectual property law, for example, ship hull designs have achieved a unique category of protection and are "*sui generis*" within copyright law. CORNELL LAW SCHOOL, LEGAL INFORMATION INSTITUTE, https://www.law.cornell.edu/wex/sui_generis.

[135] Navajo Nation v. Urban Outfitters, Inc., 918 F. Supp. 2d 1245, 1250 (D.N.M. 2013).

Alaska Native arts and crafts products within the United States.[136] Allegations of violations of the Act are overseen by the United States Indian Arts and Crafts Board, an agency of the Department of the Interior.[137] The Board is made up of Native Americans from different tribes.[138] Who better to decide if there has been a misrepresentation of native culture than those who are a part of that culture? Additionally, the existence of the Act, and the oversight of the Board, not only protect their products, but also empower the indigenous peoples to be self-regulating. This law and its board are a useful model or framework for other countries and tribes that will assist with the ability to adjudicate infringement and empower indigenous peoples to mobilize.

However, there are drawbacks to this law too. As it stands, the Indian Arts and Crafts Act only recognizes products and goods made by federally recognized tribes, which puts those tribes who are not recognized at a disadvantage and allows their culture to be misappropriated without consequence.[139] Other countries that have, or may implement, similar schemes protecting a subset of specified tribes, rather than all tribes, should consider the consequences for the excluded tribes. Indian rights experts also claim that this law has had the unintended consequence of sanctioning discrimination against Native Americans whose tribal affiliation was not officially recognized.[140] Also, this Act does not apply extra-territorially and would not preclude foreign corporations from infringing on the

---

[136] *Id.*

[137] *Id.* The Indian Arts and Crafts Board was created by Congress pursuant to the Act of August 27, 1935 (49 Stat. 891; 25 U.S.C. 305 et seq.; 18 U.S.C. 1158-59)

[138] Navajo Nation, 918 F. Supp. at 1250.

[139] Gail K. Sheffield, The Arbitrary Indian: The Indian Arts and Crafts Act Of 1990, 11 (1997).

[140] *Id.*

rights of domestic indigenous rights as long as the infringing behavior occurred outside of the United States.[141]

New Zealand, which hosts a large indigenous population has both legal and nonlegal mechanisms in place to protect the intellectual property right of indigenous people.[142] In 1993, New Zealand held the first International Conference on the Cultural and Intellectual Property Rights of Indigenous Peoples.[143] This conference resulted in the Mataatua Declaration which asked for all UN member states to continually protect indigenous intellectual and cultural property and made recommendations for both the indigenous tribes and their countries of origin to protect these rights.[144] Although declarations have no legal enforcement, they do serve to educate and make countries aware of the needs of indigenous people. However, this is not the only mechanism employed by New Zealand. The Treaty of Waitangi, created in 1840 by representatives of the British Crown and Māori chiefs, was created, in part, to protect property so that the Maori would not be alienated from their own land.[145] The English version of treaty acknowledges Māori rights to "properties," which seems to imply physical, and perhaps intellectual, property.[146] The Māori version uses the word "taonga," meaning "treasures" or "precious things."[147] The term Taonga can be applied more broadly than the English concept of legal property, and since the 1980s, courts have

---

[141] *Id.* At 57.

[142] NEW ZEALAND MĀORI CULTURE, TOURISM NEW ZEALAND, IN NEW ZEALAND, https://www.newzealand.com/us/maori-culture/.

[143] MATAATAU DECLARATION ON CULTURAL AND INTELLECTUAL PROPERTY, http://ankn.uaf.edu/iks/mataatua.html.

[144] *Id.*

[145] NEW ZEALAND HISTORY, https://nzhistory.govt.nz/politics/treaty/the-treaty-in-brief.

[146] *Id.*

[147] *Id.*

defined it in such a way so as to include intangible things like language and culture.[148]

Declarations are empowering and can aid indigenous tribes to mobilize and enact change. For instance, if a tribe located in Central Africa could connect with other regional tribes to make a declaration to their respective countries or the UN, then not only would they have strength in numbers, they would be fostering relationships and gaining allies that are intimately familiar with their struggles. However, as mentioned, declarations are not legally binding and do not necessarily lead to any change. Although they bring awareness, with no enforcement provisions and no push for actual change in intellectual property laws, their effectiveness is difficult estimate. It might be preferable for countries and tribes alike to instead utilize a legally binding mechanism such as the Treaty of Waitangi.

The Treaty of Waitangi was possible because New Zealand was a part of the Commonwealth of the United Kingdom and thus had powerful international states involved. Without sovereign states, *i.e.* international governments, a treaty cannot form. Since most tribes are not sovereign states, they are unable to make a treaty with their own home countries. Instead, tribes should work with their home countries to pass legislation and laws that will protect their intellectual property right. This, of course, can only happen if the countries are receptive to doing so. The financial ramifications are certainly relevant. Since intellectual property right would lead to bigger revenue streams for indigenous tribes, it would be financially beneficial to home countries in that the tribes would potentially no longer be dependent on national funds. Many indigenous tribes find themselves in a vulnerable position, often as a vestige of colonization, which has left them marginalized and disenfranchised, with no access to

---

[148] *Id.*

education and no prospects for employment. The tribes have, for centuries, lacked the political clout and other resources necessary to pass necessary legislation.

These examples from the U.S. and New Zealand, and in some ways the Maasai too, can be extremely helpful to tribes who are looking to ensure their TK and TCE is not appropriated, specifically with regard to indigenous fashion. However, the tribes face a battle on two fronts - not only against those who are infringing, but also their home countries who do nothing to protect them.

B. WIPO & TRIPS

WIPO has numerous initiatives to help indigenous groups. This includes the IGC-GRTKF, which continually pushes for intellectual property right for indigenous peoples, and the Creative Heritage Project which is helping to digitize TK and TCE.[149] Yet, if WIPO truly seeks to be effective, the IGC-GRTKF's initiatives need to come to fruition. The IGC-GRTKF is in negotiations to have legal instruments in place. This committee has met three to four times per year since 2001, and yet no legal treaty explicitly protecting the intellectual property right of TKs and TCEs has been created.[150] There are, however, as of November 2018, twenty-six WIPO-administered treaties.[151] WIPO does have the authority, initiative and ability to make international, binding legal agreements. Although it may take several years (or decades) of effort to make a treaty, from negotiating, drafting, revising and obtaining ratification of member states, there has been little progress towards this goal by the IGC-GRTKF. The committee notes for the IGC-GRTKF show that a treaty of some sort is an eventual goal, however,

---

[149] IGC, *supra* note 17.
[150] *Id.*
[151] *Id.*

it is not close to becoming a reality.[152] WIPO, if it was to be truly helpful to indigenous communities, needs to put a significant amount of effort into laying the groundwork for a treaty.

WTO will either need to revise TRIPS Article (27.3) (b), or create an additional article specifically for TK and TCE. Focusing on biological diversity is indeed important, however remaining silent on other indigenous intellectual property rights is counter-productive. Because there exists no treaty for TK and TCE, if TRIPS were to add a TK- and TCE-specific article, there would finally be a treaty that explicitly speaks to, and protects, TK and TCE.[153] Although TRIPS may not be the best place to help to protect indigenous tribes' intellectual property right, the products that indigenous people make, especially clothing and fashion, is continually growing. TK and TCE can be viable, and valuable, sources of revenue streams. Since TRIPS is an agreement of the WTO, consideration should be given to the potential economic impact of the protection of TK and TCE. Because of the ability to have legally binding laws on TK and TCE, and its growing economic impact, TRIPS is the appropriate place for TK and TCE to be protected.

C. Sui Generis System

The variations in TK and TCE and in fashion intellectual property right generally, will undoubtedly have some considering a *sui generis* system as the best way to protect indigenous fashion intellectual property right. Although *sui generis* forms of protection could be helpful for indigenous fashion and TK and TCEs, it is perhaps premature to begin the development of such a system. As the *Navajo Nation* case has demonstrated, domestic law can,

---

[152] *Id.*
[153] TRIPS Agreement, *supra* note 9.

under some circumstances, be effective. If a *sui generis* system was going to be effective, it would likely look first to domestic laws. WIPO shares this assessment. A 2002 WIPO report stated that "defining *sui generis* protection at an international level is less likely to succeed if it is shaped without reference to the experience gained from operational national systems that provide practical models for functioning TK protection, whether through *sui generis* protection or application of existing intellectual property systems to TK subject matter."[154]

The flexibility of the *sui generis* system would work in accordance with the variation of fashion intellectual property and indigenous fashion particularly, but more work on a domestic level is needed. Indigenous *sui generis* needs a reference point. The Maasai and the Navajo Nation could certainly be a paradigms, but more successful instances would be required.

Speaking more broadly, a *sui generis* system solely for TK and TCE seems too unwieldy because of the wealth of differences in TK and TCE. As WIPO goes on to say in their 2002 report, "Members must still decide whether, if a future *sui generis* system were to be developed, such a system would cover all manifestations and expressions of TK..."[155] Thus, a paradox is formed where a *sui generis* system would be helpful to encapsulate the variations in TK and TCE, but the variety in TK and TCE might be too broad to for a *sui generis* system to effectively protect. Thus, a paradox is formed where *sui generis* would be helpful to encapsulate the variations in TK and TCE, but the variations in TK and TCE might be too broad to effectively protect using *sui generis*.

---

[154] WIPO, Rep. of the Intergovernmental Comm. on Intellectual Property and Genetic, Resources, Traditional Knowledge, Folklore on Its Forth Session, U.N. Doc. WIPO/GRTKF/IC/4/8.
[155] *Id.*

D. Organizations & Fashion Activism

Another potential solution that indigenous people can use to protect their TK and TCE is activism. Light Years IP is a group which has decided itself to assisting indigenous peoples "reposition for power."[156] Ethical Fashion Initiative (EFI), rather than looking to protect intellectual property rights, is a group of indigenous and non-indigenous designers who want to use fashion as a way to promote change.[157] EFI connects indigenous designers with international fashion houses, giving the indigenous designers jobs and a livable wage, while the non-indigenous fashion designers benefit from a wealth of new and exciting material and inspiration without infringing on the indigenous intellectual property rights.[158] EFI also works with upcoming fashion designers in Africa and provides them mentorship to grow their brands and encourages collaborations with other designers in the region. By doing this, EFI has made fashion a means of development for indigenous people. Organizations like Light Years IP and EFI, although having different methods and results, are still working towards the betterment of indigenous groups and their intellectual property rights. If more organizations like these existed and were easily accessible to indigenous groups, transformation can occur as indigenous fashion becomes recognized, celebrated and protected. With broader recognition of the issue will come compensation or attribution to the indigenous creators.

---

[156] LIGHT YEARS IP, http://lightyearsip.net/.
[157] INTERNATIONAL TRADE INSTITUTE,
http://www.intracen.org/itc/projects/ethical-fashion/.
[158] *Id.*

CONCLUSION

IPR for indigenous clothing and fashion is a complicated and varied part of intellectual property law that is not afforded the same protection as other facets of intellectual property. TRIPS and WIPO, in their current forms, do not provide enough protection, either for TK and TCE in general, or for indigenous fashion specifically. Without having international legal safeguards in place, indigenous fashion designers will have to look beyond TRIPS and WIPO for assistance. As the Maasai case study illustrates, outside organizations are the most helpful and can give different indigenous groups the opportunity to mobilize but be educated on the different forms of intellectual property available to them.

Sometimes, as the Navajo Nation case study highlighted, litigation based on national laws may be the best course of action where such laws exist. Until WIPO and WTO are able to assist indigenous members with specific and effective means of protection, it may be up to indigenous groups to mobilize and to carve a path themselves.

CONTRACTS AND THE COVID-19 VIRUS PANDEMIC

HENRY LOWENSTEIN[*]
LAURA L. SULLIVAN[**]

I. INTRODUCTION

It is April 6, 2020, and at time of this writing the United States along with the world is facing the greatest and most deadly viral pandemic since the *Spanish Flu* of 1918 to 1920.[1] The 1918 pandemic resulted in more deaths, estimated up to 50 million worldwide, than casualties in World War I.[2] Beyond the obvious human tragedy, the coronavirus crisis (known as COVID-19) poses severe implications to the economy and the laws of transactions and contracts, which are critical to the function of our economic system.

As the United States grapples with immediate emergency responses to the COVID-19 crisis, government powers have been used to shut down businesses, involuntarily redirect/ discharge contracts, redistribute

[*] Henry Lowenstein, PhD is Professor of Management and Law, Vereen Endowed Professor of Business at Coastal Carolina University, Conway, S.C. and former business dean.

[**] Laura L. Sullivan, J.D. is Professor of Business Law at Sam Houston State University and Executive Director of the Southern Academy of Legal Studies in Business (SALSB). The authors express their appreciation for the assistance of Anthony Sullivan, J.D., General Counsel, Petroleum Wholesale, L.P., The Woodlands, Texas, in the development of this article.

[1] *Influenza Pandemic 1918-1920*, ENCYCLOPEDIA BRITANNICA, Mar. 20, 2020. https://www.britannica.com/event/influenza-pandemic-of-1918-1919

[2] Estimated to be around 20 million war deaths.

medical products and even commandeer industry under the Defense Production Act (1950) passed by Congress during the Korean War.[3] The powers of government utilized to date are and continue to be controversial both on federal and state constitutional grounds. What impact does this emergency, unprecedented in the twenty-first century, have on business contracts, and their implementation, discharge or modification? Powers now being utilized by Congress, and the President (and states) unquestionably impinge on the U.S. Constitution's guarantee of privacy of contract. These powers range from stopping loan interest, lease or loan payments, evictions, repossessions, shipment of goods, and all manner of aspects of contracted interstate and foreign commerce. In fact, as often noted by U.S. President Donald Trump and others, United States commerce is, for the most part, at a standstill throughout the pandemic period.

This article provides a contemporaneous summary overview of the COVID-19 crisis as it impacts contracts, as a reminder to legal scholars, information for business law students, and for the benefit of non-attorney business managers and consumers. This article provides readers context, and an overview of the legal mechanisms at work during this critical national emergency and a rapidly evolving legal and contractual environment. It also provides food for thought on the potentially lasting impacts and implications for the law of contracts after the immediate crisis has abated.

II. BUSINESS CONTRACTS AND LAW

It is often noted that contracts in the United States take the form of property rights that cannot be taken away

---

[3] Pub.L. 81-774, 64 Stat. 798 (1950) (also see: 50 U.S.C.)

except by due process of law.[4] Indeed, the U.S. Constitution specifically protects the integrity of contracts under most conditions. The U.S. Constitution Article I, Section 10 states: "No state shall enter into any Treaty, Alliance or Confederation; ...or Law impairing the Obligation of Contracts...."[5]

This provision, in 1789, was ahead of its time in western civilization, and has become a key incentive within the U.S. market as businesses normally enjoy the assurance that agreements meeting all the legal requirements of contracts are protected as a matter of law. Such protections do not always exist in other nations by their judiciaries or their economies.

There are those who would suggest that the law of contracts must be interpreted differently than it has historically been interpreted due to the "unique pandemic" currently facing the U.S. and world. Such assumptions are belied by history. To the contrary, because such rights as the Constitution's Contract Clause and Bill of Rights were enacted in the face of continuous fatal health outbreaks in Colonial America, the legal intent of constitutional rights could be argued to apply even in the face of a pandemic. Indeed, Dr. Benjamin Rush, founder of the medical school at University of Pennsylvania, who dealt with frequent epidemics of smallpox in Philadelphia was, himself, an active member of the Constitutional Convention. During the eighteenth century (1699-1799), Philadelphians experienced sixty-six epidemics (thirteen smallpox, six measles, nine respiratory illnesses, eleven scarlet fever, thirteen yellow

---

[4] Leonard Kreynin, *Breach of Contract as a Due Process Violation: Can the Constitution Be a Font of Contract Law?,* 90 COLUM. L. REV. 1098, 1102-1117 (1990).

[5] U.S. Const., Art. I, §10. Note however, that a constitutional exception to government abrogating contracts falls under the bankruptcy power, U.S. Const. Art. I, §8, cl.4.

fever, one flux, two typhoid, three typhus, two diphtheria and six unclassified).

The Yellow Fever Epidemic of 1793, coming just four years after enactment of the Constitution, caused 20,000 people to flee Philadelphia including Congress, the Supreme Court, President George Washington and his government (including Thomas Jefferson and Alexander Hamilton). The epidemic killed over 10% of the city's population (approx. 5,000). Based on the city's 2020 population, this death rate would be equivalent to more than 159,000 deaths today.[6] Notwithstanding, both daily life and the American economy throughout the nation continued in spite of these fatal outbreaks.

It is clear, at least in the context of original intent, that the Framers of the Constitution did not provide for, nor anticipate, a power either of Congress, the Executive or the Judiciary to compromise or suspend fundamental rights of the Bill of Rights, nor the Contract Clause of Article I (or the later application of these provisions to states under the 14th Amendment) in the event of an epidemic or pandemic event. Thus, the use of "Stay at Home" or "Stay at Work" lockdown orders and other strict restrictions is a post- constitutional, or more modern interpretation by judicial review, is often controversial. In the 2020 COVID-19 crisis, those constitutional conflicts as to the limits and interpretation of strict scrutiny standards are already brewing and will ultimately be decided by state and U.S. supreme courts in years to come.

Consequently, the exposure of the American population to the current COVID-19 pandemic is not a unique circumstance in the nation's history, nor is its impact

---

[6] *The Great Fever: Epidemic in Philadelphia*, The American Experience, PBS, https://www.pbs.org/wgbh/americanexperience/features/fever-epidemic-philadelphia-1793/. The U.S. Census estimate for 2020 shows City of Philadelphia population to be 1,591,800, www.census.gov.

on the state of contracts in commercial transactions unique. What differs is the national public policy response, and the judicial interpretation in the instant environment. How the American legal system adapted to these conditions in the past could provide direction, if not understanding, of the path forward as courts deal with the mass of contract disputes already arising in the COVID-19 Crisis.

III. ROAD TO ABSOLUTE PRIVITY OF CONTRACT: GOVERNMENT EXCEPTIONS

Of course, the question is asked by those reading the "plain meaning" text of the Constitution, if the federal and state governments are banned from impairing contract rights, how have those governments been allowed to do so? Judicial review became a post-constitutional power just a few years after the enactment of the Constitution, beginning a long road of constitutional jurisprudence that has changed with changing society norms and, often, the political expediency of the moment. Beginning in 1803, the Supreme Court made clear that, notwithstanding the Constitution's "plain words," what is considered "constitutional" was to be determined by the Supreme Court as the last word.[7]

A. Privacy of Contract: War Exceptions

The initial exceptions to contract enforcement occurred during times the nation was involved in declared wars. In these exigencies, U.S. presidents, state governors by executive orders, or Congress by legislation granted powers to address the emergency of the moment, leaving issues of constitutionality to be debated far after the crisis had passed.

---

[7] As famously stated by Chief Justice John Marshall, "It is emphatically **the province and duty of the judicial department to say what the law is,**" *Marbury v. Madison*, 5 U.S. 137 (1803).

1. Revolutionary War

The Constitution's *contract clause* was enacted in the aftermath of the American Revolution (1775-1781) to prohibit states, federal government and other debtors from reneging on contracts and resultant "IOU" debts issued by states, their agents and militias during times of conflict.[8] Indeed, one of the earliest Supreme Court cases dealt with such an attempt by the State of Georgia to breach a contract in the case of *Chisholm v. Georgia* (1793).[9] Chisholm was the executor for a South Carolina merchant, Farquhar, who had supplied provisions to the Georgia Militia fighting during the Revolutionary War.[10] When it came time to pay for the provisions, Georgia refused claiming "sovereign immunity."[11] Controversial in its time, and perceived as a threat to federalism, the Court, nevertheless, ruled Georgia could not breach the constitutional right of privity of contract, an interest superior to state sovereign immunity.[12]

---

[8] The Contract Clause also served to incorporate provisions established by Congress in the Northwest Territory Ordinance, and as part of the peace treaty with Britain. It also played a key role in protecting individuals' private property against states, as well as prohibiting states from interfering with essential federal obligations. *See,* James W. Ely, Jr., *The Contract Clause: A Constitutional History*, U OF KAN. PRESS, 2016.

[9] 2 U.S. 419.

[10] Doyle Mathis, *Chisholm v. Georgia: Background and Settlement,* 54 Journal of Amer. Hist. 19, 20 (June 1967).

[11] *Id.*

[12] 2 U.S. 419 (1793). The case became highly controversial, not necessarily for the issue of privity of contract but the fact that the State of Georgia was forced to appear in a Federal Court which, at the time, was viewed as a federalism issue. Many legal scholars of the day believed that Georgia, as a sovereign, could not be hailed into the nascent nation's federal court system. To nullify this jurisdictional aspect of the case, Congress passed and the states ratified Const. Amend. XI (1795), banning a state from being sued by "citizens of the state or of foreign states" in federal court.

2. Civil War (1861-1865)

During the Civil War both President Lincoln and Union Generals, as a matter of necessity, invalidated contracts made in the Confederate states. The most obvious destruction of privity of contract was the abolition of slavery and nullification of related contracts by President Lincoln's Executive Order, The Emancipation Proclamation (1862).[13] Questions about the constitutionality of this proclamation were quickly resolved at war's end by the enactment of the 13th Amendment to the Constitution.[14]

Yet, in other cases, privity of contract was such a strongly held legal tenet that it was upheld even in contracts made within states in open rebellion against the Union at the time. Post war, the U.S. Supreme Court ruled in cases such as *Thorington v. Smith* (1868)[15] that "such contracts in the ordinary course of business, and not in aid of the rebellion," could be enforced in federal court "to the extent of their just obligation."[16]

3. World War I (U.S. Involvement-1917-1918)

Congress became so angered at the deterioration of the U.S. railroad system and its impediment to the war effort that it passed the Army Appropriations Act of 1916, giving the President authority to seize the railroads and their contracts from private ownership.[17] President Woodrow Wilson did so in 1917. The railroads were not returned to private control until the Transportation Act of 1920

---

[13] Presidential Proclamation 95, Sept. 22, 1862.
[14] U.S. Const. Amend. XIII.
[15] 75 U.S. 1 (1868).
[16] James Ely, Jr., *The Contract Clause During the Civil War and Reconstruction*, J. S.CT. HIST., 41(3), 2016 at 5.
[17] 39 Stat. 649 (1916).

(Cummins-Esch Act).[18]   The Supreme Court, in 1917, upheld the action, not based on war powers, but on Congress' constitutional power to regulate interstate commerce, including railroads already under federal regulation since 1887.[19] Contract rights were not addressed in the decision.

4. <u>World War II (1941-1945)</u>

In what remains today one of the most notorious violations of not only privity of contract, but also property rights and liberty, during World War II, President Franklin Roosevelt on February 19, 1942, ordered the exclusion and removal of any person (U.S. citizen or not) of Japanese descent from the West Coast.[20] Private property was seized or sold at forced sales for confiscatory prices while the individuals were dispersed to detention camps in interior, rural western states throughout the rest of the war. The constitutionality of the act was challenged in the famous case *Korematsu v. U.S* (1944).[21] In what is considered one of the worst decisions of the U.S. Supreme Court, the majority upheld the President's action on the grounds that national security outweighed these individual rights, including the

---

[18] 41 Stat. 456 (1920).
[19] Wilson v. New 243 U.S. 332 (1917): The court found that U.S. Const. Art. I, Sec. 8, Cl. 3 "Commerce Clause" power was a sufficient legal basis. (Railroads had been federally regulated since enactment of the Interstate Commerce Act of 1887, Pub.L. 49-104, 24 Stat. 379.
[20] EXEC. ORDER, 9066, Feb. 19, 1942.
[21] 323 U.S. 314 (1944). Although by the 1980s there were various apologies from the U.S. government to affected citizens, the case has never been officially overturned by the U.S. Supreme Court. (It was, however, formally condemned seventy-four years later in Trump v. Hawaii, 585 U.S. ___ (2018).

contractual and property rights of American Citizens of Japanese ancestry.[22]

5. Korean War (1950-1952)

In 1950, the United States was embroiled in war in Korea. President Harry S. Truman was at the same time grappling with using a Wage Stabilization Board to avoid the economic problems of World War II including wage and price controls that constrained contracts. In 1951, the United Steel Workers union threatened a nationwide strike which the President believed would imperil defense production and hence, have a major negative impact on the war effort. The steel industry and its labor unions failed to heed the President's warnings of dire consequences to the country and defense, and President Truman on April 8, 1952, proceeded by Executive Order to seize the entire U.S. steel industry.[23] This effectively impaired privity of contract to labor and other contracts of the steel companies. The U.S. Supreme Court quickly intervened in the case of *Youngstown Sheet & Tube Co. v. Sawyer* (1952).[24]

The U.S. Supreme Court, with extraordinary speed, reviewed the entire history of government war seizures, including a recitation of the overriding of privity of contract from the Revolutionary War through World War II.[25] The majority opinion ruled that Truman's actions were unconstitutional and lacking any statutory basis war powers or other) granted by Congress.[26]

---

[22] Scott Bomboy, *The Supreme Court's 'Worst Decision' Lives on in 2016 Campaign,* CONSTITUTION DAILY, (December 18, 2015) https://constitutioncenter.org/blog/the-supreme-courts-worst-decision-lives-on-in-2016-campaign.

[23] EXEC. ORDER 10340, Apr. 8, 1952.

[24] 343 U.S. 579 (1952).

[25] *Id.* at 598 and Appendix 1.

[26] *Id.* at 655.

B. Peace Time: Privity of Contract

As we have seen in this summary, outside of war, and even in the aftermath of war (war being a temporary expedient), the U.S. Supreme Court has held firm to the privity of contract up until the 1930s. An early challenge came in the Supreme Court case *Allegeyer v. Louisiana* (1897), in which a challenge to state restriction on contracting with certain marine insurers was ruled unconstitutional.[27] The court held that the word "liberty" in the Constitution's 14th Amendment buttressed freedom or liberty to contract.[28]

1. Lochner Era: Privity of Contract

The more famous and still controversial Supreme Court contract ruling today came in the case *Lochner v. New York* (1905).[29] Lochner challenged a New York labor law as interfering with his constitutional liberty right to contract.[30] The Supreme Court agreed and for the next 30 years, government attempts to impose social or other contract restrictions were struck down as unconstitutional.[31] This became known as the *Lochner* Era.

2. Post-Lochner Era

---

[27] 165 U.S. 578 (1897).

[28] U.S. Const. Amend. XIV: (1868) "All persons born or naturalized in the United States, and subject to the jurisdiction thereof, are citizens of the United States and of the state wherein they reside. No state shall make or enforce any law which shall abridge the privileges or immunities of citizens of the United States; nor shall any state deprive any person of life, *liberty,* or property, without due process of law; nor deny to any person within its jurisdiction the equal protection of the laws." (1868) (emphasis added).

[29] 198 U.S. 45.

[30] *Id.* at 52.

[31] *Id.* at 64.

With the Stock Market Crash of 1929 and ensuing Great Depression, the Supreme Court began to change its view of contracts in response to the dire national economic conditions. This change was also hastened by the confirmation of President Franklin Roosevelt's more progressive judges to the U.S. Supreme Court. Congress and the President attempted to enact economic safety net programs, such as the minimum wage, to mitigate the continuing negative economic effect of the Depression's impact on the public. *Lochner* became a significant impediment to these objectives as any government mandate to employment contracts or other contracts under *Lochner* would be viewed as violation of liberty to contract.

In 1937, the Supreme Court heard a new challenge to *Lochner* that ultimately ended the Lochner Era. In *West Coast Hotel Co. v. Parrish* (1937), West Coast Hotel challenged a new minimum wage law as interfering with its liberty right to contract, claiming it was an unconstitutional infringement on its right to contract. [32] In *West Coast Hotel*, the Supreme Court overturned precedent. [33]

The Supreme Court upheld the minimum wage law, putting an end to the *Lochner* Era. Chief Justice Charles Evans Hughes' majority opinion explained such liberty is not absolute and in effect, privity of contract is also not absolute:

> But it was recognized …that freedom of contract is a qualified, and not an absolute, right. There is no absolute freedom to do as one wills or to contract as one chooses. The guaranty of liberty does not withdraw from legislative supervision that wide department of activity which consists of the making of

---

[32] 300 U.S. 379 (1937).
[33] *Id.* at 400.

contracts, or deny to government the power to provide restrictive safeguards. Liberty implies the absence of arbitrary restraint, not immunity from reasonable regulations and prohibitions imposed in the interests of the community.[34]

IV. 2020 COVID-19 EMERGING IMPACTS ON CONTRACTS

The current pandemic poses at least two major categories of contract legality issues during the crisis. First is the government's use of emergency powers to invoke or revoke existing contracts in the public interest during an emergency. Such power generally flows at the federal level from the Defense Production Act (DPA) (1950), which provides the President extraordinary powers over the economy in the event of a national defense emergency.[35] Although the national defense emergency has traditionally been considered a *war* in the conventional sense, the COVID-19 pandemic has been deemed to be a war against a deadly pathogen.[36] Thus, the DPA has been activated to date without objection from Congress or any court.

The DPA contains three major sections or presidential powers. The first provides the power to prioritize, accept and, to great extent, impose on industry, contracts necessary for the national defense regardless of the financial impact on the firm. The second provides that the

---

[34] *Id.* Note: Chief Justice Hughes ironically was a Republican appointee, former Governor of New York, former Secretary of State and had run for President in 1916. (The fact that he was convinced to overturn *Lochler* showed the gravity of the Depression's impact on judicial thinking.)

[35] PUB.L. 81-774 (1950).

[36] Philip Wegman, *A Changed Trump Declares War on Coronavirus*, REAL CLEAR POLITICS, Mar. 19, 2020, https://www.realclearpolitics.com/articles/2020/03/19/a_changed_trump_declares_war_on_coronavirus_142705.html.

President may order industries to produce essential, necessary strategic items for the national defense. This has included even the commandeering of private plants to produce products. And, finally, the DPA contains presidential powers to compel the release of necessary supplies in private or public hands to stop hording of critical supplies during the national defense emergency.

The second category of contract impact from the pandemic is the invoking by industry of classic common law and statutory defenses to contract performance and discharge. This includes insurance and other business contracts with no specific provision for such a situation. These attempts to nonetheless interpret out liability will lead to much litigation in the future. The COVID-19 situation has thrown a major complication into contracts, particularly insurance, travel and hospitality companies, but almost every other industry as well. Businesses now cull through their contracts to find words that "could" be interpreted to give them cover to deny claims or enforce contractual agreements while other businesses examine their contracts to justify filing claims. Many cases are arising in which the stretching of textual terms is so extreme as to cause public officials to contemplate regulatory action and, for those receiving denials of claims, to contemplate initiating legal action. The issue has already become the subject of a *Wall Street Journal* headline, particularly with regard to business interruption insurance.[37]

---

[37]Leslie Scism, *Pressure Mounts on Insurance Companies to Pay Out for Coronavirus*, W.S.J. Mar. 30, 2020 at A1.
https://www.wsj.com/articles/pressure-mounts-on-insurance-companies-to-pay-out-for-coronavirus-11585573938?mod=djemRiskCompliance.

A. Defense Production Act (DPA) Actions

Since President Trump's activation of the Defense Production Act, the President has been careful to use the DPA sparingly. In a similar fashion to President Teddy Roosevelt, the DPA is being used as a "Big Stick," to encourage industry to voluntarily come forward knowing that the failure to do so will result in the Act being imposed upon them. Industry also realizes that failing to cooperate in this crisis becomes a public relations problem for the business both in terms of present and future business with consumers and in helping avert further regulatory legislation that may be even more costly.

The DPA is being particularly used to produce and secure essential medical items that, at writing, are life-and-death critical to dealing with the pandemic. These include ventilators, medical protective masks (N95),[38] Personal Protective Gear (PPG) including gowns and face shields, and prescription drugs. Two recent actions provide examples.

1. General Motors

During the current crisis, a number of major manufactures voluntarily announced they would cease their current product production and convert their plants to making critically important ventilators. These included auto companies such as Tesla, Ford and even vacuum cleaner manufacturer Dyson.

President Trump engaged in quick negotiations to have Detroit-based General Motors (GM), the largest auto company (and one with recently shuttered plants) convert to this effort. GM did not react promptly and was alleged to be

---

[38] N95 masks have built in respirators and are used by medical professionals and other industries (for instance, construction). The masks are essential to protect front-line medical personnel and first responders in the war against the coronavirus.

seeking excessive prices.[39] President Trump, indicating GM was wasting time, invoked DPA and ordered GM to produce the ventilators.[40]

> "Our negotiations with GM regarding its ability to supply ventilators have been productive, but our fight against the virus is too urgent to allow the give-and-take of the contracting process to continue to run its normal course," Trump said. "GM was wasting time," the president asserted. "Today's action will help ensure the quick production of ventilators that will save American lives."[41]

2. 3M And Public Policy Legal Risks of Contract

3M, based in Minneapolis, Minnesota is one of the world's largest manufacturers of protective medical masks (N95), medical gowns and other protective medical products.[42] Since the beginning of the pandemic, the demand for masks, especially in large cities such as New York City, Detroit, New Orleans, Seattle and Los Angeles, has become extremely urgent and has far outstripped supply. At the same time, 3M had international contracts for N95

---

[39] Brett Samuels, *Trump Uses Defense Production Act to Require GM to Make Ventilators*, THE HILL, Mar. 27, 2020, https://thehill.com/homenews/administration/489909-trump-uses-defense-production-act-to-require-gm-to-make-ventilators.

[40] *Id.*; Administration of Donald J. Trump, Memorandum on an Order Under the Defense Production Act of 1950 Regarding General Motors Company (March 27, 2020).

[41] *Id.*; Administration of Donald J. Trump, Memorandum on an Order Under the Defense Production Act of 1950 Regarding 3M Company (April 2, 2020).

[42] 3M, https://www.3m.com/3M/en_US/company-us/coronavirus/ (last visited March 23, 2021).

masks, and was exporting its masks while critical shortages grew in the U.S.[43]

The President requested 3M voluntarily divert its masks to needed U.S. domestic use.[44] Refusing to comply, 3M executives first claimed they were primarily obligated under their export contracts to export the masks to foreign customers first.[45] They objected diverting the masks to U.S. domestic needs would cause "humanitarian" issues overseas.[46] 3M's corporate position generated the ire of not only the President but governors and Congress of both parties (as well as the public). President Trump immediately invoked the DPA, obligating 3M to release all inventory to domestic use and expand production at its plants.[47] Future government retaliation toward 3M has also been threatened.[48] The presidential order said he invoked the DPA to make sure "all health and medical resources needed to respond to the spread of COVID-19 are properly distributed to the nation's healthcare systems and others that need them most at this time." [49]

To be sure, 3M, within the United States, created a difficult public image problem. In effect, during the crisis, 3M was telling the American public, whether intending to do so or not, that they were prepared to contribute to U.S.

---

[43] Bill Chappell, *Slammed By Trump, 3M Says N95 Mask Exports From U.S. Should Continue,* NPR, April 3, 2020, https://www.npr.org/sections/coronavirus-live-updates/2020/04/03/826629472/slammed-by-trump-3m-says-n95-mask-exports-from-u-s-should-continue.

[44] *Id.*

[45] *Id.*

[46] *Id.*

[47] *Id.*

[48] Marcy Kreiter, *Coronavirus N95 Mask Shortage: Trump Invokes Defense Production Act against 3M, Threatens Retaliation,* INT'L. BUS. TIMES, Apr. 3, 2020, https://www.ibtimes.com/coronavirus-n95-mask-shortage-trump-invokes-defense-production-act-against-3m-2952222

[49] *Id.*

citizen deaths to secure future international business.[50] Such a position is a problematic business optic to the public and public policy during a domestic emergency. Such a business decision in the midst of a public crisis is fodder for government to react with restrictive laws (*e.g.* the Defense Production Act) and, as a practical matter, may adversely impact its business model long after the crisis has abated.

The public and potential public consequences of 3M's position were not lost on its management, which quickly changed position, ramping up major production for domestic consumption.[51] 3M also began an aggressive campaign to go after vendors engaged in mask price gouging, distribution of counterfeit products and trademark infringement worldwide.[52]

Placing contracts over public safety in a crisis may, in the long term, negatively impact the firm. Businesses that do not heed lessons from history do so at their own financial and legal peril.

V. IGNORING LESSONS OF CRISIS HISTORY: TEXACO

Texaco, in the 1930's, at that time the fourth largest oil company in the world, held large contracts to supply oil and fuel to Nazi Germany and its fascist partner, Spain.[53] By the late 1930s, in the face of Hitler's takeover of European nations and support of fascists in Spain and Italy, Congress

---

[50] Austen Hufford and Joe Palazzolo, *3M Pushes Back on President*, W.S.J., Apr. 4-5, 2020, at A1.
[51] *Id.*
[52] Austin Hufford, *3M Sues Mask-Seller for Alleged Gouging, Trademark Infringement,* W.S.J., Apr. 10, 2020, (https://www.wsj.com/articles/3m-sues-mask-seller-for-alleged-gouging-trademark-infringement-11586529025).
[53] Adam Hochschild, *Fueling Fascism: The Secret History of How Texaco Supplied Oil to Fascists in Spain*, NPR, March 31, 2016, https://www.democracynow.org/2016/3/31/fueling_fascism_the_secret_history_of.

passed a series of Neutrality Acts (1937, 1939) which prohibited supporting either side of the conflict thereby making contracts with those nations illegal.[54]

Notwithstanding the embargo, then Texaco Chairman, Torkid Riber, sympathetic to the Nazis, continued to secretly honor shipments of oil to Fascist Spain and other direct and indirect shipments of oil to Nazi Germany.[55]

By 1940, the U.S., though not yet in the war, was supportive of the allied effort against Hitler led by Great Britain by way of a "Cash and Carry" supply program (later the Lend-Lease Act (1941).[56] By early 1940, the public became aware of Texaco's illegal oil contracts. Texaco, based in New York City, which included a large Jewish and anti-fascist population, encountered an outraged public not the least of which being Texaco's sales were in effect supporting Hitler's murderous concentration camps. Public outcry called for politicians to put Texaco out of business.

In August 1940, the Board of Directors of Texaco removed Chairman Riber and cancelled all contracts and shipments of oil to Nazi Germany and its fascist partners.[57] To repair its thoroughly damaged public image, reputation, even its business survival, Texaco financially bailed out a beloved New York City institution, the Metropolitan Opera, which was on the verge of bankruptcy at the time. Beginning December 7, 1940 (exactly one year prior to Pearl Harbor and U.S. entry into WWII) Texaco generously sponsored the Met and its radio broadcasts.[58] Texaco's sponsorship of this

---

[54] 22 U.S.C. 441, *et. seq.*

[55] Tierney, Dominic, *FDR and the Spanish Civil War: Neutrality and Commitment in the Struggle that Divided America*, Duke University Press, (June 11, 2007).

[56] Pub.L. 77-11, Stat.31 (1941).

[57] Oil Exit Rieber, TIME MAGAZINE, Aug. 26, 1940.

[58] Anthony Sampson, *The Seven Sisters: The Great Oil Companies & the World They Shaped*, PENGUIN PUB., 1975. Texaco's formal support ended in 2004, four years after it was acquired in 2000 by Chevron,

major arts institution endured long after its original desperate purpose faded in public memories.[59]

VI. CARES ACT AND STATE GOVERNORS' EMERGENCY DECLARATIONS

Congress, in the current pandemic emergency, passed the coronavirus, Aid, Relief and Economic Security Act, also known as CARES Act.[60] This $2 trillion stimulus law was the second in a series of emergency measures to bolster the economy during the coronavirus shutdowns. The Act contains elements impacting contracts, but to date, mainly those in which the federal government is a principal party. Thus, it seems, there is unlikely to be resultant constitutional litigation. Impacted contracted payments include deferring interest on federally guaranteed student loans and mortgages as well as deferring lease payments in federally funded housing. Where the federal government subsidizes housing, such as through Federal Housing Authority (FHA) mortgages, rent subsidies and the like, contractual non-payment evictions have been halted. The law also contains unique provisions whereby small businesses may borrow funds necessary to cover their payroll. Provided the business does not lay off the covered employees, the loan will be forgiven after one year.[61]

Standard Oil of California; 64 years after its legal and public relations debacle.

[59] Robin Pogrebin, *ChevronTexaco to Stop Sponsoring Met's Broadcasts*, N.Y. TIMES, https://www.nytimes.com/2003/05/21/arts/chevrontexaco-to-stop-sponsoring-met-s-broadcasts.html (May 21, 2003).

[60] PL 116-136, Mar. 17, 2020.

[61] See: CARE Act of 2020: Business Provisions, Principal, https://www.isvma.org/wp-content/uploads/2020/03/CARES-Act-Business-Provisions-002.pdf (last visited Apr. 7, 2020).

VII. STATE GOVERNORS' EMERGENCY ORDERS

Under the U.S. system of federalism, all states and territories retain inherent police powers which in most cases have been codified in their constitutions and enacted statutes. Typically, these statutes grant extraordinary emergency powers to governors under certain conditions and limitations. These powers often come into play during natural disasters such as hurricanes, floods, earthquakes or tornados, as well as civil riots and insurrections.[62] Throughout the COVID-19 crisis, governors have issued various States of Emergency orders in accordance with their state constitutions and statutes. While these are fully intended to deal with immediate emergency situations, the states are, indeed, abrogating privity of contract. In the *Lochner* Era, no doubt these orders would be constitutionally viewed as improper, albeit *post hoc,* as observed in the aftermath of wars.

However, post-*Lochner*, the orders, if challenged, would more likely fit the *West Coast Hotel* doctrine as prudent and necessary police powers of the state. It will remain to be seen once the instant crisis abates if litigation attempts to challenge state-induced contract breaches or interference with contract in the current national pandemic emergency. As but one example, in the State of South Carolina under statutory Emergency Health Powers,[63] in the case of a severe health emergency the Governor may issue a *State of Health Emergency* at which point, emergency powers are delegated to the state Department of Health and Environmental Control (DHEC) to use virtually unlimited power to abrogate or take over pharmaceutical, health care

---

[62] *See, Federalism 4-4*, Constance E. Bagley, MANAGERS AND THE LEGAL ENVIRONMENT, 9TH ED., Cengage, 2019 at 91.
[63] S.C. Code §44-4-300.

supply or facilities regardless of prior contract provisions, with impunity from liability.[64]

Under a State of Emergency a South Carolina Governor's Executive Order has the further power:

> … when a state of emergency has been declared, the undersigned "may further, cope with such threats and danger, order and direct any person or group of persons to do any act which would in his opinion prevent or minimize danger to life, limb or property, or prevent a breach of the peace; and he may order any person or group of persons to refrain from doing any act or thing which would, in his opinion, endanger life, limb or property, or cause, or tend to cause, a breach of the peace, or endanger the peace   and good order of the State or any section or community thereof, and he shall have full power by use of all appropriate available means to enforce such order or proclamation"[65]

Accordingly, on March 13, 2020, South Carolina Governor Henry McMaster, using such emergency powers declared a *State of Emergency* by Executive Order (and subsequent additional orders)[66] which among other things declared:

---

[64] *See, e.g.*, S.C. Code §44-4-330.

[65] S.C. Code § 1-3-430.

[66] S.C. Gov. E.O. 2020-8 through 10 as of 4/3/2020. https://governor.sc.gov/executive-branch/executive-orders (last visited Apr. 5, 2020).

- All state government offices shall remain open for operation during their normal business hour;
- Visitation at state and local correctional facilities in all 46 counties shall be suspended immediately;
- DHEC shall immediately restrict visitation to nursing homes and assisted living facilities with the exception of end of life situations;
- State price gouging laws shall go into effect immediately;
- The State Emergency Management Plan shall be activated[67]

Effective April 7, 2020, a further Executive Order mandated individuals "Stay In Place" at home, visit only "essential" businesses, and only travel for essentials (food, medicines and the like).[68] Furthermore, his order continued temporary closure of a list of "non-essential" businesses.[69] Violation of the orders are criminal misdemeanors which carry enforcement fines of $100 or 30 days in jail.[70]

If litigation were to result from these orders, it is unlikely, given the extraordinary circumstances, that the South Carolina Supreme Court or any federal court would find this exercise of the state's emergency powers resulted in damages arising from the interference with privity of contract. Rather, the disposition of contracts negatively

---

[67] *South Carolina Governor Declares State of Emergency in Response to Covid-19,* WJBF NEWS, Mar. 13, 2020, https://www.wjbf.com/lifestyle/health/coronavirus/south-carolina-governor-declares-state-of-emergency-in-response-to-covid-19/.

[68] S.C. Gov. E.O. 2020-21 "Home or Work Order;" S.C. Gov. E.O. 2020-17 and 18, "Closure of Non-Essential Businesses" https://governor.sc.gov/executive-branch/executive-orders (last visited Apr. 8, 2020).

[69] *Id.*

[70] S.C. Code § 16-7-10(A).

impacted would fall on the common law defenses which have long been to discharge contracts.

VIII. COMMON LAW CONTRACT DEFENSES: COVID-19 CRISIS

A. *Discharge of Contract by Operation of Law*

Courts have allowed contracts to be "discharged" based upon certain legally recognized circumstances. Here are some selected examples most likely to be encountered by businesses during the COVID-19 shutdown and crisis that are recognized in common law, under the Uniform Commercial Code or statutes within each state or territory.

While these defenses are similar and can sometimes be interchangeable depending on the facts, they have specific differences. Of primary importance is the contract itself, and it is important to read the contract to see if any of these defenses are addressed and/or defined. If not, then the parties must look to the common law, statutes and the UCC for guidance.[71]

1. Impossibility of Performance (Doctrine of Impossibility)

The doctrine of impossibility applies when supervening events occurring after the creation of the contract (*e.g.*, the COVID-19 pandemic) make objective performance impossible. Here, parties would argue they could not have anticipated or reasonably foreseen this event at the time of the contract and could not have guarded against

---

[71] Amy E. Murphy, Christopher J. Schneider and Laci V. Resendiz, *Evaluating Whether COVID-19 Excuses Nonperformance Based on Impossibility, Frustration of Purpose, or Impracticability*, https://millerjohnson.com/publication/evaluating-whether-covid-19-excuses-nonperformance-based -on-impossibility-frustration-of-purpose-or-impracticability.

it. "Where the obligation to perform is absolute, impossibility of performance occurring after the contract is made is not an excuse for nonperformance if the impossibility might have reasonably been anticipated and guarded against in the contract."[72]

What exactly is "impossibility?" As a preliminary matter, it requires that the performance be objectively impossible, not just financially unfavorable or impracticable.[73] If a party can render performance with additional time, money or energy, then impossibility will not be an effective defense.[74] If the doctrine is successfully invoked, the contract is rescinded without liability. The standard explanation for the doctrine is that nonperformance is not a breach if it is caused by a circumstance "the non-occurrence of which was a "basic assumption on which the contract was made."[75]

"Impossibility" is thus a doctrine "for shifting risk to the better able to bear it,

either because he is in a better position to prevent the risk from materializing

or because he can better reduce the disutility of the risk (as by insuring) if the

risk does occur."[76]

---

[72] Huffines v. Swor Sand & GravelCo., Inc., 750 S.W.2d 38, 40 (Tex.App.—Fort Worth, 1988, no writ). *See also,* Northern Indiana Public Service Co. v. Carbon County Coal Co., 799 F.2d 265, 276-78 (7th Cir.1986).

[73] Murphy, *supra.* note 49.

[74] *Id.*

[75] Wisconsin Electric Power v. Union Pacific RR, 557 F.3d 504 (7th Cir, 2009) at 505, *citing* Restatement (Second) of Contracts, introductory note to ch. 11, preceding § 261 (1981), quoting UCC § 2-615.

[76] Wisconsin Electric, *supra.* note 51 at 506, *citing* Associated Gas Distributors v. FERC, 824 F.2d 981, 1016-17 (D.C.Cir. 1987).

Impossibility as a contract defense is applied narrowly by the courts "due in part to judicial recognition that the purpose of contract law is to allocate the risks that might affect performance and that performance should be excused only in extreme circumstances such as when destruction of the subject matter of the contract by an act of God or by law makes performance objectively impossible."[77]

2. Commercial Impracticability

Unlike impossibility, commercial impracticability takes into consideration performance that becomes unreasonably more difficult or expensive than parties contemplated at the time of contracting. Thus, grossly adverse financial impacts of an event causing the contract breach are taken into consideration under this doctrine to avoid major loss. This standard is less rigid and more easily demonstrated than the common law impossibility defense because it does not require a showing that performance is objectively impossible. In theory, the defense of commercial impracticability will excuse performance where performance may be possible, but prohibitively expensive (at least as interpreted through the eyes of a judge and jury).

Courts define this doctrine narrowly, typically where there is: (1) death or incapacity of a person for whom performance is required, (2) destruction of the object contracted; or (3) obstruction or prohibition by legal action. In the context of COVID-19, there are a host of situations which could trigger a contract discharge based upon commercial impracticability or impossibility doctrines:

---

[77] *Kel Kim Corp. v. Cent. Markets, Inc.*, 70 N.Y.2d 900, 902, 519 N.E.2d 295, 296 (1987).

- A severe shortage of raw materials or supplies because an unforeseen shutdown of major sources of supply causes a marked increase in cost or prevents performance altogether;
- A company may no longer be able to ship product to its customers due to forced closure or closures within its supply chain;
- A contractor cannot enter the premises because someone is infected with COVID-19;
- A restaurant may no longer be able to host an event because the government is restricting gatherings of more than 10 people; or
- A hotel may have to cancel reservations because of government-issued travel restrictions.[78]

The United States Supreme Court has defined the doctrine of commercial impracticability in a government contract as "where, after a contract is made, a party's performance is made impracticable without his fault by the occurrence of an event the nonoccurrence of which was a basic assumption on which the contract was made, his duty to render that performance is discharged, unless the language or the circumstances indicate the contrary."[79]

3. Frustration of Purpose

Many states recognize the defense of frustration of purpose, which releases a party from its contractual obligations where an intervening event occurs that

---

[78] Sarah J. Odie and Scott O. Luskin, *Frustration of Purpose and Impracticability of Contracts Due to COVID-19,* PAYNE & FEARS INSIGHTS, Mar. 30, 2020,
https://www.paynefears.com/insights/frustration-purpose-and-impracticability-contracts-due-covid-19.
[79] *Id., see also,* United States v. Winstar Corp., 518 U.S. 839, 904 (1996).

substantially frustrates the purpose of the underlying contract. Similar to commercial impracticability, frustration of purpose involves a supervening, unforeseen event makes it impossible for the contract to meet its purposes. For instance, the doctrine may apply where you have contracted with an officiant for a beach wedding planned for this weekend, but the Governor of South Carolina declares a state of emergency and bans public access to the beach.

The concept first entered common law in the early twentieth century from the 1903 landmark British case, *Krell v. Henry* [Coronation Cases][80] and has since been adopted into American common law. To discharge performance under the doctrine of frustration, three requirements must usually be met:

1. The frustration must relate to the principal purpose of the party in making the contract (both parties must understand that the contract makes little sense without the object that has been frustrated);
2. The frustration must be substantial – it is not enough that the transaction has become less profitable; and
3. The non-occurrence of the frustrating event must have been a basic assumption on which the contract was made.[81]

"In other words, this doctrine applies when the frustrated purpose is so completely the basis of the contract that, as both parties understood, without it, the transaction would have made little sense."[82] Unlike impossibility, this contract

---

[80] 1903, 2 KB 740.

[81] Odie and Luskin, *supra.* note 56. *See also,* Felt v. McCarthy, 922 P.2d 90, 130 Wash.2d. 203, (Wash. Sup. Ct., 1996), *citing* Restatement (Second) of Contracts § 265 (1979).

[82] Jennifer Ancona Semko, *No Force Majeure Clause? Other Potential Options to Excuse Contractual Performance under US Law in the Face of COVID-19,*

defense is available only when the event rendered the contract pointless for both parties.[83] This is a key distinction because courts have been careful not to find commercial frustration if it would only result in allowing one party to withdraw from a poor bargain.[84] In addition, frustration does not offer a defense when the parties had some ability to mitigate to protect the value of the contract, or, the parties had some prior knowledge that allowed them to decide to assume the risk.

B. *Rules of Interpretation*

1. Plain Reading Rule

The importance of using precise contract language cannot be understated. In disputes, the courts read the actual words used in a contract in terms of their plain meaning to a "reasonable person." So a word used in a contract does not mean what a PhD in English, or an accountant, or an engineer would define it. Instead, the court will interpret the word as the "reasonable" general population would fairly read and understand it. The defense, "that's not what we meant" is rarely granted or even considered (based in part on the parole evidence rule).[85] This is demonstrated in the Massachusetts court decision on whether a burrito was defined as a sandwich in a restaurant contract dispute.[86]

---

www.bakermckenzie.com/en/insight/publications/2020/03/no-force-majeure-clause

[83] *Id.*

[84] *Valencia Center, Inc. v. Publix Super Markets, Inc.*, 464 So.2d 1267, 1269 (Fla. 3d DCA 1985).

[85] *Interpreting Contracts: Understanding the Plain Meaning Rule*, https://contract-law.laws.com/interpreting-contracts/plain-meaning-rule (Dec. 22, 2019).

[86] White City Shopping Center, LP. V. PR Restaurants, LLC, 21 Mass. L. Rptr. 565, 2006 WL 3292641 (Mass. Super. 2006) (relying on the common dictionary definition to rule a burrito was not a sandwich.]

2. Construction Against the Drafter

Under this doctrine, the terms of a contract when ambiguous or otherwise in dispute, are interpreted by the principle of *contra proferentem* against the party that wrote it, and in favor of the party that did not write it. (Just as with your home and auto policy, businesses rarely get to write the terms of their insurance policy.)[87]

3. Insurance Rule

For insurance policy contracts, most state insurance laws state all perils for which a policy insures are covered *except* those specifically excluded. [88] Thus, you'll see your auto insurance covers everything *except*, the specific exceptions going on at length for pages and pages in the rest of the policy.[89] As stated by the Court of Appeals of Georgia:

> Insurance is a matter of contract, and the language used is to be accorded its general ordinary meaning, bearing in mind that the contract is to be construed in accordance with the intention and understanding of the parties, and in construing it the court cannot go further than a fair construction of the language used will permit. The contract

---

[87] *Rule of Construction Law and Legal Definition*, US LEGAL.COM, https://definitions.uslegal.com/r/rule-of-construction/ (last visited May 25, 2020)

[88] Where the contract is unambiguous, it must be construed to mean what it says. This rule applies to language limiting coverage. *State Farm Mut. Auto. Ins. Co. v. Sewell*, 223 Ga. 31 (153 SE2d 432).

[89] Barry Zalma, *There is an Obligation for the Insured to Read an Insurance Policy,* MERLIN LAW GROUP, Nov. 21, 2019, (https://www.propertyinsurancecoveragelaw.com/2019/11/articles/insurance/there-is-an-obligation-for-the-insured-to-read-an-insurance-policy/)

must be construed by the words, unless there be some reason for taking the case out of this first great rule for the construction of contracts. There is no greater sanctity and no more mystery about a contract of insurance than any other. The same rules of construction apply to it as to other contracts, and the true rule for their interpretation may be stated to be, that stipulations and conditions in policies of insurance like those in all other contracts, are to have a reasonable intendment, and are to be so construed, if possible, as to avoid forfeitures and to advance the beneficial purposes intended to be accomplished.[90]

Already, insurance executives are raising fears of losses to the industry, claiming that the COVID-19 pandemic and its losses were not anticipated and somehow should be exempted from the very insurance coverage purchased by business and consumers to protect against unforeseen risks and for which insurers profit by spreading risk over vast number of individuals and businesses. The President of Chubb Insurance, Evan Greenberg, in a *Wall St. Journal* Op-Ed article made the argument that "The loss potential in practical terms is infinite, but insurance companies have finite balance sheets."[91]

While there is no doubt that the payment of claims could be catastrophic to insurers who did not prepare exclusionary language in their contracts, it may not diminish

---

[90] Cherokee Credit Life Ins. Co. v. Baker, 119 Ga. App. 579, 168 S.E. 2d. 171 (Ga. Ct. App., 1969) at 579 (internal citations and references omitted).
[91] Evan G. Greenberg, *What Won't Cure Corona: Lawsuits*, W.S.J. Apr. 21, 2020, https://www.wsj.com/articles/what-wont-cure-corona-lawsuits-11587504920.

the fact that pandemics and epidemics were a known liability risk to the industry, even in the immediate era prior to the onset of COVID-19. The law does not normally protect an insurer from its own omissions in contract.[92]

To be sure, government assistance to Chubb and other major insurers may be appropriate to protect the financial stability of the industry as has been done to date with airlines but an across-the-board industry defense to contract liability to their insureds that the insurer lacked knowledge or contingency for such events stretches credibility.

Consider the industry risk exposure of recent past events including SARS (2003) and MERS (2012) (both variants of coronavirus), H1N1 "Swine Flu," and Zika Virus (2015-16) among others. Chubb states it is "the world's largest publicly traded P&C insurance company and a leading commercial lines insurer in the U.S."[93] Ironically, Chubb was founded in 1792 (a year before the Philadelphia Yellow Fever 1793 pandemic) and has survived centuries of experience with epidemics and pandemics, including the famous "Spanish Flu" of 1917-18.[94]

4. *Force Majeure* Clauses

Force Majeure (from the French: superior force) is generally defined as an event or an effect that can be neither anticipated nor controlled and includes both acts of nature (sometimes called acts of "God") and acts of people.[95] Most, if not all, commercial contracts contain a

---

[92] Prudential Insurance v. United States Lines 686 F. Supp. 469 (S.D.NY, 1988) holding Prudential liable for the over $90 million loan contract mistake it made by recording the wrong amount of ship loans.
[93] Chubb, https://www.chubb.com/us-en/about-chubb/who-we-are.html (last visited March 21, 2021).
[94] *Id.*
[95] Black's Law Dictionary (7th ed. 1999).

"*force majeure*" clause, which aims to apportion liability or exclude certain liabilities resulting from the above-mentioned acts of nature (for example, hurricanes, tornadoes, earthquakes, etc.) and/or acts of people (such as riots, strikes, wars, etc.). (For example, since September 11, 2001, most insurance policies now exclude damages from terrorism and even nuclear damages. (Even here, the event not excluded must be unforeseen and outside the contract language.

> Modern contracting parties often do contract around the doctrine [of impossibility], though not by making the promisor liable for any and every failure to perform rather by specifying the failures that will excuse performance. The clauses in which they do this are called *force majeure* ("superior force") clauses. ...But it is essential to an understanding ... that a *force majeure* clause must always be interpreted in accordance with its language and context, like any other provision in a written contract, rather than with reference to its name. It is not enough to say that the parties must have meant that performance would be excused if it would be "impossible" within the meaning that the word has been given in cases interpreting the common law doctrine.[96]

The *force majeure* clause is usually viewed as an obscure contract clause or simply "boilerplate" that most people have come to largely ignore. But when some

---

[96] Wisconsin Electric, *supra*. note 51, at 507 (internal citations omitted).

catastrophic event occurs, one party will look to its contract assuming that it will be able to recover its loss, only to realize after reading the *force majeure* clause (usually for the first time) that the loss does not quite fit into the definition set forth in the contract. Some may just assume that the coronavirus is an "act of God," but is it? How is an "act of God" defined in the contract itself? Does it include an epidemic or a pandemic, and does it reference a particular standard (e.g. WHO or CDC)?[97] Most will find this is not the case. Is there a distinction between naturally occurring disasters and government actions in anticipation or response? [98]

This point will likely see litigation in the near future. Why? Because the actual cause of the loss will be determinative. For example, suppose a business seeks to recover for losses under its commercial insurance policy, citing its "business interruption clause" resulting from being shut down during the COVID-19 pandemic. The insurance company then cites the *force majeure* clause that excludes "acts of God" from coverage. Case closed, right? Perhaps not. Does the business owner have a case? The owner may argue that the covered loss was not caused by the pandemic at all; rather, it was caused by the local government ordering businesses to be shut down. The other side may argue that COVID-19 was not an "Act of God" at all but rather an act of human negligence, the allegation being that it escaped from a virus lab in Wuhan, China. Such allegation is under active investigation by the U.S., U.N. agencies and other nations.[99]

---

[97] David S. Robinson, "*Force Majeure*: is COVID-19 an Act of God?", https://www.nexsenpruet.com/insights/force-majeure-is-covid-19-an-act-of-god.
[98] *Id.*
[99] Alex Berezow, PhD, *Best Evidence Yet that Coronavirus Came from Wuhan BSL-4 Lab*, AM. COUNCIL ON SCIENCE AND HEALTH, Apr. 13,

The same scenario can be envisioned if one party to a contract tries to avoid a contractual obligation delivery of product, performance of a service, etc. due to the pandemic. Attorneys say a multitude of companies have found themselves unable to perform services because their employees are sick, at home with children, or prevented from coming to work due to state or local order.[100] Manufacturers that receive parts in the global supply chain from China have also been affected, as well as any company that planned an event with more than ten people present.[101] Weddings, birthday parties, meetings, conventions and countless other gatherings have been cancelled and/or postponed indefinitely as people wait out their local stay at home orders.

Who is the "breaching" party in such a case? Are the deposits refunded? Are the venues obligated to reschedule events? These are issues and disputes that will play out in the near future among a variety of state and federal courts and ultimately to the appellate levels.

IX. THE CORONAVIRUS CONTRACT CONUNDRUM

Insurance is a form of contract. As is often the case, insurance companies go to great lengths to write contract policies for auto, homes, buildings and business interruption, with extraordinarily specific terms that minimize their risk (claims) and maximize the premiums acquired (revenue). The former Kemper Group Insurance, in the 1980's one the largest insurers in America, hired English majors only as policy underwriters rather than business majors for this

---

2020 (https://www.acsh.org/news/2020/04/13/best-evidence-yet-coronavirus-came-wuhan-bsl-4-lab-14712)
[100] Lydia Wheeler, "Coronavirus Threatens to Flood Courts with Contract Disputes" (https://news.bloomberglaw.com/health-law-and-business/coronavirus-threatens-to-flood-courts-with-contract-disputes.)
[101] *Id.*

specific purpose.[102] The goal is to come up with language sufficient to "cap" liability to the maximum extent possible.[103]

As a result, for centuries, the process of insurance claims has manifested as a "cat and mouse" game in contract interpretation. An insurer's "interpretation" of a word or phrase can often defy the English language, hence the courts step in. Contract interpretation disputes fuel litigation, including the proverbial accident attorneys replete with TV advertising and other categories of trial lawyers in America's contingent fee legal system. Not surprisingly, a major percent of South Carolina Supreme Court and other state Supreme Court cases each year are insurance contract disputes over the definition and interpretation of words.

Now comes the first pandemic since 1918 shutting down businesses; those businesses are now, in desperation, turning to their business interruption insurance policies. When the SARS epidemic hit some years ago, many insurers added the exclusion for "viruses and bacteria." But as we can see, the context of the sentences are subject to a different interpretation which lawyers will doubtless argue.

The "pathogen clauses" frequently seen today in home, business or rental insurance normally apply to shutting down one's home or business for "virus, mold or bacteria" specific to the business premises, not all commerce in all areas. The policy holder business will argue in favor of coverage, claiming that a pathogen specific to their business did not shut down the business, rather, the international pandemic did. Therein will be the conflict in courts. The second business argument for coverage would be those noted

---

[102] Co-author Henry Lowenstein during the 1980's period was Corporate Director of Management Development and Training worldwide for Kemper Group.

[103] Wisconsin Electric, *supra.* note 51 at 506 "The analogy is to a provision in a fire insurance contract that excepts from coverage a fire caused by an act of war."

previously, namely, the loss of business shutdown was due to an act of the government (emergency orders) as a defensive response to the pandemic. And, the impossibility and impracticality doctrines may apply.[104]

X. CONTRACT LAW REALITY AND ETHICS JUDICIAL

The insurance companies or other businesses with contracts attempting to enforce questionable clauses and denials in the COVID-19 crisis face this reality: court decisions are made by judges and juries, real people, all affected by the same emergency. Any jury pool would be comprised of people who have lost their jobs, have lost someone they know, had the virus themselves and have been all manner of inconvenienced, and are unlikely to hold favorable opinions on unreasonable litigation positions. Jury selection *voir dire* won't be able to protect from it. There simply is not a pool of jurors who have not been affected by COVID-19. Likewise, the judges have all experienced the impact of the pandemic on their courts. The courts in South Carolina were closed from March to early May 2020 for COVID-19.) As a result, insurance companies, never popular with the courts even in the best of times, face a steep hill to climb in seeking to have claim denials upheld.

Even if insurers win in the short term, long term would likely result in a backlash. State regulators and legislators may seek to level the playing field by enacting regulations and laws banning the practice in question in the future. This could, in turn, raise the cost of doing business

---

[104] *Id.* "So it is no surprise that in *Allanwilde Transport Corp. v. Vacuum Oil Co.,* 248 U.S. 377, 385-86, 39 S. Ct. 147, 63 L. Ed. 312 (1919), the doctrine of impossibility was successfully invoked when a wartime embargo prevented the performance of a shipping contract because the ship could not complete its voyage. See also *Israel v. Luckenbach S.S. Co.,* 6 F.2d 996 (2d Cir. 1925)."

and lower insurer profits. Let's face it, insurance is a necessary but often unpopular product.

XI. MARKETING STRATEGY / BUSINESS-SMART RESPONSES

Smart firms and insurers play the long game and realize, outside of the immediate panic, that the customers impacted today are their customers tomorrow—and customers can have long memories. On television, consumers are bombarded with daily ads for auto insurance: Geico, Liberty Mutual, Allstate, State Farm, Farmers. The moment of truth is when the business has to deliver on its promises. A business that unfairly denies a claim is likely to lose a customer to a competitor. We already see smart businesses and insurers implementing positive long-term strategies despite the short term costs.

A. Humana, Aetna and Medicare

Some of the largest medical insurers, despite their contract policy terms, voluntarily waived all co-payments and deductibles for any medical claim caused by COVID-19.[105] Government programs, including MEDICARE and MEDICAID, also relaxed various provisions to accommodate COVID-19 cases.

B. Viking Cruise Line

The cruise ship-travel industry has taken a major blow due to COVID-19. Rather than throw passengers to the terms of their "Travel Insurance Policies," Viking Cruises added an option for cancellations allowing the choice of a

---

[105] Health Insurance Providers Respond to Coronavirus (COVID-19) AHIP, May 22, 2020, https://www.ahip.org/health-insurance-providers-respond-to-coronavirus-covid-19/.

voucher for 125% of the cruise cost to be applied to a future Viking Cruise.[106] This offer preserved and enhanced future business, while conserving desperately needed cash that would have had been paid out as refunds.

C. Airlines

Almost all air carriers are waiving "No cancellation, no refund clauses" and allowing future rebooking with no additional change-fees. Airlines, buoyed by financial assistance from the federal government, have also liberalized cash refund policies to passengers who cancelled flights.[107]

D. Auto Insurance

In recognition of the substantial drop in driving during the COVID-19 crisis and thus a substantial reduction in risk exposure, major auto insurers began issuing voluntary refunds to auto insurance policy holders as a good faith attempt to share the savings of lower auto accidents during the crisis. This policy has become a major marketing tool.[108]

E. Voluntary Business Conversions

Much like Janzen transitioned from making sports, underwear and T-shirts to making parachutes for the military during World War II, during the COVID-19 crisis, Janzen

---

[106] Torstein Hagen, Chairman, *Viking, Letter to Cruise Guests,* Mar. 30, 2020.

[107] *COVID-19 response: Airline industry struggles to come up with a standard approach*, GULF NEWS, May 19, 2020, https://gulfnews.com/business/aviation/covid-19-response-airline-industry-struggles-to-come-up-with-a-standard-approach-1.1589862179113.

[108] *See, e.g.,* SAFECO Insurance, *Personal Auto Customer Relief Refund*, provided 15% auto insurance refund on two months auto premium from April 7 to May 15, 2020.

and other clothing-textile manufacturers have converted their plants to making "Made in the USA" personal protective equipment. Other luxury brands have likewise converted to making COVID-19 related products.[109] The positive public outreach efforts are being made without legal coercion.

CEOs of major firms such as Walmart, United Technologies, Abbot Labs, Proctor and Gamble, Dyson, Ford, UPS, and FedEx are flocking to state and presidential press conferences to voluntarily suspend their contract restrictions and convert to helping solve problems. No doubt, in the short term, the goal is to avoid Defense Production Act mandates, but savvy strategic thinking is also creating positive public relations and consumer loyalty. Whether the rethinking of contract modification, refund or other policies permanently alters major industries and insurance policies after the current crisis has abated remains to be seen. Industries that are inflexible during the crisis face a steep and costly litigation future, drawing the ire of public policy makers and, no doubt, the public at large.

Because the COVID-19 pandemic presents a catastrophic event unseen in over 100 years, many businesses were lulled into a sense of complacency that such an event would not happen or would not have any strategic impact on particular contracts. It was not uncommon to see *force majeure* clauses silent on the matter, even in the later 1990's with the Ebola, MERS and SARS epidemics that were primarily confined overseas.

---

[109] Ingrid Schmidt, Fashion brands are making face masks, medical gowns for the coronavirus crisis, *L.A. Times*, Mar. 24, 2020, https://www.latimes.com/lifestyle/story/2020-03-24/fashion-brands-face-masks-medical-surgical-gowns-coronavirus.

XII. CONCLUSION

COVID-19 and its aftermath will see commercial attorneys quickly revising contract forms with *force majeure* clauses to exclude "Pandemics and Epidemics" or to include specific contract discharge provisions. Such exclusions and limitations will quickly be found in newly issued insurance policies of all kinds; with insurers petitioning state regulators for approval where necessary. Perhaps our long-held law of contracts in each state may, too, emerge differently than the past; new legal precedents will doubtlessly emerge. The post COVID-19 era legal environment of business will certainly result in a landscape of legal changes. It will test longstanding legal doctrines, precedents and the judicial review between strict constructionist interpretation of contracts and novel interpretations of this twenty-first century.

How business reacts to these unprecedented circumstances may have a huge effect on future legislation by Congress, state legislatures and local government bodies. To what extent such future legislation complicates contracting, ultimately increasing transaction costs, is unknown.

To be sure, the crisis has planted seeds of major legal changes to come. COVID-19 is neither the first, nor the last, global conundrum of contracts to be faced in the dynamic legal environment of business.

KISOR V. WILKIE: CABINING ADMINISTRATIVE AGENCIES' DEFERENCE IN INTERPRETING REGULATIONS

EDWARD J. SCHOEN *
DIANE Y. HUGHES **

I. INTRODUCTION

Kisor v. Wilkie[1] was one of the most anticipated and closely watched cases of the U.S. Supreme Court's 2018-2019 term. As noted in SCOTUSblog, the *Kisor* case "could be one of the most consequential of the term, because the justices will decide whether to overrule a line of cases instructing courts to defer to an agency's interpretation of its own regulation." The Court's ruling, the blog noted, "could have a significant impact far beyond veterans' benefits, from the environment to immigration, and it could also shed more light on when and whether the justices are willing to overrule their prior cases."[2] Moreover, *Kisor* is "significant because it is part of a broader conservative attack on the administrative state, and the consequences of that attack, if successful, could be tremendous." Likewise, the recent additions of Justices Gorsuch and Kavanaugh to the Court heightened expectations that the Court would

---

* Professor of Management, Rohrer College of Business, Rowan University, Glassboro, New Jersey
** Associate Professor of Accounting, Rohrer College of Business, Rowan University, Glassboro, New Jersey
[1] Kisor v. Wilkie, 139 S. Ct. 2400 (2019).
[2] Amy Howe, *Justices To Tackle Important Agency-Deference Question*, SCOTUSBlog (Mar. 20, 2019, 11:55 AM), https://www.scotusblog.com/2019/03/argument-preview-justices-to-tackle-important-agency-deference-question/.

terminate the deference accorded agencies in interpreting their own regulations,[3] particularly because the U.S. Supreme Court in granting certiorari stipulated the sole issue to be addressed was whether its two prior decisions establishing deference should be overruled.[4] Finally, *Kisor* clearly attracted the keen interest of business groups and conservatives who want to weaken federal regulators and have targeted the deference precedents for overturn, because, in their view, the deference theory "gives agencies too much power."[5]

This article closely examines: (1) the two major U.S. Supreme Court decisions—*Seminole Rock* and *Auer*—which recognized and launched the judicial deference granted to agency interpretation of its own regulations; (2) two U.S. Supreme Court decisions—*Gonzales v. Oregon*

---

[3] Brianne Gorod, *Why Kisor is a Case to Watch*, SCOTUSblog (Jan. 31, 2019, 11:14 AM), https://www.scotusblog.com/2019/01/symposium-why-kisor-is-a-case-to-watch/. *See,* Erwin Chemerinsky, *What SCOTUS rulings are we still waiting for?*, ABA JOURNAL (May 2, 2019), https://www.abajournal.com/news/article/chemerinsky-remaining-rulings-to-address-administrative-state-stare-decisis. "Many have suggested that the conservative majority on the Supreme Court wants to impose greater judicial oversight of the actions of federal administrative agencies. Both of the two newest justices, Neil M. Gorsuch and Brett Kavanaugh, advocated this in their decisions as federal court of appeals judges. This has led to much discussion of whether the high court might reconsider its ruling in *Chevron*, which held that courts should defer to federal agencies in their interpretation of the statutes that they are implementing. (Although no case this term is likely to reconsider *Chevron* deference, in *Kisor v. Wilkie*, the court will consider a related doctrine: the principle that courts should defer to agencies in interpreting their own regulations.")
[4] Kisor, 239 S. Ct. at 2409.
[5] Debra Cassens Weiss, *Auer Deference Precedent Targeted By Business Groups May Be Overturned by SCOTUS,*" ABA JOURNAL (December 10, 2018), https://www.abajournal.com/news/article/supreme_court_to_consider_overruling_auer_deference_precedent_targeted_by_b.

and *Christopher v. SmithKline Beecham Corp.*—which have imposed limitations on judicial deference to government agencies' interpretation of their own regulations; (3) the U.S. Supreme Court's decision in *Kisor*; and (4) the reactions of legal experts and commentators to the *Kisor* decision. The article also examines the U.S. Supreme Court decision in *Chevron*, which decided that regulations developed by government agencies interpreting genuinely ambiguous statutes are also entitled to judicial deference, contrasts *Chevron* deference to *Kisor* deference, and predicts that *Kisor* will have little substantive influence on *Chevron* deference.

II. (*SEMINOLE ROCK* AND *AUER'S* DEFERENCE TO AGENCIES' INTERPRETATION OF AMBIGUOUS REGULATIONS

The judicial doctrine of granting deference to an administrative agency's interpretation of its own genuinely ambiguous regulation stems from two U.S. Supreme Court decisions: *Bowles v. Seminole Rock & Sand Co.*[6] and *Auer v. Robbins.*[7] In *Seminole Rock*, the U.S. Supreme Court reviewed price control regulations issued by the Administrator of the Office of Price Administration ("OPA") under Section 2(a) of the Emergency Price Control Act of 1942,[8] the central component of which prohibited sellers from charging any more than the prices charged during the selected base period of March 1 to 31, 1942.[9]

---

[6] Bowles v. Seminole Rock & Sand Co., 325 U.S. 410 (1945).

[7] Auer v. Robbins, 519 U.S. 452 (1997).

[8] 56 Stat. 23, 24, 50 U.S.C.A. Appendix s 902(a); Seminole Rock, 325 U.S. at 411.

[9] Seminole Rock, 325 U.S. at 413 ("On April 28, 1942, . . . [the Administrator] issued the General Maximum Price Regulation. (This brought the entire economy of the nation under price control with certain minor exceptions. (The core of the regulation was the requirement that each seller shall charge no more than the prices which

OPA made subsequent refinements of this restriction for specific groups of commodities.[10] One such refinement was Maximum Price Regulation 188, which covered specified building materials and consumer goods:

> [T]he maximum price for any article which was delivered or offered for delivery in March, 1942, by the manufacturer, shall be the highest price charged by the manufacturer during March, 1942 as defined in s 1499.163 for the article. Section 1499.163(a)(2)6 in turn provides that for purposes of this regulation the term: Highest price charged during March, 1942 means (i) The highest price which the seller charged to a purchaser of the same class for delivery of the article or material during March, 1942; or (ii) If the seller made no such delivery during March, 1942, such seller's highest offering price to a purchaser of the same class for delivery of the article or material during that month; or (iii) If the seller made no such delivery and had no such offering price to a purchaser of the same class during March, 1942, the highest price charged by the seller during March, 1942, to a purchaser of a different class, adjusted to reflect the seller's customary

---

he charged during the selected base period of March 1 to 31, 1942. While still applying this general price 'freeze' as of March, 1942, numerous specialized regulations relating to particular groups of commodities subsequently have made certain refinements and modifications of the general regulation. (Maximum Price Regulation No. 188, covering specified building materials and consumers' goods, is of this number.")

[10] *Id.* at 413.

differential between the two classes of purchasers.[11]

Respondent, Seminole Rock and Sand Co. ("Seminole"), a manufacturer of crushed stone which was subject Maximum Price Regulation No. 188, had several relevant sales of crushed stone.[12] In October 1941, prior to the effective date of Maximum Price Regulation No. 188, Seminole agreed to sell crushed stone to Seaboard Air Line Railway ("Seaboard") on a demand basis at 60 cents per ton, and actually delivered the stone to Seaboard in March 1942.[13] In January 1942, Seminole also agreed to sell crushed stone to V. P. Loftis Co., for $1.50 a ton.[14] Some of the crushed stone was delivered in January 1942; the remainder of the crushed stone was delivered in August 1942.[15] After the effective date of Maximum Price Regulation No. 188, Seminole agreed to sell crushed stone to Seaboard at 85 cents and $1.00 per ton.[16]

OPA challenged the price Seminole charged Seaboard (85 cents and $1.00 per ton) in Federal District Court, claimed the maximum price Seminole could charge was 60 cents per ton (the price Seminole charged for the crushed stone when it was delivered in March 1942), and sought an injunction preventing Seminole from violating Maximum Price Regulation No. 188.[17] The District Court determined that the highest price charged by Seminole during March, 1942, was $1.50 per ton, and that Seminole's sale of crushed stone to Seaboard did not exceed that ceiling

---

[11] *Id.* at 414-15 (internal quotation marks omitted).
[12] *Id.* at 412.
[13] *Id.*
[14] *Id.*
[15] *Id.*
[16] *Id.*
[17] *Id.* at 412-13.

price.[18] The Fifth Circuit Court of Appeals affirmed, and the U.S. Supreme Court granted certiorari.[19]

The U.S. Supreme Court noted that the central issue to be resolved was the meaning and applicability of Rule (i) of Maximum Price Regulation 188.[20] Seminole took the position that, in order for Rule (i) to apply, both the establishment of the sales price and the delivery of the crushed stone must have been occurred in March, 1942, and hence applying the 60 cents price ceiling was erroneous.[21] The OPA claimed that Rule (i) was applicable and controlling because there was an actual delivery of crushed stone in March, 1942.[22]

In resolving this issue, the Court observed that "more than one meaning may be attached to the phrase 'highest price charged during March, 1942' . . . and [that] the phrase might be construed to mean only the actual charges or sales made during March, regardless of the delivery dates . . . or

---

[18] *Id.* at 412.

[19] *Id.* at 413.

[20] *Id.* at 415.

[21] *Id.*

[22] This position was promulgated by OPA in a bulletin issued by the Administrator entitled "What Every Retailer Should Know About the General Maximum Price Regulation," and made available to manufacturers, wholesalers and retailers, in which the Administrator stated: "The highest price charged during March 1942 means the highest price which the retailer charged for an article actually delivered during that month or, if he did not make any delivery of that article during March, then his highest offering price for delivery of that article during March" and "It shall be carefully noted that actual delivery during March, rather than the making of a sale during March is controlling." This position was also published in the Administrator's First Quarterly Report to Congress, in which he defined the "highest price charges" as follows: "(1) It means the top price for which an article was delivered during March 1942, in completion of a sale to a purchaser of the same class .... (2) If there was no actual delivery of a particular article during March, the seller may establish as his maximum price the highest price at which he offered the article for sale during that month." *Id.* at 417.

to charges made for actual delivery in March."[23] The Court agreed with the position advanced by OPA: "We can only conclude, therefore, that for the purposes of rule (i) the highest price charged for an article delivered during March, 1942, is the seller's ceiling price regardless of the time when the sale or charge was made."[24] This conclusion was facilitated by the Court's earlier statement that, in interpreting an administrative regulation, "a court must necessarily look to the administrative construction of the regulation if the meaning of the words used is in doubt" and "the ultimate criterion is the administrative interpretation, which becomes of controlling weight unless it is plainly erroneous or inconsistent with the regulation."[25]

In *Auer*, police sergeants and a lieutenant employed by the St. Louis Police Department brought suit against members of the St. Louis Board of Police Commissioners ("Board") to obtain overtime pay under § 7(a)(1) of the Fair Labor Standards Act of 1938.[26] The Board denied their eligibility for overtime pay, reasoning that the police officers were exempt "bona fide executive, administrative or professional" employees.[27] Under Department of Labor (DOL) regulations, one requirement for exempt status was that "the employee earn a specified minimum amount on a 'salary basis,' " *i.e.*, the employee must "regularly receive[] each pay period on a weekly, or less frequent basis, a predetermined amount constituting all or part of his compensation, which amount is not subject to reductions because of variations in the quality or quantity of the work

---

[23] *Id.* at 415.

[24] *Id.* at 416.

[25] *Id.* at 414. This statement of deference was made with neither legal authority nor even limited reasoning. Linda D. Jellum, *Will the Supreme Court Retain, Cabin, or Eliminate Seminole Rock and Auer Deference?*, 46 ABA PREVIEW 35, 37 (2019).

[26] Auer, 519 U.S. at 455; 29 U.S.C. § 207(a)(1).

[27] Auer, 519 U.S. at 455.

performed."[28] The police officers argued that, because their compensation could be cut for a variety of disciplinary infractions which were related to the "quality or quantity" of the work performed, they did not qualify as salaried employees and were entitled to overtime compensation.[29] The District Court found the police officers were paid on a salary basis and were not entitled to overtime pay; the Eighth Circuit of Court of Appeals affirmed; and the U.S. Supreme Court granted certiorari.[30]

The U.S. Supreme Court noted (1) the Department of Labor ("DOL") policy manual lists a total of 58 possible rule violations and a corresponding range of disciplinary penalties for each violation (some of which involve deductions in pay); (2) all department employees are nominally covered by the manual; and (3) the manual does not single out a category of employees (salaried or non-salaried) for whom pay deductions are a form of punishment.[31] The Secretary of Labor in an *amicus* brief argued that the imposition of pay deduction penalties would undermine the exemption for salaried employees only if the pay deduction penalties are employed "as a practical matter," *i.e.*, there is an actual practice of making pay deductions or the agency's policy creates a "significant

---

[28] *Id.*, citing 29 C.F.R. §§ 541.1(f), 541.2(e), 541.3(e), 541.118(a) (1996). The U.S. Supreme Court summarized the history of the salary-basis test as follows:

> The FLSA did not apply to state and local employees when the salary-basis test was adopted in 1940. In 1974 Congress extended FLSA coverage to virtually all public-sector employees, and in 1985 we held that this exercise of power was consistent with the Tenth Amendment. The salary-basis test has existed largely in its present form since 1954, and is expressly applicable to public-sector employees.

Auer, 519 U.S. at 457 (internal citations omitted).
[29] *Id.* at 455.
[30] *Id.* at 455-56
[31] *Id.* at 462.

likelihood" pay deductions will be made.[32]   Because there was no indication of either an actual practice of deducting police officer's pay,[33] or an employment policy which makes the imposition of pay deductions significantly likely in the case of police officers, it was possible (1) that pay deduction penalties apply only to non-salaried employees, or (2) that the pay deduction policy was not or would not be invoked against salaried employees.[34] Hence, the existence of pay deduction penalties was insufficient to disqualify the police officers as salaried employees.[35] Moreover, the Court noted, the Secretary of Labor's interpretation of the DOL's own regulations is controlling unless it is "plainly erroneous or inconsistent with the regulation," and hence is entitled to judicial deference.[36] Furthermore, the Court stated, there is no reason to doubt the Secretary's interpretation actually reflects the agency's "fair and considered judgment" on the issue, and there is no need to require the Secretary to interpret his own regulations narrowly, because he is "free to write the regulations as broadly as he wishes, subject only to the limits imposed by the statute."[37]   Hence, judicial deference to the agency's interpretation of its own regulation carried the day, and the Court upheld the police officers' exempt status under the overtime provisions of FLSA.[38]

Seminole Rock and *Auer* provide substantial deference to the government agency's interpretation of its

---

[32] *Id.* at 461.

[33] The record showed that the salary of one police officer, Sergeant Guzy, was voluntarily reduced. Because Sergeant Guzy did not reside in St. Louis, he violated the police department's residency requirement. In order to keep his job, he agreed to a one-time reduction in his pay. Because this pay reduction was not related to a disciplinary matter, it did not disqualify him as a salaried police officer. *Id.* at 463.

[34] *Id.* at 462.

[35] *Id.* at 461.

[36] *Id.*

[37] *Id.* at 462-63.

[38] *Id.* at 464.

own regulations: the regulation is entitled to "controlling weight unless it is plainly erroneous or inconsistent with the regulation."[39] In *Seminole Rock*, the Court gleaned the government agency's interpretation of the regulation from a bulletin issued by OPA prior to its challenge to the price Seminole charged Seaboard for the crushed stone and from an annual report issued by OPA.[40] In *Auer*, the Court gleaned the government agency's interpretation of the regulation from the DOL's *amicus* brief drafted well after the police officers initiated their claim for overtime pay.[41] Regardless of the source and the timing of the interpretation, substantial deference was due.

A succinct summary of the arguments in support of and in opposition to *Seminole Rock* and *Auer* deference appears in SCOTUSblog.[42] Supporters of deference claim that it derives from the *Chevron* doctrine,[43] under which courts will generally accept the agencies' interpretation of ambiguities in its enabling legislation as long as that interpretation, appearing the agencies' regulations, is reasonable. Similarly, supporters contend deference should be accorded to agencies in interpreting ambiguities in their regulations, because the agency which wrote the regulation likely knows best what it means. Supporters also argue that granting *Seminole Rock* and *Auer* deference facilitates courts' reviews of challenges to an agency's interpretation of its regulation, because the sole question to be resolved by the court is whether the agency's interpretation is reasonable, avoiding the struggle of determining the best interpretation. Likewise, supporters argue, granting deference to the agencies' interpretation of their own

---

[39] Seminole Rock, 325 U.S. at 414, and Auer, 519 U.S. at 461.

[40] Seminole Rock, 325 U.S. at 414.

[41] Auer, 519 U.S. at 461.

[42] Howe, *supra* note.

[43] Chevron U.S.A. Inc. v. Natural Resources Defense Council, Inc., 467 U.S. 837 (1984). (*See, infra,* text accompanying notes 175 - 197.

regulations likely produces greater consistency in court decisions, because courts throughout the country are more likely to uphold the agency's interpretation.[44]

Opponents of *Seminole Rock* and *Auer* claim that deference confers too much power on administrative agencies to announce its interpretation of its regulations without engaging in rule-making procedures involving notice, comment, and rule resolution; deference also short circuits the Administrative Procedures Act which assigned the role of resolving ambiguities in regulations to the courts, rather than administrative agencies.[45] Moreover, opponents argue, deference stymies individuals who struggle to comply with the agencies' regulations only to discover later that the agency has a different interpretation of the regulation. Most importantly, opponents contend, deference raises constitutional concerns, because (1) an agency's interpretation of its own regulations does not give adequate and fair notice to individuals affected by the regulation in violation of due process, and (2) deference improperly skews the separation of powers, because courts abdicate their responsibility to interpret the law and act as a check on the political branches of the government.[46]

---

[44] Howe, *supra* note. *See,* Gillian Metzger, *The puzzling and troubling grant in Kisor*, SCOTUSblog (Jan. 30, 2019, 10:22 AM), https://www.scotusblog.com/2019/01/symposium-the-puzzling-and-troubling-grant-in-kisor.

[45] 5 USC §551 *et seq.* (1946).

[46] Howe, *supra* note. *See,* Jonathan Adler, *Government agencies shouldn't get to put a thumb on the scales*, SCOTUSblog (Jan. 31, 2019, 2:36 PM), https://www.scotusblog.com/2019/01/symposium-government-agencies-shouldnt-get-to-put-a-thumb-on-the-scales/; Elizabeth Murrill, *Reverse Seminole Roc and Auer*, SCOTUSblog (Jan. 30, 2019, 1:40 PM), https://www.scotusblog.com/2019/01/symposium-reverse-seminole-rock-and-auer/; Adrian Vermeule, *Tampering with the structure of administrative law*, SCOTUSblog (Jan. 29, 2019, 10:23 AM), https://www.scotusblog.com/2019/01/symposium-tampering-with-the-structure-of-administrative-law/; and Kimberly Hermann, *The Supreme Court and the forgotten "Three Ring Government"*,

III. U.S. Supreme Court Limitations on *Auer* and *Seminole Rock*

Since deciding *Seminole Rock* and *Auer*, the U.S. Supreme Court has twice re-examined and narrowed their scope: (1) deference is not due when "the underlying regulation does little more than restate the terms of the statute itself," and (2) deference is not due when the agency's interpretation would "impose potentially massive liability...for conduct that occurred well before [an agency's] interpretation was announced."[47]

The first limitation was recognized in *Gonzales v. Oregon*,[48] in which the Court refused to grant deference to an interpretive rule of the United States Attorney General threatening criminal action against physicians who assist in the suicide of terminally ill patients pursuant to Oregon's Death With Dignity Act ("ODWDA").[49] Under ODWDA, upon the request of a terminally ill patient, physicians are permitted to dispense or prescribe lethal doses of drugs which are regulated under the Controlled Substances Act ("CSA").[50] The drugs prescribed under ODWDA are

---

SCOTUSblog (Jan. 29, 2019, 2:19 PM), https://www.scotusblog.com/2019/01/symposium-the-supreme-court-and-the-forgotten-three-ring-government/.

[47] Jellum, *supra* note, at 37.

[48] Gonzales v. Oregon, 546 U.S. 243 (2006).

[49] *Id.* at 249; Ore. Rev. Stat. § 127.800 *et seq.* (2003). In order to be eligible to request a prescription under ODWDA, patients must receive a diagnosis from their attending physician that they have an incurable or irreversible disease that, within reasonable medical judgment will cause death within six months. Gonzales, 546 U.S. at 252. ODWDA was enacted in 1994 and survived a ballot measure seeking its repeal in 1997. *Id.*

[50] Gonzales, 546 U.S. at 252; 84 Stat. 1242, as amended, 21 U.S.C. § 801 *et seq.* The attending physician is required to confirm the patient's request is voluntary and informed, and, if not, to refer the patients to counseling to ascertain whether they are suffering from a psychological disorder or depression causing impaired judgment. If the attending

Schedule II drugs which, in order to prevent the diversion of controlled substances, may be prescribed only pursuant to a written, nonrenewable prescription issued by a physician registered with the Attorney General.[51] Notably, CSA explicitly does not preempt state law unless the specific provision of the state law is in "positive conflict" with a provision of CSA.[52]

On November 9, 2001, seven years after the enactment of ODWDA, the Attorney General, John Ashcroft, issued an interpretive rule intended to restrict the use of controlled substances in physician-assisted suicide.[53] The interpretive rule stated: (1) assisting suicide is not a

---

physician determined the request is voluntary and informed, a second, consulting physician must examine the patient and the patient's medical records and confirm the attending physician's conclusion. (The physicians must keep detailed medical records of the process leading to the final prescription, and are prohibited from administering the lethal drug. The patients end their lives by ingesting the medication prescribed. Gonzales, 546 U.S. at 252.

[51] "When deciding whether a practitioner's registration is in the public interest, the Attorney General shall consider:
(1) The recommendation of the appropriate State licensing board or professional disciplinary authority.
(2) The applicant's experience in dispensing, or conducting research with respect to controlled substances.
(3) The applicant's conviction record under Federal or State laws relating to the manufacture, distribution, or dispensing of controlled substances.
(4) Compliance with applicable State, Federal, or local laws relating to controlled substances.
(5) Such other conduct which may threaten the public health and safety."
Id. at 251 (internal quotation marks omitted.)

[52] *Id.* ("No provision of this subchapter shall be construed as indicating an intent on the part of the Congress to occupy the field in which that provision operates . . . to the exclusion of any State law on the same subject matter which would otherwise be within the authority of the State, unless there is a positive conflict between that provision . . . and that State law so that the two cannot consistently stand together. § 903")

[53] Gonzales, 546 U.S. at 249.

valid medical practice and is unlawful under the CSA, and (2) the registration of physicians who prescribe, dispense or administer federally controlled substances may be revoked or suspended.[54] Because a physician is prohibited from prescribing controlled substances unless he is registered with the Attorney General, the revocation or suspension of the physician's registration threatened to "substantially disrupt the entire ODWDA regime."[55] In response, the State of Oregon challenged the interpretive ruling in Federal District Court, which issued a permanent injunction against its enforcement.[56] A divided panel of the Ninth Circuit Court of Appeals affirmed, because either the interpretive rule impermissibly made a medical procedure authorized under Oregon law a federal offense or the interpretive rule could "not be squared" with the language of the CSA.[57] The U.S. Supreme Court granted the Attorney General's petition for certiorari.

The U.S. Supreme Court addressed two principal issues in affirming the decision of the Ninth Circuit: (1) whether the Attorney General was authorized to interfere with Oregon's assisted suicide regimen, and (2) whether the interpretive rule was entitled to judicial deference.[58] In resolving the first issue, the Court observed that CSA gives the Attorney General limited powers to promulgate rules relating solely to the "registration" and "control" of identified controlled substances.[59] Because the interpretive rule did not relate to the addition or deletion of a drug to or from one of the five schedules established by CSA, it cannot fall under the Attorney General's control authority.[60] Nor

---

[54] *Id.* at 249, 254.
[55] *Id.* at 254.
[56] *Id.* at 255.
[57] *Id.*
[58] *Id.* at 260.
[59] *Id.* at 260-261.
[60] *Id.*

does the power to control substances authorize the Attorney General to promulgate his view of legitimate medical practice.[61]   Likewise, CSA restricts the authority of the Attorney General to deregister a physician's registrations to only circumstances involving (1) physicians who falsified their application, were convicted of a felony relating to controlled substances, or had their state license revoked, or (2) physician registrations that may be "inconsistent with the public interest," which is resolved by considering five factors, including the state's recommendation, compliance with state, federal and local controlled substances law, and public health and safety.[62]   Because none of the factors identified in the first circumstance occurred, and because the interpretive rule did not consider the five required factors, the Court held that the Attorney General's interpretive rule cannot be supported by his authority to register.[63]

Addressing the second issue, the Court observed that the language in the regulation under which the Attorney General issued his interpretive rule was identical to the language appearing in CSA and hence there was no ambiguity to be resolved.[64]   The Court noted:

> Simply put, the existence of a parroting regulation does not change the fact that the question here is not the meaning of the regulation but the meaning of the statute. An agency does not acquire special authority to interpret its own words when, instead of using its expertise and experience to

---

[61] *Id.* at 260-61

[62] *Id.*

[63] *Id.* at 261.

[64] *Id.* at 257. The regulation uses the terms "legitimate medical purpose" and "the course of professional practice." Because these terms are identical to two statutory phrases in CSA, the regulation fails to provide an interpretation of the statute.

formulate a regulation, it has elected merely to paraphrase the statutory language.[65]

Hence, the Court decided that "the CSA's prescription requirement does not authorize the Attorney General to bar dispensing controlled substances for assisted suicide in the face of a state medical regime permitting such conduct,"[66] and that judicial deference is not owed to administrative regulations that merely parrot the language of the enabling legislation because there is no ambiguity requiring interpretation.[67]

The second limitation imposed on *Seminole Rock* and *Auer*—namely, that deference is not due when the agency's interpretation imposes a potentially massive liability on parties relying on an agency's prior interpretation of a regulation—was recognized in *Christopher v. SmithKline Beecham Corp*,[68] in which the U.S. Supreme Court ruled that salespersons employed as pharmaceutical sales representatives by SmithKline Beecham ("SKB") qualified as outside salespersons and were exempt from the overtime pay provisions of the Fair Labor Standards Act.[69] Under regulations issued by the Department of Labor ("DOL") in 1938, 1940, 1949, and 2004, outside salespersons employed by pharmaceutical companies were deemed to be exempt employees not entitled to overtime pay, because they "in some sense made a sale."[70]

Nonetheless, two pharmaceutical representatives ("petitioners") employed by SKB initiated an action in Federal District Court seeking compensation for overtime

---

[65] *Id.*

[66] *Id.* at 274-75.

[67] *Id.* at 258.

[68] Christopher v. SmithKline Beecham Corp., 567 U.S. 142 (2012).

[69] *Id.* at 147.

[70] *Id.* at 148-49, citing 69 Fed.Reg. 22122 (2004).

pay.[71] The District Court agreed the two employees were exempt from overtime pay provisions and granted summary judgment in favor of SKB.[72] After the District Court entered its order, the petitioners filed a motion to amend the judgment based on the DOL's assertion in an uninvited *amicus* brief filed in a similar action pending in the Second Circuit that pharmaceutical representatives were not exempt employees, because they did not actually "make a sale" with the meaning of the regulations.[73] The petitioners asked the District Court to grant deference to the DOL's interpretation of the regulation appearing in the *amicus* brief, but the District Court denied the motion.[74] The Court of Appeals for the Ninth Circuit agreed the interpretation was not entitled to deference and affirmed, and the U.S. Supreme Court granted certiorari.[75]

The U.S. Supreme Court ruled that the interpretation of the regulation appearing in the *amicus* brief was not entitled to deference, because the DOL's revised interpretation imposed "potentially massive liability" on SKB and other pharmaceutical companies for conduct that transpired well before the interpretation was announced, contrary to the principles that agencies should provide regulated parties "fair warning of the conduct" mandated or prohibited by the regulation and that agencies should not change an interpretation of a regulation that imposes a "new liability" on individuals for past actions undertaken in good-faith reliance on an interpretation of a regulation.[76] Because (1) the pharmaceutical industry had no reason to suspect the DOL's longstanding interpretation would change, (2) the DOL never initiated any enforcement actions to suggest the

---

[71] *Id.* at 152.
[72] *Id.* at 153.
[73] *Id.*
[74] *Id.*
[75] *Id.* at 151-53.
[76] *Id.* at 156-57.

drug industry was acting unlawfully, (3) the DOL's announcement of its revised interpretation was preceded by a prolonged period of inaction, and (4) the nature of the work of pharmaceutical sales representatives had not materially changed for decades, the Court held that granting deference would constitute unfair surprise on the industry.[77] Hence, "whatever the general merits of *Auer* deference, it is unwarranted here."[78] Instead, the Court stated, the DOL's revised interpretation must be evaluated by "the validity of its reasoning, its consistency with earlier and later pronouncements, and all those factors which give the power to persuade."[79] The Court stated the revised interpretation, so evaluated, "lacks the hallmarks of thorough consideration" and is flatly inconsistent with the FLSA's definition of a sale to mean a consignment for sale.[80] Hence the Court determined that the DOL's revised interpretation is "neither entitled to *Auer* deference nor persuasive in its own right."[81] Employing "traditional tools of interpretation" to ascertain whether petitioners are exempt outside salespersons, the Court determined the DOL's revised interpretation is inconsistent with the text of FLSA, the definition of "sales" in related DOL regulations, and the intent of Congress to define "sale" in a broad manner.[82] Given this broader interpretation, the Court easily concluded "the petitioners made sales for the purposes of FLSA" and therefore are exempt outside salesmen not entitled to overtime compensation.[83]

---

[77] *Id.* at 157-58.
[78] *Id.* at 159.
[79] *Id.*, citing U.S. v. Mead Corp., 533 U.S. 218, 228, 121 S.Ct. 2164, 150 L.Ed.2d 292.
[80] *Id.* at 159-60; 29 U.S.C.A. § 203(k).
[81] *Id.* at 160-61.
[82] *Id.* at 161-63.
[83] *Id.* at 165.

IV. *KISOR V. WILKIE*'S PROCEDURAL HISTORY

In 1982, Petitioner, James Kisor, a Vietnam War veteran, applied for disability benefits from the Department of Veterans Affairs ("VA"), claiming he suffered from post-traumatic stress disorder ("PTSD") stemming from his participation in a military action called Operation Harvest Moon.[84] Because the VA's evaluating psychiatrist determined that he did not suffer from PTSD, the VA denied Kisor's application for benefits.[85] Twenty-four years later, Kisor moved to reopen his claim, and, based on a new psychiatric report, the VA agreed that Kisor suffered from PTSD, but granted him benefits prospectively from the time of his motion to reopen rather than from the date of his first application.[86] The Board of Veterans Appeals ("the Board") affirmed the VA's timing decision on the basis of an agency rule permitting retroactive benefits if there were "relevant official service department records" which were not considered in its initial decision denying benefits.[87] While the Board recognized Kisor submitted two new service records that confirmed his participation on Operation Harvest Moon, the Board determined those records were not "relevant" to the previous psychiatrist's finding that he did not have PTSD.[88]

The Court of Appeals for Veterans Claims affirmed the Board's decision.[89] Granting deference to the Board's interpretation of the VA rule, the Court of Appeals for the

---

[84] *Kisor*, 139 S. Ct. at 2409.
[85] *Id.*
[86] *Id.*
[87] *Id.*
[88] *Id.* ("[The] documents were not relevant to the decision in May 1983 because the basis of the denial was that a diagnosis of PTSD was not warranted, not a dispute as to whether or not the Veteran engaged in combat.")
[89] *Id.*

Federal Circuit affirmed.[90] In his argument to the Federal Circuit, Kisor claimed a service record is deemed "relevant" if it relates to some other criteria for obtaining disability benefits.[91] Facing Kisor's and the VA's differing interpretations of the VA rule, the Federal Circuit agreed the VA rule was ambiguous, because the VA rule did not specifically address whether "relevant" records must cast doubt on VA's prior decision denying benefits (the VA's interpretation) or may more broadly support the veteran's claim (Kisor's interpretation).[92] Because both Kisor's interpretation and the VA's interpretation were reasonable, the Federal Circuit granted deference to the VA's interpretation of the rule.[93] Hence, the VA's construction of its regulation prevailed, because it was not "plainly erroneous or inconsistent with the VA's regulatory framework."[94] Applying that standard, the Federal Circuit upheld the VA's interpretation and affirmed the denial of retroactive benefits; the U.S. Supreme Court granted certiorari.[95]

V. U.S. SUPREME COURT DECISION IN *KISOR V. WILKIE*

While the U.S. Supreme Court's decision in *Kisor* was unanimous in its judgment, the opinions are splintered.[96] Justice Kagan wrote the plurality opinion, in which Justices Ginsburg, Breyer and Sotomayor joined.[97] Chief Justice Robert concurred in parts I, II-B, III-A and IV.[98] Justice

---

[90] Kisor v. Shulkin, 869 F.3d 1360, 1368 (2017).
[91] *Kisor*, 139 S. Ct. at 2409.
[92] *Id.*
[93] *Id.*
[94] *Id.*
[95] *Id.*
[96] *Id.* at 2407.
[97] *Id.*
[98] *Id.* at 2424. (*See,* Sullivan and Cromwell LLP, Kisor v. Wilkie: *U.S. Supreme Court Upholds – But Limits – Auer Deference* (June 26, 2019)

Gorsuch concurred in the judgment, joined in full by Justice Thomas and in part by Justices Alito and Kavanaugh.[99] Justice Kavanaugh concurred in the judgment.[100]

---

at 4, https://www.sullcrom.com/files/upload/SC-Publication-Kisor-v.-Wilkie-U.S.-Supreme-Court-Upholds%E2%80%93But-Limits%E2%80%93Auer-Deference.pdf Chief Justice Roberts "suggested that the distance between the majority . . . and the concurrence in the judgment by Justice Gorsuch . . . is not as great as it may initially appear." He further observed that *Auer* raises concerns distinct from those raised by *Chevron*, which governs judicial deference to agency interpretations of statutes."

[99] *Id.* "Justice Gorsuch argued that *Auer*'s rule of deference should be overturned because it requires judges to 'abdicate their job of interpreting the law' in violation of both the APA and constitutional separation-of-powers principles. (He also contested the majority's invocation of *stare decisis*, arguing that the doctrine did not apply where, as here, the precedent at issue announced a general interpretive methodology rather than a specific holding about the meaning of a particular law. Justice Gorsuch also criticized the majority for appealing to *stare decisis* while simultaneously changing *Auer* by limiting its application.")

[100] *Kisor*, 139 S. Ct. at 2448. Justice Kavanaugh agreed with Chief Justice Roberts that *Auer,* as cabined by the plurality opinion, reduced the distance between the majority view and Justice Gorsuch's view, but "not a great as it may initially appear." He stated that, if a reviewing court employed all of the traditional tools of construction, it will ascertain the best interpretation of the regulation. He thought, however, that formally reversing *Auer* would have been a more direct approach, noting "[u]mpires in games at Wrigley Field do not defer to the Cubs manager's in-game interpretation of Wrigley's ground rules. (So too here." *Id.* (Justice Kavanaugh also agreed with Chief Justice Roberts that the decision in *Auer* is distinct from *Chevron* ("[i]ssues surrounding judicial deference to agency interpretations of their own regulations are distinct from those raised in connection with judicial deference to agency interpretations of statutes enacted by Congress.") *Id.* at 2449. Justice Alito concurred in Justice Kavanaugh's concurring opinion, putting Justice Alito in favor of the "cabined" *Auer* deference and the differentiation of *Auer* from *Chevron*. *Id.* at 2448. In her opinion, Justice Kagan cites *Chevron* seven time in support of *Auer*. *Id.* at 2414, 2415, 2416, and 2417.

In *Kisor*, the U.S. Supreme Court upheld but significantly restricted the deference an administrative agency can employ in interpreting its own regulations.[101]

---

[101] *Kisor* was one of three important administrative law decisions handed down by the U.S. Supreme Court during its 2018-2019 term, an indication, perhaps, that the Court is increasingly interested in the administrative state. Erwin Chemerinsky, *How the Roberts Court Could Alter the Administrative State*, ABA JOURNAL (September 4, 2019, 6:00 AM), https://www.abajournal.com/news/article/chemerinsky-the-roberts-court-could-alter-the-administrative-state.

In Gundy v. United States, 139 S. Ct. 2116 (2019), the Court considered an "impermissible delegation" challenge to the Sex Offender Registration and Notification Act ("SORNA"), 120 Stat. 590, 34 U.S.C. § 20901 *et seq.*, under which a convicted sex offender must register in every state where the offender resides, works or studies. Any sex offender who knowingly fails to do so and travels in interstate commerce may be imprisoned for up to ten years, 18 U.S.C. § 2250(a). (Section 20913(d) of SORNA authorized the Attorney General to specify the applicability of the registration requirements to offenders convicted before the enactment of SORNA. The Attorney General did so, issuing a final rule in December 2010 providing SORNA applies to all pre-Act offenders, 75 Fed. Reg. 81850. *Gundy*, 139 S. Ct. at 2122. Petitioner, Herman Gundy, pleaded guilty under Maryland law to sexually assaulting a minor. After his release from prison, he moved to and resided in New York, but failed to register in New York as a sex offender, and was convicted of violating § 2250. Gundy claimed that authorizing the Attorney General to apply SORNA to pre-Act offenders was an unconstitutional delegation of legislative power. The District Court and the Court of Appeals for the Second Circuit rejected that claim, "as had every other court (including eleven Courts of Appeals) to consider the issue," and the U.S. Supreme Court granted certiorari. *Id.* at 2122. Justice Kagan, joined by Justices Ginsburg, Breyer and Sotomayor, wrote the plurality opinion upholding Gundy's conviction, in which she determined that the delegation of that authority to the Attorney General "easily passes constitutional muster" and that,"[i]ndeed, if SORNA's delegation is unconstitutional, then most of the government is unconstitutional." *Id.* at 2121, 2129, 2130. Justice Alito concurred in the judgment, writing: "If a majority of this Court were willing to reconsider the approach we have taken for the past 84 years, I would support that effort. But because a majority is not willing to do that, it would be freakish to single out the provision at issue here for special treatment." *Id.* at 2131.

The other administrative law decision issued by the U.S. Supreme Court in its 2018-2019 term is Department of Commerce v. New York, 139 S. Ct. 2551 (2019), in which the Court addressed the citizenship question that, in March 2018, Secretary of Commerce Wilbur Ross decided to reinstate on the 2020 census forms. In response, two groups of plaintiffs filed suit in Federal District Court in New York challenging his decision. The actions were consolidated. *Id.* at 2562-64. The District Court decided that the Secretary's action was "arbitrary and capricious, based on a pretextual rationale, and violated the Census Act." The District Court vacated the Secretary's decision and enjoined him from including the citizenship question on the census. *Id.* at 2564-565. The Government appealed to the Second Circuit and also asked the U.S. Supreme Court for expedited review because the census form had to be finalized by the end of June, 2019. *Id.* at 2565. In a 5-4 decision authored by Chief Justice Roberts, and joined by Justices Ginsburg, Breyer, Sotomayor and Kagan, the Court decided that including the citizenship question did not violate either the Enumeration Clause of the Constitution or the Census Act. *Id.* at 2567, 2568, 2573-574. The Court concluded that the Government failed to provide a sufficient justification for its decision to reinstate the citizenship question to meet the requirements of the Administrative Procedures Act, namely "[r]easoned decision making" which explains the agency's action. *Id.* at 2576. The Court determined that the reason advanced by the Government – obtaining census-based citizenship data which would permit better enforcement of the Voting Rights Act ("VRA") – "seems to have been contrived," and that "viewing the evidence as a whole" the Government failed to adequately explain how improved citizenship data leads to better enforcement of the VRA. "What was provided here" the Court said, "was more of a distraction" than reasoned decision making. *Id.* at 2575-576. Hence the Court remanded the case to give the Commerce Department the opportunity to justify the inclusion of the citizenship question. *Id.* at 2576. The Trump Administration subsequently decided not to proceed further in order to have the census forms printed on a timely basis. Chemerinsky, *supra.*

While the Court noted that permitting administrative agencies to exercise such deference "retains an important role in construing agency regulations," it also recognized "deference is sometimes appropriate and sometimes not" and "[w]hether to apply it depends on a variety of considerations that we have noted now and again, but compile and further develop today" in order that such deference may be "potent in its place, but cabined in its scope."[102]

The Court addressed the multitude of reasons agency regulations may genuinely be ambiguous (such as not clearly analyzing an issue, being susceptible to more than one reasonable reading, careless drafting, awkward wording or opaque construction),[103] and provided insightful examples of ambiguous regulations: (1) whether Americans with Disabilities Act regulations mandating that people with disabilities have lines of sight at sporting events comparable to members of the general public means the Washington Wizards must construct seating so that wheelchair seating can see the game with lines of sight over spectators when they rise to their feet or when they remain seated; (2) whether the Transportation Security Administration regulations, which requires that liquids, gels, and aerosols in carry-on baggage be packed in containers smaller than 3.4 ounces and carried in a clear plastic bag applied to a packed jar of truffle pâté in the same way; or (3) whether a Mine Safety and Health Administration regulation requiring employers to report occupational diseases within two weeks after they are diagnosed clearly defines the term "diagnosed." [104]

---

[102] *Id.* at 2408. "Cabined" is frequently defined as "confined to close quarters." *See*, Your Dictionary, https://www.yourdictionary.com/cabined; *see also*, Merriam Webster Disctionary, https://www.merriam-webster.com/dictionary/cabin ("to confine or restrain").

[103] *Kisor*, 139 S. Ct. at 2410.

[104] *Id.* at 2410.

Deference, the Court explained, presumes that the agency will carry out the intent of Congress, that the agency which wrote the regulation has better insight into its meaning, and that the agency's judgment is grounded in policy concerns underlying the regulatory ambiguity.[105]   Furthermore, deference leads to greater consistency in interpreting genuinely ambiguous rules, because judges are far less likely to know the meaning of the regulation and bypassing piecemeal judicial interpretations likely leads to greater uniformity,[106] illustrated by *Auer* itself:

> [F]our Circuits held that police captains were "subject to" pay deductions for disciplinary infractions if a police manual said they were, even if the department had never docked anyone. Two other Circuits held that captains were "subject to" pay deductions only if the department's actual practice made that punishment a realistic possibility. . . Had the agency issued an interpretation before all those rulings (rather than, as actually happened, in a brief in this Court), a deference rule would have averted most of that conflict and uncertainty.[107]

The Court then examined "some of the limits inherent in the *Auer* doctrine."[108]   "First and foremost, a court should not afford *Auer* deference unless the regulation is genuinely ambiguous," *i.e.*, after exhausting all of the "traditional tools" of construction, the court must conclude

---

[105] *Id.* at 2412-13.

[106] *Id.* at 2413-14.

[107] *Id.* at 2414. Because the legal principles examined by the Court in Part II-A of the decision did not garner a majority vote, they do not represent binding precedent. *See, supra,* text accompanying notes 89-95.

[108] *Id.* at 2415.

"the meaning of the words used is in doubt" and more than one "reasonable construction of a regulation" exists.[109] Second, the agency's reading must be reasonable, *i.e.*, it falls "within the bounds of reasonable interpretation." Third, the court "must make an independent inquiry into whether the character and context of the agency interpretation entitles it to controlling weight," *i.e.*, the agency's regulatory interpretation (1) is the agency's "authoritative" or "official position" rather than an *ad hoc* statement not reflecting the agency's views, (2) emanates from agency officials or staff, (3) implicates in some way the agency's substantive expertise, (4) is the agency's "fair and considered judgment," and (5) does not create "unfair surprise" to the regulated parties."[110]

The Court next rejected the two statutory arguments advanced by Kisor to abandon *Auer* deference: (1) *Auer* is inconsistent with the judicial review provision found in Section 706 of the Administrative Procedures Act (APA),[111]

---

[109] *Id.*

[110] *Id.* at 2416-18.

[111] 5 U.S.C. § 706, Pub.L. 89-554, Sept. 6, 1966, 80 Stat. 393. "To the extent necessary to decision and when presented, the reviewing court shall decide all relevant questions of law, interpret constitutional and statutory provisions, and determine the meaning or applicability of the terms of an agency action. The reviewing court shall--
(1) compel agency action unlawfully withheld or unreasonably delayed; and
(2) hold unlawful and set aside agency action, findings, and conclusions found to be--
  (A) arbitrary, capricious, an abuse of discretion, or otherwise not in accordance with law;
  (B) contrary to constitutional right, power, privilege, or immunity;
  (C) in excess of statutory jurisdiction, authority, or limitations, or short of statutory right;
  (D) without observance of procedure required by law;
  (E) unsupported by substantial evidence in a case subject to sections 556 and 557 of this title or otherwise reviewed on the record of an agency hearing provided by statute; or

and (2) *Auer* wrongfully circumvents the APA's notice and comment procedures required in rulemaking under Section 553 of the APA.[112] The Court determined that granting

---

    (F) unwarranted by the facts to the extent that the facts are subject to trial de novo by the reviewing court.
In making the foregoing determinations, the court shall review the whole record or those parts of it cited by a party, and due account shall be taken of the rule of prejudicial error."
[112] 5 U.S.C. § 553, Pub.L. 89-554, Sept. 6, 1966, 80 Stat. 383:
    "(a) This section applies, according to the provisions thereof, except to the extent that there is involved—
        (1) a military or foreign affairs function of the United States; or
        (2) a matter relating to agency management or personnel or to public property, loans, grants, benefits, or contracts.
    (b) General notice of proposed rule making shall be published in the Federal Register, unless persons subject thereto are named and either personally served or otherwise have actual notice thereof in accordance with law. The notice shall include--
        (1) a statement of the time, place, and nature of public rule making proceedings;
        (2) reference to the legal authority under which the rule is proposed; and
        (3) either the terms or substance of the proposed rule or a description of the subjects and issues involved.
Except when notice or hearing is required by statute, this subsection does not apply--
        (A) to interpretative rules, general statements of policy, or rules of agency organization, procedure, or practice; or
        (B) when the agency for good cause finds and incorporates the finding and a brief statement of reasons therefor in the rules issued that notice and public procedure thereon are impracticable, unnecessary, or contrary to the public interest.
    (c) After notice required by this section, the agency shall give interested persons an opportunity to participate in the rule making through submission of written data, views, or arguments with or without opportunity for oral presentation. After consideration of the relevant matter presented, the agency shall incorporate in the rules adopted a concise general statement of their basis and purpose. When rules are required by statute to be made on the record after opportunity for an agency hearing, sections 556 and 557 of this title apply instead of this subsection.

deference to an agency's interpretation of its own regulations is perfectly consistent with Section 706 of the APA.[113] The Court noted that deference cannot be granted unless, after using the traditional methods of interpretation and performing a "thoroughgoing" review, the court finds that the regulation is "genuinely susceptible to multiple reasonable meanings" and that the agency's interpretation lines up with one of those meanings and is "authoritative, expertise-based, considered, and fair to the regulated parties."[114] Performing this task, the Court states, provides "meaningful judicial review" required by Section 706.[115] Furthermore, the practice of granting deference existed at the time of the APA's enactment, and the APA did not suggest that that the practice should be curtailed.[116] Hence, the APA did not "significantly alter the common law of judicial review of agency action."[117]

The Court also determined that *Auer* does not circumvent the notice and comment procedures of the APA's rulemaking requirements under Section 553.[118] The Court noted that, unlike the issuance of "legislative rules," the APA permits agencies to issue "interpretive rules" without

---

(d) The required publication or service of a substantive rule shall be made not less than 30 days before its effective date, except--
  (1) a substantive rule which grants or recognizes an exemption or relieves a restriction;
  (2) interpretative rules and statements of policy; or
  (3) as otherwise provided by the agency for good cause found and published with the rule.
(e) Each agency shall give an interested person the right to petition for the issuance, amendment, or repeal of a rule."

[113] *Kisor*, 139 S. Ct. at 2418-19.
[114] *Id.* at 2420.
[115] *Id.* at 2419.
[116] *Id.*
[117] *Id.* at 2419-20. The legal principles examined by the Court in Part III-A of the decision did not garner a majority vote, and are therefore not binding precedent. *See, supra,* text accompanying notes 96 - 100.
[118] *Id.* at 2420.

notice and comment,[119] because interpretive rules, unlike legislative rules, do not "have the force and effect of law" and do not otherwise "bind private parties."[120] Rather, interpretive rules merely advise the public of the agency's understanding and likely application of its legislative rules, and granting deference to interpretive rules does not confer the "force and effect of law," because interpretive rules can never form "the basis for an enforcement action."[121] In contrast, an enforcement action can be undertaken only pursuant to a legislative rule, which must go through notice and comment in order to be valid.[122] Likewise, when a court decides to grant deference to an agency's interpretation of its regulations, the court must comply with the same "procedural values" which are contained in the notice and comment requirements of Section 553, and hence *Auer* deference "reinforces, rather than undermines, the ideas of fairness and informed decision making at the core of the APA."[123]

The Court also rejected Kisor's policy argument that regulatory agencies are encouraged to issue vague regulations so that the agency can later impose whatever interpretation of those rules it prefers.[124] The Court stated that there was "[n]o real evidence – indeed, scarcely an anecdote" - to support the assertion, and two noted scholars who closely studied the claim wrote: '[W]e are unaware of, and no one has pointed to, any regulation in American history that, because of *Auer*, was designed vaguely.'"[125] Likewise, regulatory agencies have strong incentives to

---

[119] *Id.*

[120] 5 U.S.C. § 553 explicitly provides that notice and comment provisions do not apply to interpretive rules. *See, supra,* note 99.

[121] *Kisor*, 139 S. Ct. at 2420.

[122] *Id.*

[123] *Id.* at 2420-21.

[124] *Id.* at 2421.

[125] *Id.* citing Sunstein & Vermeule, *The Unbearable Rightness of Auer*, 84 U. CHI. L. REV. 297, 308 (2017).

write clear and precise regulations.[126] Regulators "want their regulations to be effective and clarity promotes compliance," and the issuance of ambiguous regulations poses two long-term risks to the agency: increasing the chance of an adverse court decision overturning the regulation and facilitating the ability of "future administrations, with different views, to reinterpret the rules to their own liking."[127] Similarly, "regulated parties often push for precision from an agency so that they know what they can and cannot do."[128] The Court concluded, "Add all of that up and Kisor's ungrounded theory of incentives contributes nothing to the case against *Auer*."[129]

The Court also rejected Kisor's constitutional argument that *Auer* violates the "separation of powers principles" in two respects: usurping the interpretative power of the courts and improperly commingling legislative and judicial functions within an agency.[130] With respect to the former, the Court noted: "[T]his opinion has already met [this argument] head-on. Properly understood and applied, *Auer* does no such thing. In all the ways we have described, courts retain a firm grip on the interpretive function."[131] With respect to the latter, the Court noted that commingling of legislative and judicial functions within an agency has been going on "since the beginning of the Republic," and "does not violate the separation of powers . . . because . . . even when agency activities take legislative and judicial forms, they continue to be exercises of the executive power."[132]

---

[126] *Id.* at 2421.

[127] *Id.*

[128] *Id.*

[129] *Kisor*, 139 S. Ct. at 2421.

[130] *Id.* at 2421.

[131] *Id.* at 2422.

[132] *Id.* (internal quotation marks omitted)

Nor, the Court determined, does *stare decisis*, adherence to which is "a foundation stone of the rule of law," support Kisor's position.[133] "Overruling precedent is never a small matter."[134] It requires "special justification," which exceeds "an argument that the precedent was wrongly decided."[135] Overruling *Auer* would reverse not only "a single case, but a long line of precedents . . . going back 75 years or more," in which the Court has applied *Auer* deference.[136] Reversing *Auer* would also unleash the relitigation of, and force courts to wrestle with, *Auer*'s impact on those decisions, and introduce "so much" instability into many areas of the law, "all in one blow."[137] Indeed, Congress has "chosen acceptance" of the Court's deference decisions.[138] While Congress could have amended the APA to require *de novo* interpretation of regulatory interpretations, "it has let our deference regime work side-by-side with the APA and the many statutes delegating rulemaking power to agencies."[139] There being no indication *Auer* is "unworkable" or that *Auer* is a "doctrinal dinosaur," and the Court having "taken care today to reinforce the limits of *Auer* deference," the Court declined to reverse *Auer*.[140]

Having addressed the arguments raised by Kisor against *Auer* deference, the Court returned to the issue of Kisor's retroactive VA benefits and the meaning of the term "relevant records" in the VA regulation.[141] The Board understood records to be relevant if they related to the reason for denying VA benefits; Kisor argued records were relevant

---

[133] *Id.*
[134] *Id.*
[135] *Id.*
[136] *Id.*
[137] *Id.*
[138] *Id.*
[139] *Id.* at 2423.
[140] *Id.*
[141] *Id.*

if they addressed any benefit criterion.[142] Relying on *Auer* deference, the Federal Circuit upheld the Board's interpretation, "casually" remarking "that [b]oth parties insist that the plain regulatory language supports their case, and neither party's position strikes us as unreasonable."[143] In doing this, the Federal Circuit "jumped the gun" by declaring the regulation ambiguous without employing all of its interpretive tools to "make a conscientious effort to determine, based on indicia like text, structure, history, and purpose, whether the regulation really has more than one reasonable meaning."[144] Second, the Court noted, *Auer* deference does not automatically apply when the court determines a genuine ambiguity exists.[145] Rather, the court "must assess whether the interpretation is of the sort that Congress would want to receive deference."[146] The Solicitor underscored the need to make this assessment when he explained that the 100 or so members of the Board make about 80,000 decisions individually each year, none of which has precedential value.[147] That being so, a Board member's ruling might not qualify as the "considered judgment" of the VA as a whole.[148] That question, the Court noted, is "exactly the kind [of issue] the court must consider in deciding whether to award *Auer* deference to the Board's interpretation."[149] Accordingly, the Court vacated the judgment below and remanded the case for further proceedings.[150]

---

[142] *Id.*
[143] *Id.*
[144] *Id.* (
[145] *Id.*
[146] *Id.*
[147] *Id.* at 2424.
[148] *Id.*
[149] *Id.*
[150] *Id.*

VI. REACTIONS TO *KISOR*

Commentators' responses to the U.S. Supreme Court decision in *Kisor* are divided. Some applaud but others deplore. Falling into the latter category, Eric Schmitt, the Attorney General of Missouri, claims *Kisor* "missed a golden opportunity to restore the role of federalism and the separation of powers in federal administrative law," and, the federal courts having whiffed, "state courts . . . should work to restore the place of these fundamental principles to agency-deference doctrines under state law."[151] He opines that the significant restrictions imposed on courts before they are permitted to grant deference will surely "generate voluminous 'threshold' litigation over whether *Auer* applies at all," similar to the 'threshold' litigation that already bedevils the application of *Chevron* deference."[152] In light of *Kisor*'s majority having failed to respect the principles of federalism and the separation of powers, Attorney General Schmitt issues "a call to action to state courts and state attorneys general to clarify agency-deference doctrines at the state level," where courts can "carefully consider whether *Kisor*'s splintered opinions and multi-factored tests properly safeguard constitutional structure and the separation of powers at the state level."[153]

Similarly, Cory Andrews and Corbin Barthold, respectively Senior Litigation Counsel and Litigation Counsel at the Washington Legal Foundation, which filed an *amicus* brief in support of the petitioner in *Kisor*, lament that *Kisor*'s "fight to abolish Auer deference - and to check the

---

[151] Eric S. Schmitt, *Kisor v. Wilkie – A swing and a miss*, SCOTUSblog (Jun. 27, 2019, 12:46 PM),
https://www.scotusblog.com/2019/06/symposium-kisor-v-wilkie-a-swing-and-a-miss/.
[152] *Id.* at 2.
[153] *Id.* at 3.

administrative state - is lost, at least for now."[154] *Auer*, they insist, forces the judge to interpret binding regulations to mean "not what he thinks they mean, but what an executive agency says they mean," putting "the power to make, enforce and interpret laws into the same hands" and blurring separation of powers under the Constitution.[155] "Under that venerable scheme," they conclude, "Congress enacts laws; executive branch agencies promulgate rules to implement those laws; and courts interpret the meaning of the words that comprise both the laws and the rules." *Auer*, they complain, "confuses—or worse, ignores—these distinctions."[156]

Thomas Merrill, the Charles Evans Hughes Professor at Columbia Law School, described the *Kisor* decision as "shadow boxing with the administrative state."[157] The decision, he says, reveals "very broad agreement among the justices. No one defended the unadorned standard in *Auer*."[158] Justice Kagan's approach retained "the label '*Auer*' deference but crafted new standard of review;" Justice Gorsuch wanted *Auer* overruled and replaced by "the contextual standard of review associated with *Skidmore v. Swift & Co.*[159] While Gorsuch's approach adopts *Skidmore*,

---

[154] Corbin K. Barthold and Cory L. Andrews, *A Small Win For James Kisor; A Big Loss For The Constitution*, SCOTUSblog (Jun. 27, 2019, 2:19 PM), https://www.scotusblog.com/2019/06/symposium-a-small-win-for-james-kisor-a-big-loss-for-the-constitution/.
[155] *Id.*
[156] *Id.*
[157] Thomas W. Merrill, *Shadow Boxing With The Administrative State*, SCOTUSblog (Jun. 27, 2019, 7:00 AM), https://www.scotusblog.com/2019/06/symposium-shadow-boxing-with-the-administrative-state/.
[158] *Id.*
[159] *Id.* at 2. (Skidmore v. Swift & Co., 323 U.S. 134 (1944). (Under the *Skidmore* approach:

    [D]eference exists on a sliding scale, rather than an all-or-nothing conclusion that emerges after a sequential inquiry. (The court remains responsible for the interpretation, and whether the court

which has been around since 1944, Justice Kagan's approach, which draws roughly upon the same factors as

---

adopts the agency view depends on how the various contextual factors stack up, either for or against the agency. (The more the factors favor the agency, the more 'persuasive' the agency view becomes, but at no point is the court compelled to adopt the agency view. (Merrill, *supra* note **Error! Bookmark not defined.**. (

In *Skidmore*, some of the workers engaged in fire hall duties stayed in the fire hall overnight three or four days per week. (They sought overtime compensation under FLSA for their night duty, during which time they were provided with sleeping quarters, a pool table, a domino table, and a radio, but no fires occurred and few alarms rang. (The workers were paid their normal compensation plus additional compensation for each alarm. (The trial court ruled that the overnight fire hall duty did not constitute working time as interpreted by the Administrator, and the Circuit Court of Appeals affirmed. (U.S. Supreme Court said courts were not bound by the Administrator's determination:

> [T]he rulings, interpretations and opinions of the Administrator under this Act, while not controlling upon the courts by reason of their authority, do constitute a body of experience and informed judgment to which courts and litigants may properly resort for guidance. (The weight of such a judgment in a particular case will depend upon the thoroughness evident in its consideration, the validity of its reasoning, its consistency with earlier and later pronouncements, and all those factors which give it power to persuade, if lacking power to control. (*Skidmore*, 323 U.S. at 140.

Chief Justice Roberts captured the main difference between *Skidmore* and *Kisor* as follows:

> That is not to say that *Auer* deference is just the same as the power of persuasion discussed in *Skidmore v. Swift & Co.*, 323 U.S. 134, 65 S. Ct. 161, 89 L.Ed. 124 (1944); there is a difference between holding that a court ought to be persuaded by an agency's interpretation and holding that it should defer to that interpretation under certain conditions. (But it is to say that the cases in which *Auer* deference is warranted largely overlap with the cases in which it would be unreasonable for a court not to be persuaded by an agency's interpretation of its own regulation. (*Kisor*, 139 S. Ct. at 2424-25.

Skidmore, is untried.[160] Hence, *Kisor* "is likely to produce significant uncertainty among lower court judges, agencies and persons contemplating a challenge to agency interpretations."[161] Moreover, Merrill claims, agencies should be free to change their interpretation under Kagan's approach, provided they engage in the extensive review envisioned in *Kisor*. In contrast, under *Skidmore,* the interpretation is ultimately the court's, which means the agency might not be able to change its interpretation.[162]

Michael Hertz, the Arthur Kaplan Professor of Law at Yeshiva University's Cardozo School of Law, notes that the Court's opinion catalogues all of the limitations and weaknesses of *Auer*, "rests solely on *stare decisis* as the reason not to overrule it," and does nothing to cut back or overrule *Auer*."[163] Lower courts, he opines, will "likely be more circumspect applying *Auer* going forward," because *Auer*, like the doctrine of *stare decisis*, forces judges to set aside their own view of the best result in light of some other decision maker's judgment."[164] Liberal administrations might use *Auer* to expand the reach of regulations, just as conservative administrations might use *Auer* to cut back on the reach of regulations, and doing so is much easier than "undoing rules," as the "Trump administration is currently learning the hard way."[165] Hence, "a robust *Auer* doctrine should make it easier for agencies to reverse course. If that

---

[160] Merrill, *supra* note 144, at 3.

[161] *Id.*

[162] *Id.*

[163] Michael Herz, *Auer survives by a vote of 4.6 to 4.4,* SCOTUSblog (Jun. 27, 2019, 11:30 AM),
https://www.scotusblog.com/2019/06/symposium-in-gundy-ii-auer-survives-by-a-vote-of-4-6-to-4, at 2, (last accessed on August 28, 2019) at 1.

[164] *Id.* at 3.

[165] *Id.* at 4.

is not the case, then there has been a lot of fuss over nothing.)"[166]

Daniel Walters, assistant professor of law at Penn State Law, says: "The first line in Justice Neil Gorsuch's partial concurrence in *Kisor v. Wilkie* says it all: 'It should have been easy for the Court to say goodbye to *Auer v. Robbins*'."[167] Instead, in a decision that surprised nearly everyone, the "court turned back the tide and declined the long awaited invitation to do away with *Auer* deference."[168] In Professor Walters' view, the Court's "failure to jettison *Auer* deference feels like a major turning point in the conservative legal movement's campaign against the administrative state."[169] Chief Justice Roberts' "stark reliance on *stare decisis* as the sole basis for retaining *Auer*," Professor Walters says, "made it crystal clear that there are immovable barriers to his participation in the actual deconstruction of the administrative state," and overcoming *stare decisis* in the future will be a barrier "in every effort to undo the administrative state by judicial fiat."[170] "There should be no mistake," he continues, "Roberts' decision to save *Auer* deference is a devastating setback for opponents of judicial deference to agency legal interpretations, and all the more so because it is based entirely on *stare decisis*."[171] Professor Walters concludes:

> *Kisor* will, I suspect, be canonical. Part of its staying power will come from the exceptionally lucid articulations of two

---

[166] *Id.*
[167] Daniel Walters, *Laying bare the realpolitik of administrative deconstruction*, SCOTUSblog (June 27, 2019), https://www.scotusblog.com/2019/06/symposium-laying-bare-the-realpolitik-of-administrative-deconstruction/.
[168] *Id.*
[169] *Id.*
[170] *Id.*
[171] *Id.*

completely different understandings of the necessity of the administrative state in Kagan's opinion for the court and Gorsuch's partial concurrence. The initial reaction of many legal scholars is that these are masterfully written and paradigmatic statements of the major perspectives in administrative law today—and I agree. But the decision will also likely come to be known as the decision that laid bare the realpolitik of administrative deconstruction. Faced with the real consequences of its actions, the Supreme Court blinked. As it turns out, the court is as frozen between 'administrativism' and 'anti-administrativism' as is the body politic.[172]

Finally, Ronald Levin, the William R. Orthwein Distinguished Professor of Law at Washington University in St. Louis, observes that *Auer* survived, but not without a plethora of mixed messages and only on the basis of *stare decisis*.[173] Kagan's plurality and Gorsuch's concurring opinion, Professor Levin notes, were "far apart on the core question of whether deference to agencies' interpretations of their own regulations is desirable."[174] Kagan's arguments in favor of retaining but restraining judicial deference "have been embraced by judges for decades" and that "track record enabled her to deploy a strong *stare decisis* argument—one that even [Chief Justice] Roberts found telling."[175] "In

---

[172] *Id.*

[173] Ronald Levin, *Supreme Court chooses evolution, not revolution*, SCOTUSblog (June 27, 2019), https://www.scotusblog.com/2019/06/symposium-auer-deference-supreme-court-chooses-evolution-not-revolution/.

[174] *Id.*

[175] *Id.*

contrast, [Justice] Gorsuch's concurring opinion . . . displays a viewpoint that, in historical terms, is relatively new at the Supreme Court level: full-scale, heated opposition to the very existence of judicial deference," which "reflects the disillusionment with the administrative state that has become such a prominent feature of our politics during the past decade."[176] In Professor Levin's view, the "refurbished" version of *Auer* is "far removed from the fundamental antipathy to deference that pervades [Justice] Gorsuch's concurring opinion," making "it fair to conclude that a majority of the Court, as currently constituted, rejects that approach."[177]

VII. *Chevron v. National Resources Defense Council, Inc.*

In contrast to *Kisor*, which retained a highly cabined judicial deference to administrative agencies' interpretation of their own regulations, *Chevron v. National Resources Defense Council, Inc.* granted judicial deference to administrative agencies' interpretation of the statutes the agencies administer, thereby creating an administrative principle known as *Chevron* deference or the *Chevron* doctrine.[178] The premise of the *Chevron* doctrine is that courts must give judicial deference to an agency's interpretation of the statute which the agency is charged with administering.[179] Two conditions must, however, must be present: (1) the intent of Congress must be ambiguous, unclear, or hidden, and (2) the agency's interpretation must be reasonable.[180]

---

[176] *Id.*
[177] *Id.* at 3.
[178] Chevron v. Natural Resources Defense Council, Inc., 467 U.S. 837 (1984).
[179] *Id.* at 842.
[180] *Id.* at 842-43.

Chevron arose out of regulations addressing national air quality standards issued by the Environmental Protection Agency ("EPA").[181] The 1977 amendments to the Clean Air Act imposed certain requirements on "nonattainment" states, *i.e.*, those states that had failed to achieve national air quality standards established by the EPA pursuant to earlier legislation.[182] As a result, the nonattainment states were required to obtain permits under a state-established permit program for the regulation of "new or modified major stationary sources" of air pollution.[183] In 1981, the EPA promulgated regulations containing a plant-wide definition of the term "stationary," under which pollution-emitting devices within the same industrial grouping were considered to be encased in a single, virtual bubble.[184] As long as the overall emission of pollutants from the bubble met the emission standard, the existence of particular pollution-emitting devices which did not meet the standard were permitted.[185]

National Resources Defense Council, Incorporated challenged the regulations in the Court of Appeals for the District of Columbia, which set aside the regulations.[186] The Court of Appeals "stated that the bubble concept was 'mandatory' in programs designed merely to maintain existing air quality, but held that it was 'inappropriate' in programs enacted to improve air quality."[187] Because the permit program, in the Circuit Court's view, was designed to improve air quality, the "bubble concept was inapplicable" and the regulations were "contrary to law." The U.S.

---

[181] *Id.* at 840.
[182] *Id.*
[183] *Id.*
[184] *Id.* at 841.
[185] *Id.*
[186] *Id.* Natural Resources Defense Council, Inc. v. Gorsuch, 685 F.2d 718 (D.C. Cir. 1982).
[187] *Chevron*, 467 U.S. at 841.

Supreme Court granted certiorari and reversed the judgment of the D.C. Circuit Court of Appeals. [188]

The question before the U.S. Supreme Court was what standard of review should be applied when a governmental agency construes a statute which the agency is charged to administer. In essence, the Court had to determine what judicial deference, if any, should be given to an agency's interpretation:

> When a court reviews an agency's construction of the statute which it administers, it is confronted with two questions. First, always, is the question whether Congress has directly spoken to the precise question at issue. If the intent of Congress is clear, that is the end of the matter; for the court, as well as the agency, must give effect to the unambiguously expressed intent of Congress. If, however, the court determines Congress has not directly addressed the precise question at issue, the court does not simply impose its own construction on the statute, as would be necessary in the absence of an administrative interpretation. Rather, if the statute is silent or ambiguous with respect to the specific issue, the question for the court is whether the agency's answer is based on a permissible construction of the statute. [189]

The U.S. Supreme Court determined the Court of Appeals "misconceived the nature of its role in reviewing" the bubble regulation. [190] Having decided that Congress had not formulated an intention with respect to the bubble

---

[188] *Id.* at 842.
[189] *Id.* at 842-43.
[190] *Id.* at 845.

concept in the permit program, the U.S. Supreme Court held that the Court of Appeals should not have decided the bubble concept was inappropriate to the permit program. Rather, the court should have decided whether the agency's view was reasonable in the context of the particular program.[191]

The U.S. Supreme Court then embarked on a detailed and lengthy review of the origins, development, and refinement of the bubble concept by the EPA,[192] the statutory language defining the term "stationary source,"[193] the "unilluminating" and "silent" legislative history of the bubble concept,[194] the likelihood that the EPA was properly motivated by the need to both allow reasonable economic growth and administer environmental protection in its rulemaking process,[195] and the multiple "policy" arguments advanced by the parties that more properly should be addressed to legislators and administrators, "but not to judges."[196] The Court then noted that judges are not environmental experts and may rely on the administrative agency's "view of wise policy to inform its judgment."[197] When Congress, either inadvertently or intentionally, did not resolve policy issues in enacting legislation, but left the resolution of those policy issues to administrative agencies, "judges have a duty to respect legitimate policy choices made by those [administrative agencies]."[198] Hence, the Court upheld the EPA's "permissible construction of the statute," and reversed the judgment of the Circuit Court of Appeals.[199] In doing so, it enshrined the two step process to determine when deference is accorded to an administrative

---

[191] *Id.*
[192] *Id.* at 846-59.
[193] *Id.* at 859-62.
[194] *Id.* at 862.
[195] *Id.* at 863-64.
[196] *Id.* at 864.
[197] *Id.* at 865.
[198] *Id.*
[199] *Id.* at 866.

agency's interpretation of the statute it is charged to administer: (1) if the court determines that the language and meaning of the statute is clear and unambiguous and that the regulatory action of the agency conflicts with the plain meaning of the statute, the court may hold that the agency's interpretation or action is unlawful; and (2) if the court determines that the language of the statute is silent or ambiguous, the court should defer to the judgment of the agency and uphold the agency's regulatory interpretation, unless it violates the arbitrary and capricious standard, *i.e.*, not based on a consideration of relevant factors, including viable alternatives available to the regulatory agency, or a result of a clear error of judgment by the agency on the basis of the information available to the agency at the time it took the action in question.[200]

VIII. *Kisor*'s Impact on *Chevron*

The U.S. Supreme Court's willingness to review the judicial deference accorded to administrative agencies' interpretations of their own regulations in *Kisor* caused some observers to believe that the Court would move on to review and possibly eliminate *Chevron* deference.[201] As Professor Walters noted, "The only question that remained was just what the result in *Kisor* would foreshadow about future challenges to *Chevron* deference."[202]

Chevron is clearly distinguishable from *Kisor*. *Chevron* provided judicial deference to agency regulations interpreting statutes whose language is silent or ambiguous;

---

[200] *Id.* at 843-44.

[201] Weiss, *supra* note 5, at 2.

[202] Walter, *supra* note 114. *See,* Barthold, *supra* note 141, at 4 "The fight over Auer deference toward ambiguous regulations may be lost; but a fight over deference under [Chevron] toward ambiguous laws is surely on the horizon." *See also*, Levin, *supra* note 173 ("Inevitably, *Kisor* raises questions about the continued viability of [Chevron].").

Kizor provides a highly cabined deference to agency interpretations of its own regulations. The foundation of *Chevron* deference is the clarity of the statute; the foundation of *Kisor* deference is the bulletin, uninvited amicus brief, interpretive rule, or Administrative Law Judge's decision in which the agency provides its interpretation. The regulations to which *Chevron* deference are granted have the force of law; the agency's interpretations of its own regulations do not. The regulations to which *Chevron* deference are granted are subject to notice and comment procedures; the agency's interpretations of its own regulations are not despite the plurality's insistence judicial review provides the same "procedural values").[203] Given the significant differences between *Chevron* and *Kisor,* it is difficult to see how *Kisor* will have any impact on *Chevron.*

Moreover, a fair reading of *Kisor* confirms this conclusion. Notably, Chief Justice Roberts "went out of his way to say that *Kisor* has no impact on *Chevron,* and Justice Kavanaugh, joined by Justice Alito in a short concurrence, agreed."[204] That augurs well for *Chevron,* because "*Kisor* is

---

[203] Kisor, 139 S. Ct. at 2420.

[204] Merrill, *supra* note 144, at 2. Chief Justice Roberts wrote:
I write separately to suggest that the distance between the majority and Justice Gorsuch is not as great as it may initially appear. The majority catalogs the prerequisites for, and limitations on, *Auer* deference: The underlying regulation must be genuinely ambiguous; the agency's interpretation must be reasonable and must reflect its authoritative, expertise-based, and fair and considered judgment; and the agency must take account of reliance interests and avoid unfair surprise. Justice Gorsuch, meanwhile, lists the reasons that a court might be persuaded to adopt an agency's interpretation of its own regulation: The agency thoroughly considered the problem, offered a valid rationale, brought its expertise to bear, and interpreted the regulation in a manner consistent with earlier and later pronouncements. Accounting for variations in verbal formulation, those lists have much in common. *Kisor*, 139 S. Ct. at 2424.
Justice Kavanaugh wrote:

strong evidence that, barring a change in the court's membership, the court will continue to adhere to that incremental process, eschewing the total overthrow that [Justice] Gorsuch would so obviously welcome."[205] Perhaps the two-step *Chevron* review[206] will be supplemented with the five steps in the *Kisor* review, but no significant change to *Chevron* is likely to occur in the absence of a major change to the composition of the U.S. Supreme Court.[207]

I agree with the Chief Justice that "the distance between the majority and Justice Gorsuch is not as great as it may initially appear. . . . If a reviewing court employs all of the traditional tools of construction, the court will almost always reach a conclusion about the best interpretation of the regulation at issue. After doing so, the court then will have no need to adopt or defer to an agency's contrary interpretation. In other words . . . courts will have no reason or basis to put a thumb on the scale in favor of an agency when courts interpret agency regulations. (*Kisor*, 139 S. Ct. at 2448.

[205] Levin, *supra* note.

[206] *Chevron*, 467 U.S. at 842-43. "When a court reviews an agency's construction of the statute which it administers, it is confronted with two questions. First, always, is the question whether Congress has directly spoken to the precise question at issue. If the intent of Congress is clear, that is the end of the matter; for the court, as well as the agency, must give effect to the unambiguously expressed intent of Congress. If, however, the court determines Congress has not directly addressed the precise question at issue, the court does not simply impose its own construction on the statute, as would be necessary in the absence of an administrative interpretation. Rather, if the statute is silent or ambiguous with respect to the specific issue, the question for the court is whether the agency's answer is based on a permissible construction of the statute.")

[207] As summarized by Chief Justice Roberts, the court must determine whether (1) the underlying regulation is genuinely ambiguous; (2) the agency's interpretation is reasonable; (3) the agency's interpretation is authoritative and expertise-based; (4) the agency's interpretation is its fair and considered judgment; and (5) the agency's interpretation takes account of reliance interests and avoids unfair surprise. *Kisor*, 139 S. Ct. at 2424.

IX. Summary

This article closely examines (1) the highly anticipated and closely watched decision of the U.S. Supreme Court in *Kisor v. Wilkie*, which significantly cabined but did not overrule judicial deference provided to government agencies' interpretation of their own regulations, (2) the two major U.S. Supreme Court decisions—*Seminole Rock* and *Auer*—which recognized and launched that deference; (3) two U.S. Supreme Court decisions—*Gonzales v. Oregon* and *Christopher v. SmithKline Beecham Corp.*—which have imposed limitations on judicial deference to government agencies' interpretation of their own regulations, namely (a) the government agency's interpretation of its regulations is not entitled to deference if it merely parrots the language of the statute, and (b) the government agency's interpretation cannot impose a potentially massive liability on parties who relied on the agency's prior interpretation of the regulation; and (4) the reactions of legal scholars and commentators to the *Kisor* decision.

The article also closely examines the U.S. Supreme Court decision in *Chevron*, which decided that regulations developed by government agencies interpreting genuinely ambiguous statutes are also entitled to judicial deference, contrasts *Chevron* deference with *Kisor* deference, and predicts that *Kisor* will have little substantive influence on *Chevron* deference.

Much to the surprise of several court observers, the U.S. Supreme Court did not reverse *Auer*, the sole issue for which the Court presumably granted certiorari. Rather, the Court converted a run-down and battered fixer-upper into a sturdy cabin which will house judicial deference to government agencies' interpretations of their own regulations for another era. Following *Kisor*, courts will be unable to grant deference to a government agency's interpretation of its own regulations unless: (1) using all of the traditional tools of construction, the court concludes a genuine ambiguity exists; (2) the agency's interpretation of its regulation is reasonable; (3) the agency's interpretation is an authoritative rendition of the agency's official position and implicates in some way the agency's substantive expertise; (4) the agency's interpretation is a fair and considered judgment of subject matter that the legislature delegated to the agency for implementation; and (5) the agency's interpretation takes into account the reliance of parties and avoids unfair surprise. Significantly, this result stemmed not from the merits of judicial deference to agency interpretation of its own regulations, but from the doctrine of *stare decisis*, adherence to which is a "foundation stone of the rule of law."[208]

---

[208] Kisor v. Wilkie, 139 S. Ct. at 2422.

THERE'S NO PLACE LIKE HOME: THE SURPRISING VARIATION IN THE ENFORCEABILITY OF "NO ORAL MODIFICATIONS" CLAUSES IN THE UNITED STATES

PAUL W. FULBRIGHT[*]

I. INTRODUCTION

A. A Story about a Project Manager, His Contract, and a Slice of Pie.

"How did things get so out of hand?" John Smith, COO and Assistant Superintendent of Programs of the Suburbia Independent School District, rubbed his fingers through his hair. He was talking to Robert Anderson, another of SISD's ASPs. "I mean, despite the impossible nature of the task, our project launch a year ago was textbook. We developed a great design for the new Student Life Center, we secured buy-in from all of the relevant stakeholders, and even the contract negotiations with all of the relevant parties went off without a hitch." Robert smiled. He remembered feeling a bit of envy at the launch John had managed.

"But now," John continued, "it's clear that the final cost is going to be way over budget, even though there was no single thing that broke the bank. I mean, we *anticipated* this kind of thing happening. We developed a 'Change Order' process to ensure that any modifications made to the Program Plan *had* to be in writing – NO oral modifications

---

[*] LL.M., J.D., M.S. (Telecom.), M.B.A., B.S. (Chem. Eng'g), Assistant Professor of Business Law, University of Houston – Downtown.

– and they had to be fully approved by everyone, or they couldn't be executed or paid for."

"What does your gut tell you? Where do you think things went wrong?" Robert asked. John knew that he could trust Robert with the truth. Though both were ASPs reporting to the Superintendent, they operated in totally different areas of administration. Furthermore, their friendship had proven itself through hotter fires than this one.

"I'll tell you what I can't tell anyone else," John began. "The problem is with our Superintendent James Mercury and the Board of Trustees. When the project was commissioned two years ago, it was understood that it would finish three years later in December of 2021. However, shortly after our official launch, the "20 by 20" initiative kicked off, and, suddenly, Mercury, the Board, and everyone else wanted the project completed by the end of 2020, so that we could wow the Alumni and secure the $20 million in fundraising that was targeted for the end of the year. So, for the last year and a half, no one has had time for the Change Order process. They just want changes here, changes there, changes everywhere, all of them expensive, all of them expanding the scope of the project. And Mercury's the worst one! I'm due to meet with our Builder Rep later this week to hear the latest final cost estimate, and I'm terrified at what the number will be. I'm wondering if it's time to talk to one of SISD's lawyers."

As John finished his diatribe, he thought about his good friend Prudence Jones. They had been friends ever since college. He had gone into education administration, and she had become a lawyer in private practice at a great local firm. They had stayed in touch over the years, and John recalled at least three occasions when a one-hour conversation with Prudence, over drinks and pie after work, had saved his neck on the job. It was fascinating talking to her. She wasn't a business executive, but she seemed to be able to predict the moves that would be made, by both sides of a dispute, farther in advance than any business executive he had ever met. Their get-togethers weren't long, but, after comparing stories on their kids and vacations, the subject would drift to work, and, right about the time the dessert came Prudence always insisted on a slice of pie at their gatherings), she would fire off some insights that would entirely change his perspectives on a problem. He wondered if she could do that again.

Robert interrupted his thoughts. "I'd probably hold off on contacting the lawyers," he said. "First of all, more legal bills just add gasoline to the fire. And, second, I can save you the trouble by telling you right now what they're going to say. 'Read the contract. Follow the contract. Rinse, lather, repeat.' What's interesting to me is that, in the end, you might end up looking like a hero, because, after all, the contract says that there can be no changes made to the contract, and no edits made to the Project Plan, unless all of that is approved pursuant to the Change Order process. Because that wasn't done, I suspect SISD will have a good argument that it doesn't owe *anything* beyond the original quote. Now, don't get me wrong, we'll probably compromise somewhere in the middle, but I think you've got a strong argument. The contract is clear – no oral modifications – no changes outside the process. I'm not sure about how I feel about it ethically, but, legally, I think you're on high ground."

Two nights later, John and Prudence were laughing together over drinks at Houston's. They had covered the kids, and John had just finished briefing her on the SLC Project. "I consulted a colleague, Robert, about the matter, and he didn't think talking to a lawyer would help. 'The contract is the contract.' he said. In fact, he thinks that I might be able to secure an advantage over the Builder, because most of the changes occurred outside the Change Order process, and many were oral. But dumping it all on the

Builder when we were as much at fault for this mess feels questionable to me, so that's why I asked to meet."

Prudence smiled. "Well, I do like one thing about Robert's advice. You're always better off when you've read, and done everything you can to closely adhere to, the contract. In that respect, we're all in agreement. However, business relationships in the real world aren't quite as simple as the four corners of a piece of paper. And our courts recognize that. That's why our law of contracts doesn't just concern itself with the *start* of the relationship, it also addresses how these relationships *change* over time. Bottom line: You *do* have a contract problem, John, but I'd add that you *also* have a managerial problem and an ethical one as well. And resolving the situation won't be quite as simple as Robert suggests."

"But, before we get into the details," she continued with a grin, "let's order some pie."

B. The "No Oral Modifications" (NOM) Clause – A Staple in Modern Contracts.

The "no oral modifications" clause hereinafter the "NOM clause" has become a staple of modern contracting. Although it presents itself in many forms, its fundamental nature is clear and its simplest formulation only requires thirteen words: "This agreement may only be modified through a writing signed by the parties."

Regrettably, the conflict that exists between the contract language and the realities of the rapid pace of modern business practice creates the potential for gamesmanship. Dan and Peter (vice-presidents of the parties B and A, respectively, to a contract) are discussing their relationship and the progress being made pursuant to the contract. Peter (who has forgotten about the NOM clause) orally proposes a modification to the agreement which Dan believes will be favorable to his own employer B.

147

Dan (who has *not* forgotten about the NOM clause) believes that one of two things will happen if he accepts the proposed modification orally. First, if the circumstances at the time of performance continue to favor B, Dan may well just accept and embrace the improved state of affairs and fully perform according to the modified terms. However, if, instead, the circumstances have changed so that the modification no longer favors B, then Dan may well reject A's proposed performance (or at least decline paying for it), pointing out that the contract contains a NOM clause.

Months later, after the matter has come to a head, Peter's initial appraisal of A's prospects in litigation may well be bleak. After all, the agreement says what it says, and "freedom of contract" is sacrosanct in the United States. However, Peter should be careful to not jump to conclusions, as his counsel may well discover (to his surprise and delight) that, under the state law governing the contract, the NOM clause that Dan is asserting is unenforceable. Much will depend on the specific state law that applies.

This paper provides an in-depth review of some of the law regarding the enforceability of NOM clauses in a handful of states. There are several reasons for this approach. First, different states have addressed the issue in different ways, and touring these varying landscapes is both interesting and developmental. A particular issue might be dealt with at great depth in California, but very lightly in New York. Just as physical travel can broaden one's cultural views, jurisprudential travel can broaden one's legal perspectives.

Second, more and more businesses are growing, and growing rapidly, beyond the borders of the states in which they were born. Seeing how different states approach important aspects of the contracting process reminds us that the "boilerplate provisions" such as the "Governing Law" provision can have more of a practical impact than one might suspect. And, third, speaking of the importance of practicality, it's also important to remember that, because the practice of law is about the resolution of disputes in an environment of rules, game theory will inevitably play its part. And, as any player at chess, poker, bridge, baseball, boxing, or even tic-tac-toe will tell you *and* as any legislator, negotiator, or litigator will tell you, all deep understanding of strategy begins with a firm grounding in tactics.

This is a paper about tactics. Specifically, it is about some very important tactics that can come into play when relationships change over the course of a contract's performance. The lesson for the litigator after a dispute has arisen is simple: assume nothing; research deeply. The array of overlapping laws, exceptions, and traps for the unwary is immense. The lesson for the executive to avoid needless, costly disputes is even simpler: Try very hard to live up to the letter and the spirit of your contract's NOM clause. Why? Because it's legal, and it's ethical. If you try modifying your agreement orally (despite the clause), you've commenced a high-stakes game that you play at your own risk. It's true that, if your counsel has thoroughly researched the relevant state law in advance, you might well enjoy a "home field" advantage of sorts, and it is fun to win at home. However, remember the flip side. Losing at home can be really embarrassing.

II. THE "NO ORAL MODIFICATIONS" (NOM) CLAUSE IN FOUR STATES

A. Texas

1. The Courts Invoke the Inherent Powers of Contracting Parties and their Agents

We begin in Texas, because an 1887 Texas Supreme Court opinion, *Morrison v. Insurance Co. of North*

America,[1] represents one of the oldest opinions in existence in the U.S. dealing extensively with the NOM clause. In that disposition, appellant Morrison alleged that the appellee insurance company had consented (through its agent) to Morrison's purchase of supplemental insurance on a property despite a specific insurance policy provision prohibiting it absent written consent. The question at hand was whether the insurance company could be deemed to have consented to the supplemental insurance when the policy clearly stated that the only way consent could be effected by the agent was via a written endorsement on the policy (which concededly was not done).[2]

To be clear, there was no question that the agent had orally consented to the supplemental insurance, and he even went so far as to urge renewal of the policy in reliance on that consent, memorializing the matter in a memo of renewal (just not in an endorsement to the policy as required by it).[3]

To the court, two issues were presented. First, could the appellee company be bound by the consent when it was crystal clear that its authorized general agent had *not* effected the consent in the manner required under the policy? The court held that it could and indeed was bound by the agent's consent despite the imperfections in its execution. The rationales cited sounded in ratification, waiver, estoppel, and acquiescence:

> "... application for consent to subsequent insurance was made to the agent, who had the power to give it. *This the company must be held to have known.* He gave consent, but not in the manner prescribed in the policy. *This the company must also be held to have known.* ... Having knowledge of the facts, it

---

[1] Morrison v. Ins. Co. of N. Am., 6 S.W. 605 (Tex. 1887).
[2] *Id.* at 607.
[3] *Id.*

was the duty of the company to manifest its intention as to this promptly; and, having failed to do so, it ought to be held to have *waived* the right to treat the policy as a null,... the company itself must be held, having knowledge of what he had done, to have *ratified* the consent given by him, though it may not have been given in the manner prescribed by the policy."[4]

The second issue picked up where the first left off. Assuming, now, that the *agent's* actions were authorized, the question arises as to whether *the appellee company itself* had the power to effect such a consent when it had previously bound itself by agreement to only effect such consents through a writing. That is, could the appellee, in a single oral act, essentially modify the agreement to allow for an oral consent and effectuate the consent itself. The court held that it could:

> "If the policy limited the power of the agent, it imposed no limitations on the power of the company itself; and, as said by the supreme court of Michigan in considering a provision in a policy similar to those found in the policy before us: '*The condition, literally applied, would prevent any unendorsed consent by the company itself, by resolution of its board, or by act of its officers*, as effectually as by anyone else; and *the case seems to settle down to the simple question whether a person, who has agreed that he will only contract by writing in a certain way, precludes himself from making a parol*

---

[4] *Id.* at 608-09 (emphasis added).

bargain to change it. The answer is manifest. *A written bargain is of no higher legal degree than a parol one. Either may vary or discharge the other...*"[5]

2. The Parol Evidence Rule and Statute of Frauds

In *Mar-Lan Industries v. Nelson,*[6] plaintiff-appellee Nelson had sued his former employer Mar-Lan Industries ("Mar-Lan") for back salary and bonuses pursuant to a written employment agreement. At trial, the facts revealed that, after Nelson had been hired, Mar-Lan fell into financial difficulties. The parties discussed the matter, and, after that discussion, Nelson's salary and bonus were paid at a reduced rate. Later, Nelson was terminated. He requested back salary and bonuses pursuant to the terms of his original written contract.[7] That contract contained a provision

> "That *no waiver or modification* of this agreement or of any covenant, condition, or limitation herein contained *shall be valid unless in writing and duly executed* by the party to be charged therewith, and that no evidence of any waiver or modification shall be offered or received in evidence in any proceeding, arbitration, or litigation between the parties hereto arising out of or affecting this agreement unless such waiver or

---

[5] *Id.* at 609 (emphasis added; quoting Insurance Co. v. Earle, 33 Mich. 143, 153 (Mich. 1876)).
[6] Mar-Lan Indus. v. Nelson, 635 S.W.2d 853 (Tex. App. 1982), *implicitly abrogated on other grounds by* Metrocon Constr. v. Gregory Constr., 663 S.W.2d 460 (Tex. App. 1983).
[7] *Mar-Lan Indus.*, 635 S.W.2d at 854.

modification is in writing, duly executed as aforesaid."[8]

Nelson secured a judgment at trial.[9] There, the judge excluded evidence offered by Mar-Lan that the contract upon which Nelson was terminated was a different (modified) contract than the one upon which Nelson based his suit. Specifically, Mar-Lan offered to prove that, when it encountered financial difficulties, it told Nelson that, if he wished to stay with the company and it was hoped that he would, his pay would be reduced. After that conversation, Nelson did stay until his contract was terminated.[10] The trial court sustained Nelson's objection to the introduction of testimony on this point, the objection being that the evidence was a violation of the parol evidence rule and of the clause prohibiting any later oral modification.[11]

The court first quickly dispensed with the parol evidence rule. The rule doesn't apply to agreements made *subsequent* to the written agreement.[12] It further doesn't prohibit a written agreement from being modified by a later oral one.[13]

The court also addressed the issue of the statute of frauds. Because this was an employment contract for an indefinite term, it was considered performable within one year.[14] As such, it lay beyond the reach of the statute.[15] The original agreement could have been written or oral; any

---

[8] *Id.* at 855 (emphasis added).
[9] *Id.* at 854.
[10] *Id.* at 855.
[11] *Id.*
[12] *Id.*
[13] *Id.*
[14] *Id.*
[15] *Id.*

modification[16] of the agreement could have been written or oral as well.

Finally, the court reaffirmed that a written contract not required by law to be in writing may be modified by a subsequent oral agreement even though it provides that it can only be modified by a written agreement, because a written agreement is of no higher legal degree than an oral one, and either may vary or discharge the other.[17]

3. Goods v. Services (and U.C.C. Article 2)

As noted, the *Mar-Lan Industries* court held that a written contract *not required by law to be in writing* may be

---

[16] It is worth noting that some courts have held that even contracts *within* the Statute of Frauds may be modified orally if the modification is a *non-material* one. *See, e.g.*, Group Hosp. Servs. V. One and Two Brookriver Ctr., 704 S.W.2d 886, 890 (Tex. App. 1986) "Even if the agreement were viewed as a modification, it would be enforceable. Not every oral modification to a contract within the Statute of Frauds is barred. The critical determination is whether the modification *materially* effects [sic] the obligations in the underlying agreements. Where the character or value of the underlying agreement is unaltered, oral modifications are enforceable. In the lease before us, the underlying obligations are not disputed. Tenant's right of possession remains unchallenged; only the obligation of payment is in issue and the dispute only runs to a comparatively small segment of the overall obligation to pay. … The agreement, at most, only changes the *number* of meters to be employed in computing the extraordinary electricity charge. (The Statute of Frauds does not render this type of modification unenforceable.") (emphasis in original; citations omitted); *cf.* Givens v. Dougherty, 671 S.W.2d 877, 878 (Tex. 1984) "It goes without saying that a contract required to be in writing cannot be orally modified except in limited circumstances such as an extension of time for performance. Our question, however, not previously addressed in Texas, is whether there may be a mutual oral rescission of a contract for a commission for the sale of real estate. (… We therefore disapprove of any language in *Nutt v. Berry* that would allow mutual oral rescissions of contracts required to be in writing.").
[17] *Mar-Lan Indus.*, 635 S.W.2d at 855.

modified by a subsequent oral agreement even though it provides that it can only be modified by a written agreement.[18] In many of the court decisions regarding NOM clauses, it is the Statute of Frauds that gets all the ink.

However, there is another important category of contracts that must not be forgotten when one considers the enforceability of NOM clauses: contracts for the purchase or sale of goods. In the vast majority of states in the U.S.,[19] contracts for a sale of goods are heavily regulated by that jurisdiction's instantiation of Article Two[20] of the Uniform Commercial Code.

Of particular relevance here are subsections (1), (2), and (3) of Section 2-209:[21]

> (1) An agreement modifying a contract within this Article needs no consideration to be binding.
>
> (2) *A signed agreement which excludes modification or rescission except by a signed writing cannot be otherwise modified or rescinded*, but except as between merchants such a requirement on a form

---

[18] *See supra* the text accompanying note 17.

[19] The Uniform Commercial Code, a joint 1952 creation of the National Conference of Commissioners on Uniform State Laws (NCCUSL) and the American Law Institute (ALI), has been adopted in fifty-two jurisdictions including all fifty states (although Louisiana has adopted only Articles 1, 3, 4, 7, 8, and 9); the District of Columbia; and the Virgin Islands.

[20] U.C.C. § 2-102 (Am. Law. Inst. & Unif. Law Comm'n 1977) ("Unless the context otherwise requires, this Article applies to transactions in goods..."); § 2-105 ("'Goods' means all things (including specially manufactured goods) which are movable at the time of identification to the contract for sale other than the money in which the price is to be paid, investment securities (Article 8) and things in action. ('Goods' also includes...").

[21] *Id.* § 2-209.

supplied by the merchant must be separately signed by the other party.

(3) The requirements of the statute of frauds section of this Article[22] must be satisfied if the contract as modified is within its provisions.

Thus, for example, as a matter of Texas law, under the corresponding Texas UCC provision,[23] a NOM clause in a contract *for a sale of goods* is enforceable, and the courts have so held.[24]

B. California

1. Solving the Problem by Statute

In contrast to the approach of other states, such as Texas, that have largely left the matter of the enforceability of NOM clauses to the courts, California passed a statute that specifically addresses the matter of modification of contracts (including a subsequent oral modification of a written

---

[22] *Id.* § 2-201(1) ("Except as otherwise provided in this section, a contract for the sale of goods for the price of $500.00 or more is not enforceable by way of action or defense unless there is some writing sufficient to indicate that a contract for sale has been made between the parties and signed by the party against whom enforcement is sought or by his authorized agent or broker.").

[23] Tex. Bus. & Comm. Code Ann. § 2.209(b) (West 1967).

[24] *See, e.g.*, South Hampton Co. v. Stinnes Corp., 733 F.2d 1108, 1117 n.13 (5th Cir. 1984) ("Texas law permits a contract to be modified by subsequent oral agreement, notwithstanding the inclusion of a no-oral-modification clause, if the contract is *not* required by law to be in writing to be enforceable. (The South Hampton-Stinnes contracts, however, are for the sale of goods, valued at well over $500.00, and therefore must be in writing to be enforceable.") (emphasis in original; citations omitted).

agreement) in some detail.[25] California Civil Code § 1698 contains the following provisions:

> (a) A contract in writing may be modified by a contract in writing.
>
> (b) A contract in writing may be modified by an oral agreement to the extent that the oral agreement is executed by the parties.
>
> (c) *Unless the contract otherwise expressly provides, a contract in writing may be modified by an oral agreement supported by new consideration.* The statute of frauds (Section 1624) is required to be satisfied if the contract as modified is within its provisions.
>
> (d) Nothing in this section precludes in an appropriate case the application of rules of law concerning estoppel, oral novation and substitution of a new agreement, rescission of a written contract by an oral agreement, waiver of a provision of a written contract, or oral independent collateral contracts.[26]

Our focus on the enforceability of NOM clauses makes it sensible to focus first on subsection (c) of § 1698.

---

[25] The reader will do well to remember that numerous statutes, both state and federal, address the subject of modification of contracts in specific subject areas, and the courts often apply the principle of *lex specialis* (*Lex specialis derogat legi generali*: "The specific law overrules the general law."). For example, the statutes and cases everywhere pronounce that a modification of a contract is itself a contract that must be supported by consideration. Yet, as adduced earlier, the UCC expressly provides that modifications of contracts for the sale of goods require no consideration in order to be binding. *See supra* the text regarding U.C.C. § 2-209(1) accompanying note 21.

[26] Cal. Civ. Code § 1698 (West 1976).

Notice the preamble: *"Unless the contract otherwise expressly provides..."* This establishes the general rule in California that NOM clauses are alive and well and fully enforceable. If there is no NOM clause, then the first three subsections of the statute evidence three ways in which a written contract might be modified: (a) a contract in writing (i.e., a written modification); (b) an oral agreement to the extent that the oral agreement is executed; and (c) an oral agreement supported by new consideration.

All of this seems simple enough, but there are a few traps for the unwary.

2. Oral Modifications "To the Extent Executed"

First, notice that an executory modification supported by new consideration is only available under subsection (c) *if* the contract is free of a NOM clause or similar restriction. However, subsection (b) is different. It lacks subsection (c)'s preamble, and so, even if there *is* a NOM clause, under California law, written agreements can be modified by an oral agreement to the extent that the oral agreement is executed.

A typical example of an oral modification being deemed effective (despite the presence of a NOM clause) because it was executed is *Miller v. Brown*.[27] In that case, Miller commissioned Brown to construct a home. (Construction cases are legion in this area of the law.) Brown's construction would be pursuant to a set of plans and specifications incorporated into the parties' "Building Agreement."[28] The NOM clause was concise and clear: "Any changes or deviations from the plans and specifications shall be in writing and signed for by both Owner and Builder."[29]

---

[27] Miller v. Brown, 289 P.2d 572 (Cal. Dist. Ct. App. 1955).
[28] *Id.* at 574.
[29] *Id.*

Regrettably, when the house was completed, its total cost was far higher than the original stated price, and a dispute arose as to whether the construction items done beyond the original scope of the agreement were (a) covered by the original total cost of the agreement or (b) were to be paid for separately as "extras".[30] The trial court ruled in favor of builder Brown, and the appellate court affirmed. The rationale was clear enough:

> ... Miller, as owner, changed the basic plans by moving the bedroom wing. This increased many of the estimated costs of construction. Thereafter, Miller ordered more millwork... changed the type of tile agreed upon and increased the amount, added a furnace room, ... ordered numerous changes in the electrical specifications... Under the law this amounted to a modification of the written contract. Miller places great reliance on the provision of the contract which provides that alterations must be in writing, and points out here that he only approved one alteration in writing. *But under section 1698 of the Civil Code, an executed oral agreement may alter an agreement in writing, even though, as here, the original contract provides that all changes must be approved in writing.* This is so because the executed oral agreement may alter or modify that provision of the contract as well as other portions.[31]

It's also worth noting that subsection (b) refers to the oral agreement modifying the written agreement "to the extent that the oral agreement is executed by the parties."

---

[30] *Id.* at 575.

[31] *Id.* at 579 (emphasis added).

Thus, in contracts where performances and considerations are severable, the courts have enforced those parts of the modification that have been "executed" while refraining from doing so regarding the parts that remain "executory."[32]

3. Oral Modifications Effected via Waiver, Estoppel, and Similar Mechanisms

The final traps reside in subsection (d). Note the laundry list of other bases upon which a recovery based on an oral modification of a written agreement containing a NOM clause might be based: estoppel; oral novation and substitution of a new agreement; rescission of a written contract by an oral agreement; waiver of a provision of a written contract; and oral independent collateral contracts. Cases involving construction disputes similar to the *Miller* case above often provide relief based on principles of waiver and estoppel, some expressly calling out § 1698(d) in support and others not.

C. New York

1. Solving the Problem by Statute (Again)

Like California, New York has explicitly addressed the enforceability of NOM clauses by statute. By comparison, the NY statute is shorter, clearer, and simpler. Whether it's better, however, is a different matter. The

---

[32] *See, e.g.*, Cirimele v. Shinazy, 268 P.2d 210, 212 (Cal. Dist. Ct. App. 1954) (holding, in the context of a lease agreement dispute in which estoppel was never raised, that, as far as rent payments made under the oral modification were concerned, the previously paid payments were "executed" and there could be no claim for recovery by the lessor; however, as far as prospective (executory) rent payments were concerned, the lessor was not bound by the oral modification and a recovery under the original written agreement was appropriate).

reason: the judicial application of some would say the "judicial gloss" over the statutory language is perhaps a bit more surprising and counterintuitive. Let's begin, as always, with the text. N.Y. General Obligations Law § 15-301(1) provides:

> A written agreement or other written instrument which contains a provision to the effect that it cannot be changed orally, cannot be changed by an executory agreement unless such executory agreement is in writing and signed by the party against whom enforcement of the change is sought or by his agent.[33]

It doesn't get much clearer than that. More than a few court decisions construing New York law state that the statute is premised on the notion that, when the contract language is clear, it should be construed and enforced in accordance with its terms.[34] The courts construing New

---

[33] N.Y. Gen. Oblig. Law § 15-301(1) (McKinney 1963); *cf.* § 15-301(2) (no oral termination); § 15-301(3) (no oral discharge or partial discharge of obligations).

[34] *See, e.g.*, Golden Archer Invests. V. Skynet Fin. Sys., 908 F.Supp.2d. 526, 532 (S.D.N.Y. 2012) (applying the statute: "New York has long adhered to the sound rule in the construction of contracts that where the language is clear, unequivocal and unambiguous, the contract is to be interpreted by its own language. *When parties set down their agreement in a clear, complete document, their writing should as a rule be enforced according to its terms.* Thus, parol evidence is not admissible to create an ambiguity in a written agreement which is complete and clear and unambiguous upon its face. Of course, if a contract is not fully integrated, the parol evidence rule does not apply and courts may consider extrinsic evidence of separate oral agreements to determine the full nature of the parties' agreements. *However, even if a contract is not fully integrated, where it requires that any modifications or amendments be made in a signed writing, the contract may not be modified orally.* In this case, the Agreement states that it 'may not be

York law have held that NOM statute is applied even when the contract isn't a fully integrated one.[35]

On its face, the statute seems to recognize only one important distinction / exception of interest. It references "executory agreements."[36] That's no accident, and the decisions construing the language are clear. An oral modification that has been *fully* executed can and will be enforced despite the presence of a NOM clause,[37] whereas a *partially* executed oral modification will only be so enforced when the performance is "unequivocally referable" to the modification.[38] That is, the conduct constituting the alleged

---

amended, changed, or supplemented in any way except by written Agreement signed by both parties.' Therefore, the Agreement can only be modified in writing.") (emphasis added; citations omitted).

[35] *Id.*

[36] *See supra* the text regarding California's similar recognition of the distinction between "executory" performance versus "executed" performance of oral modifications accompanying note 32.

[37] *See, e.g.*, Mot Parking v. 86-90 Warren Str. LLC, 962 N.Y.S.2d 116, 117 (N.Y. App. Div. 2013) ("General Obligations Law § 15-301(1) states that a written agreement... cannot be changed by an *executory* agreement... The statute does not apply to an *executed* agreement. In this case, the parties' December 2007 oral agreement was executed, not executory. (Therefore, it was enforceable, notwithstanding the no-oral-modification clause in the lease.") (emphasis in original; citations omitted).

[38] *See, e.g.*, Mooney v. AXA Advisors, 19 F.Supp.3d 486, 504-505 (S.D.N.Y. 2014) ("The New York Court of Appeals ... has recognized an exception to § 15-301(1), known as *the doctrine of partial performance*. (Under this doctrine, an oral agreement may modify a preexisting written agreement if (1) there has been partial performance of the oral modification and (2) that partial performance is *unequivocally referable* to the oral modification – that is, *the conduct constituting the alleged partial performance must not be compatible with the written agreement*. ... This doctrine applies even where the written agreement contains a prohibition against oral modification. Here, Mooney has alleged facts that indicate that there was a modification to the Associate and Representative Agreements by pleading that AXA "credited" him with years of continuous service when he returned to work for the company in 2003. He has also pled

partial performance must not be compatible with the written agreement.[39]   In *Mooney v. AXA Advisors, LLC,*[40] for example, an insurance company's former employee alleged that a written contract had been orally modified, and he adduced as evidence of that modification the partial performance that occurred when (a) the company credited him with years of service and (b) paid him commissions that he was not due under the written agreement (but which were paid pursuant to the alleged oral modification).[41]

2. Judicially Crafted Exceptions to the New York Statute

As stated, the NY NOM statute appears quite straightforward, referencing only a single exception of significant practical interest. However, the fact is that the courts construing New York law have recognized other important exceptions as well, exceptions that would not be apparent from a facial reading of the statute.

Chief among these is the judicially recognized exception for estoppel. In *Latham Four Partnership v. SSI Medical Services,*[42] a commercial landlord brought summary eviction proceedings against a tenant, arguing that an alleged oral modification of the written lease agreement was unenforceable due to the "no oral modifications" clause in

---

that AXA acted on this modification by paying him commissions and other compensation as if they had vested under the Agreements. According to AXA, Mooney was never entitled to vested commissions … under the Agreements… Because Mooney has alleged that AXA paid him these commissions anyway, he has sufficiently pled that AXA acted in a way that was inconsistent with the written Agreements yet unequivocally referable to the alleged modification.") (emphasis added; citations omitted).

[39] *Id.*

[40] *Id.*

[41] *Id.*

[42] Latham Four P'ship v. SSI Med. Servs., 581 N.Y.S.2d 891 (N.Y. App. Div. 1992).

the lease. The Justice Court dismissed the landlord's complaint, and the County Court and Supreme Court Appellate Division affirmed.[43] The appellate court specifically called out equitable estoppel as one of the "recognized exceptions" to § 15-301, noting that, *"once a party* to a written agreement *has induced another's significant and substantial reliance upon an oral modification, that party may be estopped from invoking the statute* to bar proof of the oral modification."[44] The court then provided a straightforward application of these principles to protect SSI, the defendant-tenant who canceled an imminently commencing new lease in reliance on its current landlord's assurances that it could extend and continue to enjoy its current lease for another five months.

> Here, [Tenant's Agent] clearly testified that after she explained the situation between [Tenant] and [Tenant's New Landlord], *[Landlord's Agent] agreed that it would be permissible for [Tenant] to remain at [Landlord's] premises* until April 1, 1990, when [Tenant's New Landlord]'s new premises ... would be ready for occupancy. As a result of this November 2, 1989 conversation, [Tenant] thereafter agreed to release [Tenant's New Landlord] from his original obligation to provide [instantly available] rental space to [Tenant] ... commencing December 1, 1989. ... *There is little doubt from this evidence that [Landlord] agreed to modify its lease with full knowledge of [Tenant's] situation and that [Tenant] substantially relied on this*

[43] *Id.* at 893.

[44] *Id.* (quoting Rose v. Spa Realty Assocs., 366 N.E.2d 1279, 1285 (N.Y. 1977) (emphasis added)).

modification to its detriment by releasing [Tenant's New Landlord] from his prior obligation to provide [Tenant] with leased space [instantly available] at the expiration of [Tenant]'s original lease agreement with [Landlord]. *Under these circumstances, we decline to disturb the conclusion that [Landlord] should be estopped from asserting General Obligation Law 15-301 to bar proof of this oral modification.*[45]

D. Delaware

1. The Inherent Powers of Contracting Parties (Revisited)

Delaware's approach to the issue of NOM clauses is highly reminiscent of the approach adopted in Texas. It has largely addressed the issue in its case law.

Attention should be given to the 1972 Delaware Supreme Court opinion in *Pepsi-Cola Bottling Co. of Asbury Park v. Pepsico, Inc.*[46] In that case, the plaintiffs were two independent bottlers holding appointments by (written agreements with) Pepsico dating to the mid-1940s granting them the exclusive right to bottle and sell Pepsi-Cola in their defined areas.[47] At the time, Pepsico sold its concentrate at a uniform price, based on a mark-up to its own costs, to some 500 bottling plants throughout the U.S.[48] Over time, the explicit recognition of the cost plus basis of the pricing was phased out, but, at the time of the dispute, 125 of the 500 bottlers still had provisions that recognized cost-plus as the basis of the pricing of the concentrate.[49]

---

[45] *Id.* (emphasis and bracketed material added).
[46] Pepsi-Cola Bottling v. Pepsico, 297 A.2d 28 (Del. 1972).
[47] *Id.* at 29.
[48] *Id.* at 30.
[49] *Id.* at 31.

The appointments contained provisions that no future changes to the terms of the agreements (which included absolute prices for the concentrate) would be valid except when reduced to writing and executed by both sides.[50] One might assume that, the moment Pepsico began raising the price of its concentrate, there would have been a strong, swift reaction, but that wasn't the case. In fact, it raised the price of its concentrate nine times without objection and without express mutual written agreement over a period of more than fifteen years.[51] Although the price increases began in 1946, the first bottler objection occurred in 1963.[52]

The bottlers argued forcibly that the pricing changes weren't valid, because the written agreements proscribed changes to the pricing absent mutual express written agreement.[53] The Delaware Supreme Court was unimpressed:

> We think, therefore, that a written agreement between contracting parties, despite its terms, is not necessarily only to be amended by formal written agreement. We agree with *Stanchfield* that a written agreement does not necessarily govern all conduct between contracting parties until it is renounced in so many words. *The reason for this is that the parties have a right to renounce or amend the agreement in any way they see fit and by any mode or expression they see fit.* They may, by their conduct, substitute a new oral contract

---

[50] *Id.* at 32.
[51] *Id.*
[52] *Id.* at 31.
[53] *Id.* at 32.

without a formal abrogation of the written agreement.[54]

The prohibition against amendment except by written change may be waived or modified in the same way in which any other provision of a written agreement may be waived or modified, including a change in the provisions of the written agreement by the *course of conduct* of the parties.[55]

Thus, *Pepsi-Cola*, by its terms does indeed establish that, in Delaware, despite the presence of a NOM clause, one or more of the provisions of a written agreement may in fact be waived or modified orally by the parties. However, it's also clear that the court, in making its ruling, was struck by the rather extreme facts of the case at hand. It concluded its opinion by stating that the fifteen-year course of conduct of the parties had "emasculated" the original pricing provision and established a new pricing practice by agreement.[56]

---

[54] *Id.* at 33 (emphasis added; excerpt referring to Bartlett v. Stanchfield, 19 N.E. 549, 549 (1889) "*Attempts of parties to tie up by contract their freedom of dealing with each other are futile.* The contract is a fact to be taken into account in interpreting the subsequent conduct of the plaintiff and defendant, no doubt. But it cannot be assumed, as a matter of law, that the contract governed all that was done until it was renounced in so many words, because *the parties had a right to renounce it in any way, and by any mode of expression, they saw fit.* (They could substitute a new oral contract by conduct and intimation, as well as by express words.") (emphasis added)).
[55] 297 A.2d at 33 (emphasis added).
[56] *Id.*

2. Inherent Powers that Must be Evidenced with "Specificity"

Pepsi-Cola was followed and extended in *Reeder v. Sanford School, Inc.*[57] In that case, the plaintiff, a teacher / football coach, had brought suit for breach of an employment contract.[58] The defendant school had filed a summary judgment motion alleging that it had an express right under the contract to terminate the plaintiff's employment on thirty days' notice at any time.[59] The catch in *Reeder* is that the plaintiff alleged that defendant's headmaster had orally modified the contract by assuring him that his salary would not be reduced by the recent termination of the varsity football program and that he would be assigned new work to take the place of his coaching duties an allegation the headmaster denied).[60]

The *Reeder* court noted with approval *Pepsi-Cola*'s recognition of the validity of an oral modification to a written contract based on acquiescence.[61] It then went on to extend the holding, stating: "… an oral contract changing the terms of a written contract must be of *such specificity and directness* as to leave *no doubt* of the intention of the parties to change what they previously solemnized by formal document."[62] The court's application of the principles it cited was somewhat limited as it noted in parallel that the plaintiff had clearly raised a fact issue regarding estoppel, and so it ultimately denied the defendant's motion.[63] But *Pepsi-Cola*'s foundational principle that a written contract containing a NOM clause can be modified by the parties "in

---

[57] Reeder v. Sanford School, 397 A.2d 139 (Del. Super. Ct. 1979).
[58] *Id.* at 139.
[59] *Id.* at 140-41.
[60] *Id.* at 140.
[61] *Id.* at 141.
[62] *Id.* (citation to 17A C.J.S. *Contracts* § 434, 436 (1955) omitted).
[63] *Id.* at 141.

any way they see fit," and *Reeder*'s admonition that such modifications must be supported by evidence of "such specificity and directness as to leave no doubt" that the modification indeed occurred, have been followed by later courts, including the Delaware Supreme Court.[64]

III. THE WAY FORWARD

One cannot canvas the statutes and cases in this area without reaching one firm conclusion: clarity in this area of the law benefits everyone. So, readers can consider this article to be a call for continued statutory and common law attention to the issue. The creation of the NOM clause, and the courts' reactions to it, demonstrate that society is

---

[64] *See, e.g.*, 913 North Mkt. St. P'ship v. Davis, 723 A.2d 397, *2 (Del. 1998) unpublished disposition, stating: "The Superior Court refused to view Siddig's testimony as altering the written terms of the note that expressed the time for payment. The terms of a written contract, however, may be modified by subsequent oral agreement of the parties to forbear their rights under the agreement. (The party asserting such modification bears the burden of proving the intended change with 'specificity and directness,' but the circumstances of the parties' dealings may suffice.") (citations omitted); Continental Ins. v. Rutledge & Co., 750 A.2d 1219, 1230 (Del. Ch. 2000) "A party asserting an oral modification must prove the intended change with 'specificity and directness as to leave no doubt of the intention of the parties to change what they previously solemnized by formal document.' Absent a written modification, the Court finds itself in a precarious position. In order to recognize the oral modification, the Court must take defendants at their word, despite plaintiffs' denial of any alteration. To make such a leap of faith, however, the Court must first rule out the possibility that the asserting party has alleged an oral modification in an attempt to unilaterally alter a pre-existing, but unfavorable, agreement. (In an effort to screen out parties' attempts to single-handedly change contracts under the guise of oral modifications, courts have established *a high evidentiary burden* for parties asserting such changes. (Delaware law certainly continues to recognize the viability of oral modifications of contracts, but these alterations must be proven with 'specificity and directness.'") (emphasis added; citations omitted).

continuing to try to deal with two separate important problem areas.

First, the reason the NOM clause was created in the first place was to assist in minimizing the probability that "curbstone" discussions about the course of performance of a contract would be haplessly converted into revised binding contractual commitments regardless of whether they were denominated as modifications, waivers, etc.). A natural way in which to accomplish this would seem to be to simply insist that the parties couple important changes made to their relationship with a writing. So, what's the problem?

The problem is that, as the cases in this article will attest, an extraordinary amount of time and money is lost each year dealing with changes made to contractual relationships during the performance of those relationships. If this seems like much ado about nothing, the engaged reader is invited to try doing a Google search on a single two-word phrase: "**scope creep**". You'll get over *one million* hits all relating to the problem of clients requesting changes to the objectives of the relationship and service providers struggling with how to manage those expectations.

And that is the key point – in the end, scope creep is fundamentally a *management* problem. The best contract in the world cannot save a project from a poor project manager. And one of the most important aspects of the project manager's job is finding practical, effective ways in which to cajole the parties to use the contractual "change management" frameworks contained in the contract to engage in *a structured negotiation throughout the life of the project* about which changes to the project's scope really are worth the additional time and money required to bring them about.

But, because great project managers are as rare as great lawyers, great doctors, and great politicians, as delays, expenses, and frustrated expectations mount, at least one of the parties will likely begin to look longingly at the NOM clause as the ultimate "get out of jail free" card. "Perhaps," John muses as he waits for Prudence to show up at the restaurant, "this single line of text can shift the responsibility and the costs for the delays and unmet expectations to the other side…"

And *that* is the moment, the moment when one of the parties considers using the courts to resolve a management problem replete with substantial and conflicting reliance interests, that this private matter is transformed into a matter of public concern. On the one hand, we want to protect our *contractual* interest in being able to fashion our agreements however we deem fit. On the other hand, however, we also want to recognize that there are **important non-contractual interests** at stake too, such as the obvious unfairness of a party actively inducing his counterparty to rely to her detriment on a set of mutual reciprocal promises clearly made but imperfectly memorialized.

In the end, as Prudence suggested, John has a management problem, *and* an ethical problem, *and* a legal problem. The first two problems transcend jurisdiction, and they are the kind of problems that will continue to bedevil him so long as his position features important project management responsibilities and he continues to find difficulty in managing the expectations of disparate stakeholders. (Believe it or not, some project managers enjoy (nay, thrive) on scope creep – related multiparty negotiations.) The legal problem, as the cases above will attest, will be resolved based on the idiosyncratic facts regarding precisely what was said and done by whom and when and, of course, on the law in John's own particular jurisdiction.

As he sat there, eating his pie with Prudence, he recalled the warning SISD's in-house counsel had given him when they drafted the contract that he had naively thought would eliminate any potential for mismanagement. "Remember, although contracts and projects are important matters, there are always elements of game-playing at work too, because everything (even the contract) is governed by rules. And your chances of winning at blackjack, and at baseball, *and at this massive construction project*, are always better if you understand the rules, have experienced players on your side, build a lead early, use the home-field advantage, know the refs, etc., etc., etc. *So, if things start to go sideways on this thing in any way, the earlier you call me, the better.*" As John took his last bite of pie, he wished he'd paid closer attention.

VICARIOUS SUPERVISORY LIABILITY IN THE LLP, LLC, AND CORPORATION: TIME TO DO AWAY WITH THE LAST VESTIGE OF THE GENERAL PARTNERSHIP

NICHOLAS C. MISENTI[*]

I. INTRODUCTION

The doctrine of *respondeat superior* is not applicable to the relationship between a supervisor and his subordinate employees. The supervisor occupies an economic and legal position quite different from that of the employer. It is not the supervisor's work that is being performed, nor does he share in the profits which the employees' conduct is designed to produce. In the usual situation, furthermore, he, like his subordinates, is a wage earner, and he is seldom able to respond in damages to an appreciably greater extent than they. For these reasons, the law has shifted financial responsibility from the supervisor, who exercises immediate control, to the employer, who exercises ultimate control and for whose benefit the work is done.[1]

Exceptions to limited liability may be most closely associated with the LLP. When the LLP was first created in Texas, partners were not provided full limited liability. Instead, legislators partially retained vicarious liability from the general partnership in the first version of the LLP. Specifically, partners in an LLP remained vicariously liable

---

[*] J.D., CPA.
[1] California Supreme Court Chief Justice Robert Traynor, explaining why vicarious supervisory liability is inappropriate. *Malloy v. Fong,* 37 Cal. 2d 356, 378-9, 232 P.2d 241, 254-5 (Sup. Ct. 1951).

for the acts and omissions of non-partner employees and agents, and for the general debts of the partnership.[2]

However, one exception to limited liability, in the form of vicarious liability, predates the LLP: namely, vicarious supervisory liability.[3] This exception first appeared in the corporation, in the 1960s when professionals were first allowed to incorporate. Today, this exception exists in many states in the corporation, LLC, and LLP. Vicarious supervisory liability generally applies only in entities that provide professional services, although at least one state, Connecticut, applies this exception to *all* LLPs.[4]

Recent literature has not examined the underpinnings for this exception to limited liability. It has essentially gone unnoticed and unchallenged.[5] Why vicarious supervisory liability exists at all is unclear. Different theories can be envisioned that could possibly support vicarious supervisory liability. The history of prohibitions on professionals incorporating, and the history of the first LLP in Texas, offer

---

[2] Elizabeth S. Miller, *The Perils and Pitfalls of Practicing Law in A Texas Limited Liability Partnership,* 43 Tex. Tech L. Rev. 563, 564 (2011). Another way of looking at it is that the initial version of the LLP in Texas only eliminated mutual agency, so that partners would not be vicariously liable for the acts and omissions of the other partners.

[3] A typical version of the exception makes someone vicariously liable for the acts and omissions of another person who they directly supervise and control to the person who is being rendered professional services. *See, e.g.,* 8 Del. C. 1953, §608.

[4] CGS Sec. 34-327(d). Strangely, in contrast to the LLP, CT applies vicarious supervisory liability only to corporations and LLCs that provide professional services. No explanation for this inconsistency can be found.

[5] The literature has focused solely on what is "direct supervision and control" that could trigger vicarious liability, without questioning why the exception exists. *See, e.g.,* Susan Saab Fortney, *Professional Responsibility and Liability Issues Related to Limited Liability Law Partnerships,* 39 S. Tex. L. Rev. 399, 439–40 (1998).

some insights as to its origin. However, in the end, the possible theories that could support vicarious supervisory liability lack merit. There are also inconsistencies in whether, or how, states apply vicarious supervisory liability, and inconsistencies within the same state as to how the exception applies to a corporation, LLC, or LLP. The general partnership can be seen as the basis for vicarious supervisory liability. However, in some states, vicarious supervisory liability applies to classes of supervisors in a corporation and LLC who would not have vicarious supervisory liability in a general partnership. There seems to be no well-reasoned explanation for these inconsistencies, but states which are leading the way, such a s Texas, demonstrate that the time has come to do away with vicarious supervisory liability.

II. COMMON VERSIONS OF VICARIOUS SUPERVISORY LIABILITY

A. The Professional Corporation Models

States generally limit vicarious supervisory liability to professional corporations. However, exactly who in a professional corporation is potentially subject to vicarious supervisory liability varies by state. Several different models exist.

1. The "Any Person" Model

A common version of vicarious liability in the corporation makes *any person* (director, officer, shareholder, agent, or employee) of the corporation personally liable for the acts and omissions of any person under his or her direct supervision and control. Liability extends to any persons receiving professional services from the business and harmed by the acts and omissions. or example, Delaware,[6]

---

[6] 8 Del. C. 1953, §608

Connecticut,[7] Florida,[8] New York,[9] New Jersey,[10] Illinois,[11] and Washington State[12] follow this model.

Delaware has a typical provision:

> Any officer, employee, agent or shareholder of a professional corporation shall remain personally and fully liable and accountable for any negligent, wrongful acts, or misconduct committed by such person, or by any person under such person's direct supervision and control, while rendering professional services on behalf of the professional corporation to the person for whom such professional services were being rendered.[13]

Connecticut has a slightly different provision that omits shareholders from the mix:

> . . . any officer, agent or employee of a corporation … shall be personally liable and accountable only for negligent or wrongful acts or misconduct committed by him, or by any person under his direct supervision and control, while rendering professional services on behalf of the corporation to the person for whom such professional services were being rendered . . ..[14]

---

[7] CGS Sec. 33-182e.

[8] Fl Stat. §621.07.

[9] NY Business Corporation Law §1505 (McKinney).

[10] NJ REV STAT SECTION 14A:17-8.

[11] IL 805 ILCS 10/8.

[12] Washington PC Statute §18.100. 070.

[13] 8 Del. C. 1953, §608.

[14] CGS Sec. 33-182e.

The omission of shareholders from the Connecticut statute is of no practical significance, since any shareholder directly supervising and controlling employees would also be an employee/agent of the corporation.

2. The "Shareholder" Model

Oregon takes a narrower approach and makes *only shareholders* vicariously liable for the acts and omissions of any person under his or her direct supervision and control to any persons receiving professional services:

> In the rendering of specified professional services on behalf of a domestic professional corporation to a person receiving the service or services, a shareholder of the corporation is personally liable as if the shareholder were rendering the service [ ] as an individual, only for negligent or wrongful acts or omissions or misconduct committed by the shareholder, or by a person under the direct supervision and control of the shareholder. [15]

---

[15] 2017 ORS 58.185(3).

3. The "No Vicarious Supervisory Liability" Model

Some states, such as Texas, make no liability distinction between professional and other corporations and thus do not impose vicarious supervisory liability on any corporation.[16] This model is consistent with the concept of a separate legal entity.

B. The LLC Vicarious Liability Models

States also take different approaches to vicarious supervisory liability in the LLC. States apply the "Any Person" or the "No Vicarious Supervisory Liability" models. There is no discernable explanation as to why no states appear to apply the "Shareholder" model to LLCs and instead apply vicarious supervisory liability only to Members.

1. The "Any Person" Model

Connecticut, New York, and Illinois follow the "Any Person" Model.[17] The Illinois professional LLC statute has a typical provision:

> Any manager, member, agent, or employee of a professional limited liability company shall remain personally and fully liable and accountable for any negligent or wrongful acts or misconduct committed by him or her or by any person under his or her direct supervision and control while rendering

---

[16] *See, e.g.,* Tex. Bus. & Comm. Code Sec. 301.010.

[17] CGS Sec. 34-251a(c), N.Y. P'ship Law § 26(c)i (McKinney), 805 ILCS 185/35.

professional services on behalf of the professional limited liability company.[18]
This LLC model in Connecticut, New York, and Illinois is at least consistent with the corporate models in these states, but that also means it suffers from the same faults.[19]

2. The "No Vicarious Supervisory Liability" Model

Some states apply the "No Vicarious Liability" Model to LLCs, even when they impose that vicarious supervisory liability in the corporation. Thus, while Delaware imposes the "Any Person" model in the corporation, it applies the "No Vicarious Supervisory Liability model in the LLC.[20] Similarly, Oregon applies the narrower "Shareholder" model in the corporation, but it does not impose vicarious liability at all in the LLC.[21] The most likely explanation for these inconsistencies seems to be that the corporate statutes have not been updated since the statutory creation of the LLC entities in those jurisdictions. On the other hand, the Illinois professional LLC statute that applies the "Any Person" model of vicarious supervisory liability in professional service LLCs is fairly new.[22]

C. The LLP Vicarious Liability Models

1. The "Any Person" Model

New York adopts the "Any Person" model for LLPs.[23] Thus, New York consistently applies this model across all three types entities. This due to the somewhat

---

[18] 805 ILCS 185/35.

[19] These faults are discussed below in subpart I.D, *infra.*

[20] Del Stat. Title 6 § 18-303.

[21] Or Stat. 63.165.

[22] IL P.A. 99-227, eff. August 3, 2015.

[23] N.Y. P'ship Law § 26(c)i (McKinney).

unusual fact that one statutory provision applies to all professional entities in New York. While New York has more consistency than most states, why there would be greater exposure to vicarious supervisory liability in a corporation, LLC, and LLP than in a general partnership remains unclear.

2. The "Shareholder" Model

In contrast, Connecticut imposes vicarious supervisory liability only on partners in an LLP.[24] This is consistent with the "Shareholder" model some states use for corporations and general partnerships. However, it is not consistent with the "Any Person" model that Connecticut applies to corporations and LLCs. Why Connecticut imposes liability to corporations and LLCs yet uses a different standard for LLPs defies explanation. Still stranger is the fact that Connecticut makes no distinction between professional and other LLPs, and instead imposes vicarious supervisory liability in *all* LLPs. Connecticut provides that limited liability in an LLP "shall not affect the liability of a partner in a registered limited liability partnership for his own negligence, wrongful acts or misconduct, or that of any person under his direct supervision and control."[25] This creates the anomaly that a person who will not provide professional services can form a Connecticut corporation or LLC, instead of an LLP, and thereby avoid vicarious supervisory liability all together.

---

[24] CGS Sec. 34-327(d).
[25] *Id.*

3. The "No Vicarious Supervisory Liability" Model

Ironically, Texas, the birthplace of vicarious supervisory liability,[26] no longer applies vicarious supervisory liability in the LLP. Texas law provides that:

> An owner, managerial official, employee, or agent of a professional entity . . . is not subject to the same liability imposed on the professional entity under this section.[27]

The application in Texas of a single statutory provision to all professional entities is unusual. New York also has a single statutory provision that applies to all professional entities. However, unlike Texas, New York applies the "All Persons" model to all professional entities.[28]

D. Flaws in the "Any Person" Model

The "Any Person" model reduces exposure to vicarious liability for a shareholder/owner of a corporation, as compared to a general partner in a general partnership, because vicarious liability of a shareholder is limited to vicarious supervisory liability. In a general partnership, the general partners have unlimited vicarious liability because they are in essence the business. However, that vicarious liability is limited to the general partners in a general partnership. The "Any Person" model in the corporation creates the anomaly that a nonowner (director, officer, agent, or employee) would have less exposure to vicarious supervisory liability in a general partnership than in a

---

[26] For a discussion of the history of the Texas LLP statute, see Robert W. Hamilton, *Registered Limited Liability Partnerships: Present at the Birth (Nearly),* 66 U. Colo. L. Rev. 1065 (1995).

[27] Tex. Bus. Org.'s Code Sec. 301.010(b).

[28] N.Y. P'ship Law § 26(c)i (McKinney).

corporation. It is unclear that this is a result specifically contemplated by the legislature, and instead is an illustration of the often irrational nature of vicarious supervisory liability.

E. Flaws in the "Shareholder" Model

The "Shareholder" approach is consistent with the general partnership model. But it is not free of serious faults. Multiple theories could explain the imposition of vicarious supervisory liability upon an owner of a separate legal entity, such as a corporation. One theory posits that, but for vicarious liability, a shareholder could escape personal lability for wrongdoing, such as negligently supervising an employee. However, this theory lacks merit since personal liability for wrongdoing, including direct and supervisory negligence, is a well-established exception to limited liability in a corporations, LLCs, and LLPs.[29]

Another potential theory is that professionals owe a "super duty" to patients and clients, such that they guarantee the work of persons they directly supervise. If that is the case, then this model produces a peculiar outcome in that a non-shareholder supervisors will escape vicarious liability. In short, there is no justification for vicarious supervisory liability under the Shareholder Model.

III. THE ROOT OF VICARIOUS SUPERVISORY LIABILITY: VICARIOUS LIABILITY IN THE GENERAL PARTNERSHIP

Before the 1960s, professionals were denied the right to incorporate and were therefore relegated to operating in general partnership or sole proprietorship entities.[30] A

---

[29] *See, e.g., Jane Doe, et al. v. Chad Coe, et al.,* 2019 IL 123521 (May 23, 2019). See also, Nicholas Misenti, *Personal Liability for Commission of a Tort: A Significant, and Often Overlooked, Exception to Limited Liability in the LLC and Corporation* October 2016 *Southern Journal of Business & Ethics,* Volume 8 (2016), p. 11.

[30] Thill, Debra L., *The Inherent Powers Doctrine and Regulation of the Practice of Law: Will Minnesota Attorneys Practicing in Professional Corporations or Limited Liability Companies be Denied the Benefit of Statutory Liability Shields?,* William Mitchell Law Review: Vol. 20:

general partnership is an undesirable entity in which to operate a business. Vicarious liability is the hallmark of the general partnership. Each partner in a general partnership is an agent of the partnership.[31] *Respondeat superior* makes a principal vicariously liable for all of the acts and omissions of an agent that are committed while carrying out the principal's business.[32] Partners in a general partnership have joint and several liability for the partnership's debts.[33] The result is that a partner in a general partnership is vicariously liable for the acts and omissions of all partners and employees of the partnership committed in the course of the partnership's business.[34]

State legislatures have expressed outright hostility to the idea of professionals, in particular lawyers and physicians, incorporating.[35] Even when professionals have been allowed to incorporate, this hostility has continued as states adopted varying restrictions on limited liability. The majority of states adopted vicarious supervisory liability as the exception.[36] It is this vicarious supervisory liability that

Issue. 4, Article 7, 1143 (1994).
Available at: http://open.mitchellhamline.edu/wmlr/vol20/iss4/7.
George A. Buchmann, Jr. and Ralph H. Bearden, Jr., *The Professional Service Corporation - A New Business Entity,* University of Miami Law Review XVI No. 1, p. 1, Fall 1961.
[31] UPA Section 301(1).
[32] Restatement (Second) of Agency § 219 (1958).
[33] UPA Section 306(a).
[34] Unif. Ltd. P'ship Act § 404(a) (2001). Lauris G.L. Rall, *A General Partner's Liability Under the Uniform Limited Partnership Act (2001)*, 37 Suffolk U. L. Rev. 913, 926 (2004).
[35] Will Minnesota Attorneys Practicing in Professional Corporations or Limited Liability Companies be Denied the Benefit of Statutory Liability Shields?, William Mitchell Law Review: Vol. 20: Issue. 4, Article 7, p. 1143, 1154-5, fn 68.Available at: htp://open.mitchellhamline.edu/wmlr/vol20/iss4/7.
[36] Thill, Debra L., *The Inherent Powers Doctrine and Regulation of the Practice of Law: Will Minnesota Attorneys Practicing in Professional Corporations or Limited Liability Companies be Denied the Benefit of*

exists today in the corporation, LLC, and LLP. Thus, an understanding the history of the prohibition on professionals incorporating is important.

IV. The Prohibition Against Professionals Incorporating as The Origin Of Vicarious Supervisory Liability

The lifting of the prohibition on professionals incorporating in the 1960s marks the first appearance of vicarious supervisory liability in the corporation. Therefore, it is important to understand why this prohibition existed, and why it was lifted. In his 1958 article, H. Bradley Jones examined the rationales underling the prohibition against professionals incorporating.[37]   Jones summarized this rationale as follows:[38]

1. A corporation itself cannot practice a profession because it cannot meet licensure requirements, such as minimum education and testing requirements ("corporate licensure rationale");
2. A professional relationship is personal, and a corporation itself cannot engage in a personal relationship ("personal relationship rationale");
3. Incorporation by professionals would undermine a professional's primary duty is to his client or patent because a professional would be beholden to the corporation ("primary duty rationale");

Statutory Liability Shields?, William Mitchell Law Review: Vol. 20: Issue. 4, Article 7, p. 1143, 1154, fn 68 (1994).
Available at: htp://open.mitchellhamline.edu/wmlr/vol20/iss4/7
[37] H. Bradley Jones, *The Professional Corporation*, Fordham Law Review, Volume 27, Issue 3, Article 3 (1958). (Bradley also proposed a model professional corporations statute with characteristics that were eventually adopted into law, including the requirement that all shareholders be licensed in the same profession. *Id.,* at pp 360-3.
[38] *Id.,* at pp 354-5.

4. A "middle-man" should not be inserted between a professional and his patent or client ("middle-man rationale");

5. The contract for professional services would be between the patient or client and the corporation, not the professional, thus relieving the professional of any duties to the patient or client ("contract rationale");

6. Even if all shareholders were licensed processionals, transfer of their shares to unlicensed individuals could occur ("unlicensed professionals rationale");

7. A corporation itself cannot be suspended from professional practice because it cannot be licensed to practice a profession in the first place ("professional discipline rationale"); and

8. Incorporation by professionals is unethical because a corporate limited liability shield would prevent professionals from being sued for negligence, and in particular, for medical malpractice ("personal liability shield rationale").

An examination of these rationales shows that they are, at best, questionable and many may fairly be described as specious.

A. The Corporate Licensure Rationale

The corporate licensure rationale is but a truism. It is true that an inanimate entity cannot meet educational, testing, and experience requirements to obtain a professional license, but that is not relevant. As early as 1938, commentators argued that the purpose of professional licensing statutes was being misconstrued and that there was no reason a corporation would need to be licensed to practice a profession.[39] Licensing statutes are designed to protect the public by ensuring that the individuals actually practicing the profession are competent; licensing individuals fulfills this purpose. While allowing laymen shareholders to direct professionals in a corporation could present an issue, that issue is easily resolved, and the purpose of licensing statutes fulfilled, simply by requiring that all shareholders be licensed in the same profession.[40]

B. The Personal Relationship Rationale

The personal relationship rationale is another example of a truism. It is true that an inanimate entity cannot engage in a personal relationship. However, it is also true that professionals within the corporation, and not the corporation itself, actually provide the services to patients and clients, and in this process they can, and do, establish personal relationships with patients and clients, thus making the personal relationship rationale irrelevant. It also appears that the personal relationship rationale is a different expression of some of the other rationales, including the corporate licensure and middle-man rationales, and may have been designed to provide a further underpinning for the penultimate rationale, the personal liability shield rationale.

C. The Primary Duty Rationale

The primary duty rationale posits that a professional with an employer would be beholden to the employer, and put the employer's interests, including maximizing profits, ahead of the interests of the client or patient. This rationale appears to be based on the mistaken belief that duties of the

---

[39] Note, *Right of Corporation to Practice Medicine*, 48 Yale L.J. 346, 348 (1938).
[40] *Id*, at p. 348.

professional to a corporation necessarily would supplant the duties of the professional to the patient or client.[41] This rationale also fails to recognize that a professional who has not incorporated has the same objective of making money, and may put his financial interests ahead of the patient's or client's interest. The introduction of the corporation does not change that argument. The issue, that laymen shareholders with no understanding of the profession and only a profit motive could direct professionals to put the corporation's interests before the patient's or client's interests, also presents itself here.[42]   Again, this issue is easily resolved simply by requiring that all shareholders be licensed in the same profession.

D. The Middle-Man Rationale

The middle-man rationale may be the weakest rationale of all. Simply put, it is hard to explain how an inanimate entity could physically impose itself between a professional and a patient or client. A corporation could not be in the room interfering with the professional's relationship with a patient or client. Nor could a corporation affirmatively act to undermine the professional's relationship with a patient or client. In short, this rationale is not born out in the real world. The middle-man argument is most closely related to the contract rationale.

---

[41] *See, e.g., In re Co-operative Law Co.,* 198 N.Y. 479 (1910), where the New York Appellate Court invalidated a corporation that was established to practice law. The court offered the typical rationale, including the idea that if lawyers were allowed to incorporate, they "would be subject to the directions of the corporation, and not to the directions of the client", and "the attorney would be responsible to the corporation only." *Id.*, at 483-4.
[42] *In re Co-operative Law Co., supra,* at 483.

E. The Contract Rationale

If a corporation is used to provide professional services, the contract rationale theorizes that the contract for professional services would be between the patient or client and the corporation, but not the professional. While it is also true that the corporation would be inserted between the patient or client and the professional, the professional's duties to a patient or client do not arise only from the contract. Stated differently, even if the contract were between the patient or client and the corporation, the professional would still owe duties to the patient or client.[43] The lack of contractual duties does not extinguish duties, such as those that arise under tort law. Tort duties arise and exist independently of contract duties.

The economic loss doctrine needs to be considered here. This doctrine provides that, where a contract exists between a plaintiff and defendant, and damages are solely economic in nature, a tort action is barred, and the only remedy is for breach of contract.[44] This would seem, at first glance, to provide a basis for the contract rationale. However, there are two relevant exceptions to the economic loss doctrine which are universally applied: a tort action is allowed where the professional services are involved, or where personal injuries occurred.[45] In short, the contract rationale lacks merit.

---

[43] In *In re Co-operative Law Co*, the New York Appellate Court opined that if a contract for legal services existed between a corporation and the client, "There would be neither contract nor privity between him and the client, and he would not owe even the duty of counsel to the actual litigant." *In re Co-operative Law Co., supra*, at 483.

[44] For a discussion of the economic loss doctrine, see Nicholas Misenti, *Personal Liability for Commission of a Tort: A Significant, and Often Overlooked, Exception to Limited Liability in the LLC and Corporation*, Southern Journal of Business & Ethics , Volume 8 (2016), p. 11, 27.

[45] *Id.,* at 29.

F. The Unlicensed Professionals Rationale

The unlicensed professionals rationale is easily addressed by requiring shareholders to members of the same profession, and prohibiting transfers to laymen, which is what H. Bradley Jones suggested in 1958,[46] and what ultimately became law when professionals were allowed to incorporate.[47]

G. The Professional Discipline Rationale

The professional discipline rationale is similarly without merit. It is true that a corporation itself is not licensed for professional practice because it cannot meet the education, experience, and testing requirements of a profession. Therefore, a corporation itself cannot be suspended from professional practice. However, the individual shareholders, who are actually engaged in the professional practice, are licensed and subject to discipline, resulting in the adequate protection for the public.

H. The Personal Liability Shield Rationale

This leaves the penultimate argument against professionals incorporating, and by implication for vicarious supervisory liability: the mistaken belief that limited liability shields professionals from liability for their own wrongdoing. While this fear has engendered the development of vicarious supervisory liability, it is unfounded. It is well established that personal liability

---

[46] H. Bradley Jones, *The Professional Corporation*, Fordham Law Review, Volume 27, Issue 3, Article 3 (1958) at pp 360-3.

[47] *See, e.g.,* CGS Sec. 33-182c.

applies when an owner of a corporation, LLC, or LLP commits a tort, the limited liability shield notwithstanding.[48]

V. FEDERAL INCOME TAX LAW AS THE SOLE BASIS FOR CHANGE

The assumption that professionals were finally allowed to incorporate due to a reevaluation of these rationales, while logical, is incorrect. In fact, the prohibition on professionals incorporating was lifted solely due to lobbying by professionals who wanted to obtain the federal tax benefits that were afforded at that time only to corporations and not to individuals.[49] There has never been a reconsideration of the faulty underpinnings of the prohibition. This helps explain why vicarious supervisory liability was carried over to the corporation, and then to the LLC and LLP.

A. Lobbying by Professionals for Tax Equality

It is not an exaggeration to say professionals and legislatures were fixated on the tax benefits that only corporations provided and that professionals practicing in the general partnership form were missing. During the post-World War II era, individual tax rates were significantly higher than corporate tax rates, and employee benefits, including qualified pensions, profit-sharing plans, and annuity plans were available only to corporations.[50] These

---

[48] *See, e.g.*, Nicholas Misenti, *Personal Liability for Commission of a Tort: A Significant, and Often Overlooked, Exception to Limited Liability in the LLC and Corporation* October 2016 Southern Journal of Business & Ethics , Volume 8 (2016), p. 11.

[49] 4 A.L.R.3d 383 (Originally published in 1965).

[50] Charles W. Hall et. al., *Professional Incorporation in Texas-A Current Look,* 48 Tex. L. Rev. 84, 88 (1969); 4 A.L.R.3d 383 (Originally published in 1965).

distinctions   led professionals, including doctors and lawyers, who were banned from incorporating, to form common law associations, which they argued should be classified as corporations for federal tax purposes.

In the first case of this era to consider the issue, *United States v. Kintner,* the court ruled in favor of a group of physicians who had formed a common law association to practice medicine in Montana, holding that the association was classified as a corporation for federal tax purposes, even though Montana law barred physicians from forming corporations to practice medicine.[51] The court relied on precedent from an earlier era, including *Morrissey v. Commissioner.*[52] However, the court also was persuaded by treasury department regulations, which at the time relied on state law to classify common law associations as corporations for federal tax purposes.[53]

In response to *Kitner,* the Treasury Department was quick to enact revised regulations that denied common law associations corporate tax status based on a finding that any one of the characteristics of a corporation[54] was missing.[55] For example, the new regulations provided that a restriction on transfer that gave existing members the first right to buy a member's interest before it could be sold to a qualified outsider meant that corporate characteristic of the ability to freely transfer an interest was missing.[56] The revised regulations also categorically provided that professional associations lacked continuity of life, essentially closing the

---

[51] 216 F.24 418 (9th Cir. 1954).

[52] 296 U.S. 344 (1935).

[53] Treas. Reg. § 301.7701-1(c), T.D. 6503, 1960-2 Cum. Bull. 409.

[54] The four characteristics being limited liability, continuity of interest, centralized management, and the ability to freely transfer an ownership interest.

[55] Treas. Reg. §§ 301.7701-1-2, T.D. 5697, 1965-1 Cum. Bull. 558.

[56] Treas. Reg. § 301.7701-2(h)(5)(ii), T.D. 5697, 1965-1 Cum. Bull. 553.

door on any possibility that a professional association could be classified as a corporation for federal tax purposes.[57]

States were quick to seize on the fact that the post-*Kitner* treasury regulations relied significantly on local law to classify professional associations.[58] By 1969, 47 states had statutes that allowed professionals to form professional corporations or associations.[59] Professionals were also quick to challenge the revised regulations, and courts were quick to invalidate the revised regulations on the grounds that the regulations were discriminatory and inconsistent with related tax statutes.[60]

This fairly rapid evolution in the law was based entirely on the idea that professionals were being discriminated against based on federal income tax benefits that were afforded only to corporations. Nowhere to be found in this evolution is even a suggestion that professionals were being singled out and discriminated against because they were denied any form of limited liability. This failure meant that antiquated and questionable rationales against professionals incorporating would continue even after states changed their laws to allow professionals to incorporate. This omission ultimately led to vicarious supervisory liability being carried over to the corporation, and then to the LLC and LLP.

---

[57] Treas. Reg. § 301.7701-2(h)(2), T.D. 5697, 1965-1 Cum. Bull. 553.

[58] Charles W. Hall et. al., *Professional Incorporation in Texas-A Current Look,* 48 Tex. L. Rev. 84, 92 (1969).

[59] *Id. (*at 92–93 (1969).

[60] *See United States v. Empey*, 406 F.2d 157 (10th Cir. 1969); *O'Neill v. United States,* 410 F.2d 888 (6th Cir. 1969); *Kurzner v. United States*, 413 F.2d 97 (5th Cir. 1969).

B. Hostility Toward Providing Limited Liability for Professionals: The First Professional Corporations

Many states were reluctant to provide limited liability to professionals when they were allowed incorporate.[61] States adopted different restrictions on limited liability. Four states (Colorado, Oregon, Wisconsin, and Wyoming) went so far as to continue to apply unlimited personal liability to professional corporations.[62] For example, North Carolina provided that a shareholder in a professional corporation was liable as if it were a general partnership. *Nelson v. Patrick* involved a malpractice case arising from radiology services by one physician, Patrick, in a North Carolina professional services corporation. A second physician, Flournoy, was held vicariously liable for Patrick's negligence. The court held that "defendant Flournoy could be held jointly and severally liable for any negligence of his partner, defendant Patrick, which occurred during the course of the corporation's business, and he could be made a party to the action."[63] *Nelson v. Patrick* clearly

---

[61] Thill, Debra L. (1994) *The Inherent Powers Doctrine and Regulation of the Practice of Law: Will Minnesota Attorneys Practicing in Professional Corporations or Limited Liability Companies be Denied the Benefit of Statutory Liability Shields?*, William Mitchell Law Review: Vol. 20: Issue. 4, Article 7, p. 1143, 1153, fn 66. Available at: https://open.mitchellhamline.edu/cgi/viewcontent.cgi?article=2204&context=wmlr

[62] Thill, Debra L. (1994) *The Inherent Powers Doctrine and Regulation of the Practice of Law: Will Minnesota Attorneys Practicing in Professional Corporations or Limited Liability Companies be Denied the Benefit of Statutory Liability Shields?*, William Mitchell Law Review: Vol. 20: Issue. 4, Article 7, p. 1143, 1153, fn 66. Available at: https://open.mitchellhamline.edu/cgi/viewcontent.cgi?article=2204&context=wmlr

[63] *Nelson v. Patrick*, 73 N.C. App. 1, 8–9, 326 S.E.2d 45, 50 (1985).

illustrates that the general partnership is the basis for vicarious supervisory liability.[64]

Many states adopted vicarious supervisory liability as the exception to limited liability when professionals were allowed to incorporate.[65] This vicarious supervisory liability is what is seen today in corporations, LLCs, and LLPs.

C. Continued Hostility Toward Providing Limited Liability for Professionals After Professionals Were Allowed to Incorporate

Hostility by professional organizations and courts to the idea that professionals, in particular lawyers and physicians, would have any version of limited liability continued after professionals were allowed to incorporate, even in states that provided for limited liability by statute. For example, the ABA Model Code of Professional

---

[64] N.C. Gen. Stat. Section 55B-9 now provides that:
"A shareholder, a director, or an officer of a professional corporation is not individually liable, directly or indirectly, including by indemnification, contribution, assessment, or otherwise, for the debts, obligations, and liabilities of, or chargeable to, the professional corporation that arise from errors, omissions, negligence, malpractice, incompetence, or malfeasance committed by another shareholder, director, or officer or by a representative of the professional corporation; provided, however, nothing in this Chapter shall affect the liability of a shareholder, director, or officer of a professional corporation for his or her own errors, omissions, negligence, malpractice, incompetence, or malfeasance committed in the rendering of professional services."
This clearly eliminates all vicarious liability. Why other states have not updated their statutes in a similar fashion is unclear.

[65] Thill, Debra L., *The Inherent Powers Doctrine and Regulation of the Practice of Law: Will Minnesota Attorneys Practicing in Professional Corporations or Limited Liability Companies be Denied the Benefit of Statutory Liability Shields?,* William Mitchell Law Review: Vol. 20: Issue. 4, Article 7, p. 1143, 1154, fn 68 (1994).
Available at: htp://open.mitchellhamline.edu/wmlr/vol20/iss4/7

Responsibility provided that an attorney could "limit his liability for malpractice of his associates in the corporation, but only to the extent permitted by law."[66] However, an earlier draft of this provision provided the following:

> A lawyer should not seek to limit his liability to his client for malpractice, whether by contract, limitation of corporate liability, or otherwise. Thus the liability of lawyers who are stockholders in a professional legal corporation should be the same *as it would be if they were practicing as partners* (emphasis added).[67]

This, again, is an example of how the general partnership is the basis for today's vicarious supervisory liability in the corporation, LLC, and LLP.

Some state supreme courts, from the 1970s to as late as the early 1990s, refused to allow for limited liability for attorneys practicing in professional corporations, even where statutory limited liability existed. Here, state supreme courts generally invoked their authority as the ultimate regulator of attorneys to override legislatures.[68]

In *First Bank & Trust Co. v. Zagoria,* the issue was whether an attorney/shareholder of a professional corporation in Georgia become personally liable for dishonored checks issued by the corporation when that

---

[66] EC 6-6 (1980).

[67] See American Bar Foundation, Annotated Code of Professional Responsibility 273 textual and historical notes (1979).

[68] See, eg., *First Bank & Tr. Co. v. Zagoria,* 250 Ga. 844, 845, 302 S.E.2d 674, 675 (1983), *overruled by Henderson v. HSI Fin. Servs., Inc.,* 266 Ga. 844, 471 S.E.2d 885 (1996), *In re Bar Ass'n of Hawaii,* 516 P.2d 1267,1268, *South High Development, Ltd. v. Weiner Lippe & Cromley Co.,* 445 N.E.2d 1106, 1107 (Ohio 1983), *Beane v. Paulsen,* 26 Cal. Rptr.2d 486 (Ct. App. 1993).

attorney/shareholder was not personally involved in managing the checking account.[69] The Georgia Supreme Court held that the attorney/shareholder was vicariously liable for the actions of his fellow attorney/shareholder who managed the checking account. The court noted "[t]he fact that a corporation is a legal entity separate and apart from its shareholders is so well recognized that it needs no elaboration."[70] However, the Court continued:

> We hold that when a lawyer holds himself out as a member of a law firm, the lawyer will be liable not only for his own professional misdeeds but also for those of the other members of his firm. We make no distinction between partnerships and professional corporations in this respect. We cannot allow a corporate veil to hang from the cornices of professional corporations which engage in the law practice.[71]

The Court explained its holding this way:

> We do not view this case as one in which we need to interpret the statute providing for the creation and operation of professional corporations. We rather view this case as one which calls for the exercise of this court's authority to regulate the practice of law.[72]

---

[69] *First Bank & Tr. Co. v. Zagoria,* 250 Ga. 844, 845, 302 S.E.2d 674, 675 (1983), *overruled by Henderson v. HSI Fin. Servs., Inc.,* 266 Ga. 844, 471 S.E.2d 885 (1996).
[70] *Id.*
[71] *Id.*, at 250 Ga. 846.
[72] *Id.*, at 250 Ga. 844, 845.

Cases that rejected limited liability were not limited to attorneys. Some courts also refused to apply limited liability protection to physicians.[73] In *Boyd v. Badenhausen*, a physician in a professional corporation was held vicariously liable "for the derelictions of persons employed by a corporation to carry out for him the clerical details that are necessary to the successful performance of his duty to render skillful care and attention to whomever he accepts as a patient."[74] The court applied what can be described as a loose interpretation of the Kentucky professional corporation statute, holding that the statute "provides *in substance* that the corporate existence shall not affect the relationship between the professional member and his client or patient (emphasis added)."[75] Based on that interpretation, the court held that vicarious liability applied.

What is clear from an examination of cases from this era is that there was a hostility to the very idea that professionals should have limited liability. Courts seemed to grapple with the idea that professional corporations should be, in essence, general partnerships, but with the tax benefits that were afforded only to corporations. This reluctance to accept change helps explain why vicarious liability still

---

[73] *See, e.g., Boyd v. Badenhausen*, 556 S.W.2d 896, 898 (Ky. 1977), *Nelson v. Patrick,* 326 S.E.2d 45 (N.C. Ct. App. 1985).

[74] The Kentucky professional corporation statute today contains a similar statement, but now the statute clearly renounces vicarious liability. It provides that provides "that no shareholder, director, officer or employee of a professional service corporation shall be personally liable for the negligence, wrongful acts, or actionable misconduct of any other shareholder, director, officer, agent or employee nor shall such shareholder, director, officer or employee be personally liable for the contractual obligations of the corporation." KRS § 274.055(2). This is evidence that some state legislatures have evolved on these issues. Too many states have not, however.

[75] *Boyd v. Badenhausen*, 556 S.W.2d 896, 898 (Ky. 1977).

exists in many states today, in the form of vicarious supervisory liability.

VI. THE FIRST LLP IN TEXAS AND THE RELUCTANCE TO PROVIDE A FULL LIMITED LIABILITY TO PROFESSIONALS

While the history of professional's ability to incorporate provides insights on the origin of vicarious supervisory liability, the history of the first LLP in Texas provides some insight into why vicarious supervisory liability still exists today. Robert Hamilton, a Texas State Legislator at the time, stated that "[t]he idea of limiting liability within partnerships generally was received with great skepticism."[76] Hamilton elaborated:

> Representative Steven Wolens, a Democrat from Dallas (and a lawyer with Baron & Budd, a litigation firm that conducted business as a professional corporation) viewed any change in the long-accepted characteristics of a general partnership to be a radical and undesirable proposal. Two other legislators argued to lawyer witnesses, 'You want your cake and yet you want to eat it too.'[77]

Thus, in the first version of the Texas LLP, partners remained vicariously liable for the acts and omissions of non-partner employees and agents, and for the general debts of the partnership.[78] It is clear that the mistaken notion that

---

[76] Robert W. Hamilton, *Registered Limited Liability Partnerships: Present at the Birth (Nearly)*, 66 U. Colo. L. Rev. 1065, 1073 (1995).
[77] *Id.*, at 1073.
[78] Elizabeth S. Miller, *The Perils and Pitfalls of Practicing Law in A Texas Limited Liability Partnership*, 43 Tex. Tech L. Rev. 563, 564 (2011). Another way of looking at it is that the initial version of the

limited liability would shield a professional from liability for his or her own acts and omissions played a part in the development of vicarious supervisory liability. However, the historic record makes clear that there was hostility to the very idea that professionals should have limited liability.

The 1997 amendments to the Texas LLP statute provided full shield version limited liability, with one exception: the amendments retained vicarious supervisory liability.[79] This can be understood as a reluctance by the Texas legislature to completely embrace limited liability for professionals.[80] Of the corporation, LLC, and LLP, the LLP is the newest form. Thus, the history of the LLP completes the connection to vicarious supervisory liability from the corporation to the modern day and helps explain why this exception to limited liability persists.

VII. WHY VICARIOUS SUPERVISORY LIABILITY IS UNNECESSARY

Someone who commits a tort such as negligence is personally liable for that tort. The limited liability shield provided by a corporation, LLC, or LLP does not change that outcome. This principle is so well established that it has been

---

LLP in Texas only eliminated mutual agency, so that partners would not be vicariously liable for the acts and omissions of the other partners.

[79] *See* Act of May 13, 1997, 75th Leg., R.S., ch. 375, § 113, 1997 Tex. Gen. Laws 1516, 1594-95 (amending § 3.08 of the Texas Revised Partnership Act (Article 6132b-3.08, Vernon's Texas Civil Statutes). (See also Elizabeth S. Miller, *The Perils and Pitfalls of Practicing Law in A Texas Limited Liability Partnership*, 43 Tex. Tech L. Rev. 563, 586 (2011).

[80] Elizabeth S. Miller, *The Perils and Pitfalls of Practicing Law in A Texas Limited Liability Partnership*, 43 Tex. Tech L. Rev. 563, 586 (2011).

called black letter law by one court.[81] That the person may have a principal who also is vicariously liable for that same tort under *respondeat superior* also is irrelevant to that outcome. [82]

Negligent supervision is, simply put, negligence. A person who negligently supervises is directly liable for his own omission, just as he would be liable for any other act or omission constituting negligence. Thus, vicarious supervisory liability is unnecessary to liability for wrongdoing. *Jane Doe v. Chad Coe et al.* provides a good example of liability for negligent supervision.[83] The plaintiff, a 15 year old minor at the time, was allegedly sexually molested by a 31 year old youth pastor Coe), at the First Congregational Church of Dundee (FCCD). The lawsuit included allegations of negligent hiring, negligent retention and negligent supervision of the youth pastor against both FCCD and James, the church's pastor and the youth pastor's direct supervisor.

The court identified three elements to state a claim for negligent supervision: "(1) the defendant had a duty to supervise the harming party, (2) the defendant negligently supervised the harming party, and (3) such negligence proximately caused the plaintiff's injuries."[84] These are the elements in a simple negligence case. Thus, negligent supervision is already actionable. Professionals in a corporation, LLC, or LLP cannot escape liability for

---

[81] *Kilduff v. Adams, Inc.,* 593 A.2d 478, 488 (Conn. 1991).

[82] See Nicholas Misenti, *Personal Liability for Commission of a Tort: A Significant, and Often Overlooked, Exception to Limited Liability in the LLC and Corporation* October 2016 *Southern Journal of Business & Ethics* , Volume 8 (2016), p. 11.

[83] *Doe by Doe by Doe v. Coe,* 2018 IL App (2d) 170435, ¶ 90, 103 N.E.3d 436, 456, *appeal allowed sub nom. Doe v. Coe,* 108 N.E.3d 885 (Ill. 2018), and *aff'd in part, rev'd in part and remanded sub nom. Doe v. Coe,* 2019 IL 123521, ¶ 90, 135 N.E.3d 1.

[84] Id., at IL App (2d) 170435, at ¶ 103, 103 N.E.3d at 456.

improper supervision of other employees. Vicarious supervisory liability is not necessary to achieve this outcome.

VIII. CHANGE IS POSSIBLE

Change, though it may be slow, can take place. In 1996, the Georgia Supreme Court reversed its more than a decade old decision in *First Bank & Tr. Co. v. Zagoria*,[85] which had held that limited liability did not apply to attorneys, despite statutory limited liability shields.[86] The Kentucky professional corporation statute has also been amended to affirmatively disavow vicarious liability, effectively overruling *Boyd v. Badenhausen*,[87] which had held that a physician in a professional corporation was vicariously liable for the negligence of clerical staff.[88]

The Texas LLP may be the best example of how change can occur. In the original Texas LLP statute, partners remained vicariously liable for the acts and omissions of non-partner employees and agents, and for the general debts of the partnership.[89] A 1997 amendment provided more of a full shield version of limited liability, but retained vicarious supervisory liability.[90] A subsequent amendment to the Texas LLP statute did away with vicarious supervisory

---

[85] *First Bank & Tr. Co. v. Zagoria*, 250 Ga. 844, 845, 302 S.E.2d 674, 675 (1983), *overruled by Henderson v. HSI Fin. Servs., Inc.*, 266 Ga. 844, 471 S.E.2d 885 (1996).

[86] *Henderson v. HSI Fin. Servs., Inc.*, 266 Ga. 844, 471 S.E.2d 885 (1996).

[87] *Boyd v. Badenhausen*, 556 S.W.2d 896, 898 (Ky. 1977).

[88] See the current version of KRS § 274.055(2).

[89] *See,* Act of May 25, 1991, 72d Leg., R.S., ch. 901, § 84, 1991 Tex. Gen Laws 3161, 3234 amending § 15 of the Texas Uniform Partnership Act. *See also,* Elizabeth S. Miller, *The Perils and Pitfalls of Practicing Law in A Texas Limited Liability Partnership,* 43 Tex. Tech L. Rev. 563, 564 (2011).

[90] *Id.,* at 566.

liability and provided for "full shield" limited liability.[91] Thus, the Texas LLP evolved from an extreme version of vicarious liability to a narrower version of vicarious liability that retained vicarious supervisory liability, to the current version, which is a No Vicarious Liability model. Why other states, including Delaware,[92] Connecticut,[93] Florida,[94] New York,[95] New Jersey,[96] Illinois,[97] and Washington State,[98] have not modernized their statutes in a similar fashion is unclear. The basis for these older, unamended statutes is not sound.

IX. CONCLUSION

Vicarious supervisory liability is still applied today to professional corporations, LLCs and LLPs in some states. One state, Connecticut, inexplicably applies vicarious supervisory liability to *all* LLPs. Vicarious supervisory liability may apply to "All Persons" or to "All Shareholders" models. In some states, how the exception applies will depend on whether someone is operating a corporation, LLC, or LLP. The existence of these inconsistencies cannot be explained. There are flaws in the theories that could support either of these models. Further, in some states, vicarious supervisory liability applies to classes of supervisors in a corporation and LLC who would not have vicarious supervisory liability in a general partnership. These inconstancies illustrate the irrational and haphazard nature of vicarious supervisory liability.

---

[91] See Tex. Bus. Org.'s Code Sec. 301.010(b).

[92] 8 Del. C. 1953, §608.

[93] CGS Sec. 33-182e.

[94] Fl Stat. §621.07.

[95] NY Business Corporation Law §1505 (McKinney).

[96] NJ REV STAT SECTION 14A:17-8.

[97] IL 805 ILCS 10/8.

[98] Washington PC Statute §18.100. 070.

The general partnership, and the unlimited vicarious liability it imposes on partners, forms the basis for today's vicarious liability. The hostility toward allowing professionals any version of limited liability led to vicarious supervisory liability once professionals were finally allowed to incorporate in the 1960s. The justifications preventing professionals from incorporating lack merit. In particular, the notion that limited liability shields would insulate professionals from liability from their wrongdoing is mistaken. Because professionals mounted intense lobbying efforts to be allowed to incorporate solely because of the beneficial tax treatment afforded at the time only to corporations, there was never a serious examination or abandonment of those faulty rationales. This unfortunate failure to grapple with the statutory underpinnings allowed vicarious supervisory liability to be carried forward to the LLC and then the LLP. Although some states have modernized their statutes, many have not. It is time for all states to eliminate this last vestige of the general partnership in the corporation, LLC, and LLP.

CRYPTOCURRENCY AND THE IRS: A CASE APPLYING PROPERTY TAX RULES

Lara L. Kessler [*]
Neal Vandenberg [**]

Abstract

This is an educational case developed for tax courses to expose students to the concepts of cryptocurrency, digital wallets, blockchain, and the tax consequences of various cryptocurrency transactions. As the Internal Revenue Service ("IRS") considers cryptocurrencies to be treated as property, this case should be introduced after students are exposed to the taxation of property transactions. The case includes several scenarios and suggested solutions, including four basic scenarios, with difficulty level appropriate for an introductory tax course, and two additional advanced scenarios appropriate for upper-level tax courses. The case requires students to act as tax preparers for their clients, Bob and Bonnie Bitcoin. In each scenario, the students must identify the appropriate tax treatment and consequences of the provided transaction(s). The students are expected to research the limited IRS guidance relating to the taxability of cryptocurrency transactions and then prepare professional memos advising their clients on the tax consequences in each scenario. The students learn how to research IRS guidance and apply this guidance to various circumstances, providing valuable practical experience. Students will learn how slight variations in Bitcoin

[*] J.D.,CPA Professor, School of Accounting, Grand Valley State University
[**] PhD., Assistant Professor, School of Accounting, Grand Valley State University

transactions can greatly change the tax ramifications. The case is designed to be an individual assignment or a group assignment and can be completed as an in-class activity (roughly 2.5 hours) or as an out of class activity.

The case's focus on critical thinking, research, and taxation also lends itself to other student audiences, including business law. Because business law courses require students to understand different varieties of law (i.e., contract law, labour law, or taxation), this case elicits a prime opportunity to challenge students' research skills, memo writing, and ability to reach sound conclusions. Further, the tax consequences of transactions are greatly intertwined with other areas of law, and often dictate the method in which transactions are executed. It is imperative that students possess the ability to apply their research skills to reach accurate conclusions to provide clients with accurate legal advice.

I. INTRODUCTION

You are a tax preparer in a CPA firm trying to wrap up the 2019 taxes and Form 1040 for your clients, Bob and his wife, Bonnie. You took care of their taxes last year, and they do not have anything complex going on, so they tend to be one of your easier clients. Through your knowledge of Bob and Bonnie and review of their tax documents, you have determined that their filing status is married filing jointly, and they have roughly $75,000 of taxable income, which is almost identical to their 2018 fact pattern.

As a best practice, you require all clients to fill out an annual questionnaire. However, Bob and Bonnie still had not returned their questionnaire, so you call Bob and ask him the relevant questions over the phone. When asking about investments or sales of investments, Bob initially hesitates, then assures you that they do not currently have any, and they did not sell any investments during 2019. Noticing the hesitation, you probe further, asking Bob if they bought or sold anything of value last year. Bob replies, "Well, I did have several transactions involving Bitcoin, but I did not mention that because Bitcoin isn't taxable, right?" Bitcoin was all over the news a year ago, but you had never dealt with it before, or any of the other cryptocurrencies for that matter. Bob's claim that they are not taxable caught you off-guard. Aren't they taxable? Why not? Where did he hear that? This presumption just does not feel right to you.

You admit to Bob that you are not 100% sure about the taxability of these transactions and will need to do a little research to ensure he is reporting the transactions accurately. Bob gives you the specific information, as summarized in the scenarios below, and you tell him that you will figure it out and get back to him as soon as possible.

Through this case, you will be exposed to blockchain, digital wallets, and cryptocurrencies. You will also be required to research IRS guidance to determine the proper tax treatment for cryptocurrency transactions, a topic where the IRS has released limited guidance. As an accounting professional, you will face situations with little guidance, where you are required to think critically about the economics of situations, interpret ambiguous information, and perform research on unclear topics or transactions in order to identify the most appropriate treatment and draw defensible conclusions that will protect yourself and your client.

There are many misconceptions about the legalities and tax treatment of cryptocurrencies. These misconceptions are often exacerbated by cryptocurrency advocates, bloggers & journalists, none of whom are held to the same professional standard as accountants. Due to this, you are encouraged to be skeptical of any online information that is not explicitly presented in the case. Your best sources of information include the Internal Revenue Code (IRC), IRS Notices & guidance, Treasury Regulation, Revenue Ruling,

case law, etc. You will also need to establish market values on the day of the transactions. You are encouraged to use CoinMarketCap.com to determine these values. However, this website tracks market values of over twenty-five cryptocurrencies that start with the word "Bitcoin," and it is easy to select values from the incorrect cryptocurrency. As such, you are strongly encouraged to use the following link to obtain values:
https://coinmarketcap.com/currencies/bitcoin/historical-data/.

A. Background

Cryptocurrencies, or "virtual currencies," are digital assets initially developed as a means for storing and transferring value, as a substitute for fiat currencies (*i.e.*, government-controlled currencies, such as the U.S. Dollar, or the Euro). Bitcoin, the most recognizable and most valuable cryptocurrency, was established in 2008 and made available to the public in 2009.[1]

Since inception, Bitcoin has grown in popularity, spiked and dropped in value, and can be used to purchase goods and services from various providers—Microsoft, Overstock.com, Newegg.com, among others. Although many merchants accept Bitcoin as a method of payment, this virtual currency is not currently recognized as legal tender, juxtaposed with fiat currency, which holds a value determined by the government and carries the legal tender designation.[1]

---

[1] Bernard Marr, *A Short History Of Bitcoin And Crypto Currency Everyone Should Read*, Forbes (December 6, 2017), https://www.forbes.com/sites/bernardmarr/2017/12/06/a-short-history-of-bitcoin-and-crypto-currency-everyone-should-read/#306cc2193f27

[1] Mohammed Ahmad Naheem, *Regulating Virtual Currencies – the Challenges of Applying Fiat Currency Laws to Digital Technology Services*, 25 Jou. of Fin. Crime 3 (2018).

Bitcoin is one of many different cryptocurrencies in circulation; as of March 2019, there were over 2,300 cryptocurrencies available.[2] The growing popularity surrounding cryptocurrencies has led many speculative investors to purchase these virtual currencies to capitalize on the volatility. As a result of this sudden increase in interest, a multitude of platforms referred to as "digital wallets" have been developed to act as financial custodians, safeguarding these digital assets on customers' behalf.[3]

Unlike fiat currency, the supply of cryptocurrencies is not bound by government regulation, and the exchange of cryptocurrencies does not rely on the traditional third-party banking system. In place of the banking system, traditional cryptocurrencies utilize decentralized, global peer-to-peer networks for exchange. This secured network, referred to as a blockchain, acts as a decentralized ledger tracking transactions and balances for each digital wallet on the network. The first blockchain was established in 2008 by Santoshi Nakamoto to secure, validate, and record Bitcoin transactions. One significant benefit of a public blockchain is that anyone with internet access can view past transactions between digital wallets. However, because digital wallets are only linked via alphanumeric codes, visibility is limited to the date, time, and amount of the transactions, allowing the purveyors of the transaction to achieve a level of partial anonymity.

The fact that cryptocurrency transactions are not controlled by banks or the government, coupled with the belief that cryptocurrency transactions are anonymous, has

---

Fiat currency is a term usually used to refer to money that is not linked directly to the value of a commodity (such as Gold) but is recognized as a legal system by the state.

[2] "All Cryptocurrencies", CoinMarketCap, current through August 1, 2019. https://coinmarketcap.com/all/views/all/

[3] Dennis Chu, *Broker-Dealers for Virtual Currency: Regulating Cryptocurrency Wallets and Exchanges*, 118 Col. L. Rev. 5 (2018)

led many cryptocurrency advocates to incorrectly conclude that the transactions are not regulated or taxable. This dangerous misconception has led cryptocurrency users to unknowingly, or knowingly, violate federal tax laws. According to the IRS, in 2013, 2014, and 2015, there were between 800 and 900 individual taxpayers who had appropriately reported cryptocurrency transactions on their federal tax returns. Contrary to this reporting, the U.S. based cryptocurrency exchange Coinbase, claimed that by the end of 2015, they had served 5.9 Million customers and exchanged $6 Billion ($U.S. dollar equivalent) worth of Bitcoin. [4] As a result of this gross under-reporting, in November 2016, the Department of Justice served a "John Doe" summons[5] to Coinbase on behalf of the IRS, requesting the identities of all U.S. Coinbase customers who transferred cryptocurrency during 2014 and 2015. The Supreme Court concluded that the IRS, "has a legitimate interest in investigating these taxpayers. (pg. 4)" Moreover, Coinbase was required to provide the IRS with information on certain U.S. taxpayers who conducted at least $20,000 in transactions on the Coinbase platform (about 14,000 clients) in either year.[6]

B. Required background videos

In order to further familiarize yourself with blockchain, digital wallets, and gain insights into how blockchain will likely impact the future of the accounting profession, please watch the following videos before proceeding further with the case.

---

[4] *U.S. v. Coinbase, Inc.*, No.17-cv-01431-JSC, (N.D.Ca Nov. 28, 2017), *available at* https://casetext.com/case/united-states-v-coinbase-inc
[5] 26 U.S.C. § 7609 (f). (A "John Doe" summons doesn't identify a specific person or persons, but instead requests information on a group of people that may have engaged in a specified non-complying activity.
[6] *Id.*

A. "What is Blockchain? Simply Explained in Five Minutes."[7] (https://www.youtube.com/watch?v=9gvxGVohbN E).
B. "What is a Bitcoin Wallet? – The Best Explanation EVER."[8] (https://www.youtube.com/watch?v=AD-vWx3oA84).
C. "How Blockchain technology will change auditing and accounting for good"[9] (https://www.youtube.com/watch?v=J6pzZacMj8w)
D. "Accounting on the Blockchain"[10] (https://www.youtube.com/watch?v=OiV_dwrifG4)

C. Suggested Guidance

After watching the required videos, you are ready to begin the tax portion of the case. Although cryptocurrencies have been around for over ten years and accounted for billions of dollars in digital transactions, the IRS has provided little guidance on the taxation of these transactions. Until recently, the IRS had released only one piece of guidance relating to these transactions, IRS Notice 2014-

---

[7] Devslopes. 2018. "What Is Blockchain? – Simply Explained in Five Minutes." YouTube. January 23, 2018.
https://www.youtube.com/watch?v=9gvxGVohbNE.
[8] The Cryptoverse, 2017. "What is a Bitcoin Wallet? – The Best Explanation EVER." YouTube. March 4, 2017.
[9] Sander Van Loosbroek, March 16, 2017 *How Blockchain Technology Will Change Auditing and Accounting for Good,*
https://www.cegeka.com/en/be/blog/how-blockchain-technology-will-change-auditing-and-accounting-for-good.
[10] Au, Sean, 2017. "Accounting on The Blockchain." YouTube. August 13, 2017. (https://www.youtube.com/watch?v=OiV_dwrifG4.

21.[11] This short notice essentially redirected taxpayers to Publication 544: Sales and Other Dispositions of Assets[12] and Publication 551: Basis of Assets[13] to determine the tax implications of their Bitcoin transactions. Approximately five years later, the IRS updated the Frequently Ask Questions ("FAQ") related to Notice 2014-21, providing much-needed clarity on the topic.

In addition to releasing the updated FAQs, the IRS released another pronouncement, Revenue Ruling 2019-24. This helped to clarify their positions regarding the taxable nature of "hard forks," "soft forks," and "airdrops." A hard fork is when an existing blockchain splits into two different paths, resulting in two blockchains and new virtual currency. While the new virtual currency shares an identical history with the original virtual currency, after the hard fork, the new virtual currency has a permanent divergence from the original blockchain and original virtual currency. When a hard fork occurs, all addresses and balances exist on both the old and new version of the blockchain[14]. In essence, any digital wallets holding the original virtual currency will have rights for both types of virtual currency on two separate blockchains immediately after the hard fork.

---

[11] United States. Dept. of the Treasury. Internal Revenue Service, *IRS Notice 2014-21*, Internal Revenue Service, 2014, https://www.irs.gov/pub/irs-drop/n-14-21.pdf.

[12] United States. Dept. of the Treasury. Internal Revenue Service. *Publication 544: Sales and Other Dispositions of Assets*. Internal Revenue Service, 2019, https://www.irs.gov/pub/irs-pdf/p544.pdf

[13] United States. Dept. of the Treasury. Internal Revenue Service. *Publication 551: Basis of Assets*. Internal Revenue Service, 2019, https://www.irs.gov/pub/irs-pdf/p551.pdf

[14] Dorsey, Roger, Prewett, Kyleen, and Kumar, Gaurav, "IRS Issues New Guidance on Tax Treatment of Cryptocurrencies" Practical Tax Strategies, June 2020.

D. Deliverables

A. Your initial deliverable is an overview/summary of your research. This professional memo should explicitly reply to Bob's inquiry about the taxability of his Bitcoin transaction, summarizing the perspective of the IRS and referencing the appropriate literature. The memo does not need to directly relate to any of the provided scenarios (as each scenario will have its own analysis and conclusion).

B. The second deliverable will provide your conclusions for each scenario provided below. Each scenario-specific solution should:

1. Identify the most appropriate authoritative literature—the Internal Revenue Code (IRC), Treasury Regulation, Revenue Ruling, case law, etc.—that supports your calculations and conclusion.

2. Utilize an appropriate valuation method[15] (see footnotes) to establish the market value of the cryptocurrency on the appropriate date(s). The suggested solutions use the opening market balance on each date to calculate the basis and/or proceeds.

3. Calculate the gains/losses and estimate the tax consequences ($) of the relevant transaction(s).

4. Summarize your calculations, conclusions, and provide references to the most appropriate IRS guidance that relates to your overall conclusion.

---

[15] "Bitcoin (BTC) Historical Data," CoinMarketCap, current through March 24, 2019,
https://coinmarketcap.com/currencies/bitcoin/historical-data/.

E. Basic Scenarios

A. **Scenario 1**: As an investment, Bob Bitcoin (the taxpayer) purchased a single (1) Bitcoin with cash on July 1st, 2015. On November 25th, 2019, the taxpayer sold the Bitcoin for cash, and the funds were deposited into his bank account immediately.

B. **Scenario 2**: Same situation and taxpayer from scenario 1, except the transaction dates have changed. Bob purchased a single (1) Bitcoin on December 15th, 2017, and sold it on December 20th, 2019.

C. **Scenario 3:** Same situation and taxpayer from scenario 1, except the transaction dates have changed. Bob purchased a single (1) Bitcoin on January 15th, 2018, and sold it on January 1st, 2019.

D. **Scenario 4:** The same taxpayer as in earlier scenarios, but the situation changes significantly. Instead of his annual incentive bonus, Bob's employer granted Bob one (1) Bitcoin on December 16th, 2017. The value of this non-cash award was not included anywhere in Bob's 2017 W-2, and you were not aware of the bonus when you prepared his 2017 income tax return (excluded from his 1040). Unsure of how to sell the Bitcoin, Bob held onto it. It wasn't until December 12th, 2019 that he was able to exchange the Bitcoin for US dollars.

E. Advanced Scenarios

A. **Scenario 5:** While watching his favorite team, the New England Patriots, play against the Eagles in the Super Bowl on February 4th, 2018, the taxpayer claimed that the Patriots are destined to return to the next Superbowl. His friend (taxpayer 2) disagreed and offered to place a wager. In response, taxpayer 1 bet a single Bitcoin that the Patriots would make it back to the Super Bowl the following year. They each agreed that the loser would submit payment in front of everyone during the 2019 Superbowl. To hedge their potential losses just in case the value of Bitcoin was to skyrocket), each taxpayer purchased a single bitcoin that same evening (2/4/18). The following year, the Patriots returned to the Super Bowl. Taxpayer #1 won the bet and received his victory prize of one Bitcoin during the 2019 Super Bowl party 2/3/19). (On February 6th, 2019, the taxpayer sold both bitcoins for cash. Summarize the tax consequences for each of the two individuals.

1. Additional information for taxpayer 1: No other gambling activity.
2. Additional information for taxpayer 2: Net gambling earnings throughout 2019 of $5,000.

B. **Scenario 6**: First, watch the following video to gain an understanding of why and how a 'hard fork' works in the world of cryptocurrency (it runs less than 5 minutes, but pay very close attention starting at 2 minutes and 47 seconds): https://www.youtube.com/watch?v=XCo6yyutYA M.
Next, assume the same basic information as scenario #1, including the same dates. However, the taxpayer received a single Bitcoin Cash as a result of the fork in the Bitcoin Blockchain on 8/1/2017. When he received this Bitcoin Cash, it had a market value of $380.01. When the taxpayer sold the single Bitcoin on 11/25/2019, he also sold the Bitcoin Cash for a price of $184.58.

II. TEACHING NOTES

A. Case Relevance and Literature Review

Originating roughly 12 years ago, cryptocurrencies have grown in quantity, value, popularity, media coverage, political coverage, and controversy. In recent years, adoption of, and acceptance of cryptocurrencies has increased drastically. As of mid-2020, there were over 3,500 different cryptocurrencies[16] and 330 cryptocurrency exchanges[17] across the globe. Since the start of 2018, the market capitalization for cryptocurrencies has ranged from $100 Billion to $828 Billion USD.[18] The value of cryptocurrency has been incredibly volatile in recent years. For instance, during 2017, the value of Bitcoin ranged from less than $800 to more than $19,000, then dropped below $3,300 in 2018, and spiked to over $12,000 in the first half of 2019.[19]

Cryptocurrency advocates have grown to appreciate the implied anonymity of transactions and lack of government intervention in the virtual currency space. The perceived silence from many governments around the globe led some users to conclude that cryptocurrencies are not subject to government regulations, including taxation. Despite the release of IRS Notice 2014-21 in the United States, most users of virtual currency have either improperly

---

[16] "All Cryptocurrencies," CoinMarketCap, current through October 1, 2020,
https://coinmarketcap.com/all/views/all/.

[17] "Top Cryptocurrency Spot Exchanges," CoinMarketCap, current through October 1, 2020,
https://coinmarketcap.com/rankings/exchanges/3.

[18] "Global Charts," CoinMarketCap, current through August 1, 2019,
https://coinmarketcap.com/charts/.

[19] "Bitcoin (BTC) Historical Data," CoinMarketCap, current through August 1, 2019,
https://coinmarketcap.com/currencies/bitcoin/historical-data/

reported their transactions or neglected to report them at all. The IRS recognized the repeated omission of these transactions and initiated a Virtual Currency Compliance campaign in July 2018 to address the noncompliance.

A year later, the IRS began sending letters to virtual currency owners advising them to pay back taxes and file amended returns. Taxpayers with known virtual currency holdings received one of three letters: Letter 6173, Letter 6174, and Letter 6174-A[20]. These three letters possessed varying strengths of tone, however Letter 6173 was the only one requiring taxpayer response.

Until recently, the issue of misreporting cryptocurrency transactions was due, in part, to the confusion about how to properly classify and report these transactions. In the 10 years since Bitcoin was introduced, the IRS has provided only one piece of formal guidance to clarify the tax treatment of cryptocurrency-based transactions, IRS Notice 2014-21. This guidance defined these 'virtual currencies,' such as Bitcoin, as property for income tax purposes. However, there is still broad confusion on the appropriate tax treatment of these transactions. On three separate occasions since 2017, members of congress have issued formal letters to the IRS requesting more robust guidance to clarify the tax implications of using virtual currencies.[21] However, while the IRS has continued to increase enforcement actions against cryptocurrency users

---

[20] United States. Dept. of the Treasury. Internal Revenue Service, *IR-2019-132*, Internal Revenue Service, 2019
https://www.irs.gov/newsroom/irs-has-begun-sending-letters-to-virtual-currency-owners-advising-them-to-pay-back-taxes-file-amended-returns-part-of-agencys-larger-efforts
[21] https://republicans-waysandmeansforms.house.gov/uploadedfiles/letter_irs_virtual_curren cies.pdf
https://emmer.house.gov/sites/emmer.house.gov/files/2019_IRS%20lett er_Final.pdf

who misreport, they have yet to release any additional guidance on how to properly report these transactions.

As educators, we have a responsibility to expose our students to this new and developing asset class and help them learn to navigate the IRS guidance, regardless of how ambiguous that guidance might be. This case helps achieve that objective using realistic situations our students may encounter during their career. After a thorough review of existing literature, we have come across only one case study that requires students to consider the tax implications of a Bitcoin transaction.[22] While that case study focuses on the tax implications of a single transaction, resulting in a long-term capital gain, our case includes six different scenarios, exposing students to various complexities and tax implications.

This educational case enhances student learning outcomes and achieves multiple objectives. A primary objective of this case is to expose students to the concepts of cryptocurrency, digital wallets, and the tax implications of using, trading, selling, and receiving these types of virtual currencies. The secondary benefits of the case include enhancing students comfort with researching the authoritative literature—as evidenced by the efficacy results—and reinforcing other topics students are exposed to during their tax course work—capital vs. ordinary gains (losses), short-term vs. long-term capital gains (losses), non-monetary compensation, amending prior year tax returns, and capital-loss carryforwards. Further, incorporating cryptocurrency transactions into the case creates an opportunity to expose students to the related topics of blockchain, distributed ledgers, and digital wallets. Finally, this case requires students to draft a professional memo

---

[22] Gross, A., Hemker, J., Hoelscher, J., and Reed, B., *The role of secondary sources on the taxation of digital currency (Bitcoin) before IRS guidance was issued.* 39 Journal of Accounting Education, 48-54 (2017).

summarizing the results of their research, defending their stance on various tax scenarios, and discussing conclusions reached.

The case initially directs students to IRS Notice 2014-21, the primary guidance released by the IRS that explicitly relates to cryptocurrencies. This guidance states that 'virtual currencies' should be treated as property, and taxpayers should apply the existing tax principles that are applicable to property transactions. Based on the information in this notice, students are directed to write a professional tax memo to their client, summarizing the IRS stance on cryptocurrency transactions. Following this, students in introductory tax courses are provided with four basic scenarios, while students in upper level courses are provided with two additional advanced scenarios. Based on the information provided in each scenario, the IRS Notice, and the students prior exposure to tax implications of property transactions, the students typically possess sufficient information to draw conclusions about the tax treatment of each scenario. The scenarios do not provide the USD values of the basis or proceeds of each transaction. Instead, students are directed to utilize an independent source to determine the USD value for the basis and proceeds of each transaction. The case provides the link to a website which students should use to determine the tax basis of the property and the proceeds from each sale based on the dates provided with each transaction. After obtaining the relevant values, students have all information needed to calculate the taxable gain or loss realized on the disposal of these non-traditional assets and determine whether the disposal should be treated as ordinary or capital. Students are directed to identify and reference the most appropriate Internal Revenue Code (IRC), or appropriate IRS guidance, that supports their conclusions about the realization and recognition of the gain or loss. This final requirement necessitates that students perform additional tax research, familiarizing them with the approach and the IRC.

B. Learning Objectives (Revised Blooms Taxonomy Dimension):

A. Introduce students to cryptocurrencies, digital wallets, and blockchain (Understand).
B. Exposes students to tax implications of property transactions (Understand).
C. Enhance students' ability to research through multiple associated sections of IRS guidance and independent sources based on provided scenarios (Analyze).
D. Enhance students' ability to draw appropriate conclusions about tax consequences of various complex transactions (Evaluate).
E. Cultivates professional writing skills (Create).

C. Background on Cryptocurrency

The cryptocurrency that this case utilizes is Bitcoin, the most well known and most valuable of all cryptocurrencies. Bitcoin operates through a direct peer-to-peer network, allowing individual transactions to be tracked, validated, and maintained on a public blockchain. Cryptocurrencies have served various purposes, such as a store of value or a speculative investments. However, Bitcoin was initially developed as a medium of exchange for e-commerce transactions, intended to act as a substitute, or replacement, for the traditional process of exchanging fiat currencies resulting from e-commerce transactions. [23] Traditionally, e-commerce transactions required both the

---

[23] Nakamoto, S. (2008) *Bitcoin: A Peer-to-Peer Electronic Cash System.* https://bitcoin.org/bitcoin.pdf

sender and the receiver of the fiat currency to rely on a financial intermediary (bank or financial institution) to processes the electronic payment. Both users must also agree on a fiat currency, essentially requiring both users to have faith in the government which controls the supply of that currency. Cryptocurrencies elimnate these two problems and allow users to exchange transactions independently of financial institutions and government control.

Long before Bitcoin was introduced, there were various attempts to establish virtual, or electronic, currencies dating back to the 1980s. While these currencies shared similarities with today's cryptocurrencies, none of them were broadly accepted. The lack of adoption was due in part to the absence of security around transactions. The solution to this issue was cryptography, an encryption algorithm used to protect transactions and digital wallets from outside manipulation. The concept of a cryptographically-secured electronic currency was originally theorized by members of the National Security Agency in 1996,[24] but this concept wasn't effectively implemented for over 10 years. The most notable utilization of cryptographically-secured transactions came in 2008, when a programmer, or group of programmers, using the pseudonym Satoshi Nakamoto, released a whitepaper introducing a blockchain-based, cryptographcially-secured, digital currency called Bitcoin.[25] Similar to earlier virtual currencies, Bitcoin allowed for peer-to-peer transactions without a financial intermediary, incoporating cryptography to validate and secure the transactions. Additionally, Bitcoin transactions were recorded on a publicly observable distributed ledger called a blockchain, allowing the transaction history to be

---

[24] Law, L., Sabett, S. and Solinas, J., *How to Make a Mint: The Cryptography of Anonymous Electronic Cash,*
National Security Agency Office of Information Security Research and Technology, Cryptology Division, June 1996.
[25] Nakamoto, S, *supra,* note 24.

immutable, and ensuring that individuals cannot manipulate historical transaction records. Considered by many to be the initial and most legitimate cryptocurrency, Bitcoin's initial transaction (i.e. Genesis Transaction) occurred in January 2009.

D. Determining Fair Market Value ("FMV")

Fair market value is often an imprecise concept defined differently by different people. However, the IRS provides taxpayers with a clear definition: FMV is the price that property would sell for on the open market. This price is agreed upon by a willing buyer and a willing seller, with neither party being required to act, and both having reasonable knowledge of the relevant facts.[26] Many virtual currencies are convertible, meaning they possess a corresponding value as legal tender.[27] Digital currency exchanges, such as Coinbase, provide daily pricing for convertible currencies, allowing users to quickly search and quantify the FMV of assets held.

---

[26] United States. Dept. of the Treasury. Internal Revenue Service. *Publication 561: Determining the Value of Donated Property*. Internal Revenue Service, 2020, https://www.irs.gov/pub/irs-pdf/p561.pdf

[27] United States. Dept. of the Treasury. Internal Revenue Service. *Frequently Asked Questions on Virtual Currency Transactions*. Internal Revenue Service, 2020, https://www.irs.gov/individuals/international-taxpayers/frequently-asked-questions-on-virtual-currency-transactions

E. Additional Considerations – Diversity In Application

There are various important issues that both the faculty and the students should be aware of before delving into this case.

A. The information provided to the students is both important and relevant. We strongly encourage instructors to review this student handout, and watch the videos, before proceeding.

B. Cryptocurrencies tend to have very volatile prices and there are various exchanges available to obtain reasonable estimates. Due to the lack of intra-day or hourly pricing histories, and lack of detailed information in the scenarios, there isn't a precise "correct" solution. The suggested solutions utilize the price of the cryptocurrency at the *close of the trading day.* However, it is likely some students will elect to use the opening price, or average price for the day. We do not consider this method incorrect as long as the student uses a *consistent approach* to establishing value. Some students use the highest or lowest trading price during the trading day, we consider this to be incorrect. Taking this a step further, some students may attempt to minimize gains (maximize losses) by selecting the highest trading price during the day to establish their basis, and the lowest price during the day of disposal. This approach is also incorrect.

C. IRS Publication 525 specifically addresses the tax consequences surrounding receipt of virtual currency for services rendered.[28] As previously stated in

---

[28] United States. Dept. of the Treasury. Internal Revenue Service. *Publication 525: Taxable and Nontaxable Income.* Internal Revenue Service, 2020, https://www.irs.gov/pub/irs-pdf/p525.pdf

2.4(B), students should apply a consistent approach across *all* scenarios to determine the taxable income received by the taxpayer.

D. Bitcoin is one of many cryptocurrencies available. As of March, 2019, there were over 2,000 cryptocurrencies reported. Many of these were derived from Bitcoin or the Bitcoin blockchain and these alternative cryptocurrencies often select similar names—Bitcoin Cash, Bitcoin Gold, Bitcoin Private, Bitcoin XT, Bitcoin Limited, etc. We mention this because it is incredibly easy to accidentally pull prices from an incorrect pricing index or exchange. We strongly encourage students to utilize the provided link to ensure they are obtaining accurate prices.

E. Technically, there are three basic types of cryptocurrencies—currency tokens, utility tokens, and asset/security tokens. Each type may serve a different purpose and may be subject to different regulations and financial reporting criteria. The IRS has not explicitly distinguished between these various types. For simplicity of the case, we utilize only a single currency tokens—Bitcoin (BTC)— for base scenarios, adding Bitcoin Cash (BCH) to the advanced scenarios, and assume that tax consequences of trading Bitcoin is determined by the taxpayers' actions or intent.

F. Implementation Guidance

A. Assign the case after discussion of the realized and recognized gains/losses of property transactions.

B. Make sure the students complete the preliminary assignments. If class time is available, show the videos in class and discuss Bitcoin and blockchain and how it is relevant to accounting. If class time is not available, emphasize to the students that they will be more successful answering the questions if they watch the videos and complete the reading assignments prior to attempting to answer the case questions.

C. Decide how you would like to assign the case questions. You may assign all four questions to each student or group of students. The authors suggest breaking the class into groups and assigning only one question to each group. After the groups have completed the assignment, the groups than can present their results to the class. This method will encourage a more in-depth discussion of the questions and the presented answers.

D. Allow students to either present their solutions or discuss the recommended solutions above with the class and compare them to the students' answers.

E. The authors have created a spreadsheet which automatically calculates gains/losses based on input days, allowing the instructor to adjust dates within each scenario to ensure each group/class has different dates, thus different solutions. This spreadsheet is available upon request.

F. The advanced scenarios include "treasure trove" miscellaneous income and wagering gains & losses. These are prepared so that instructors can discuss non-traditional sources of income.

G. The existence of cryptocurrency and blockchain opens a wide range of related topics that instructors might incorporate into their course. Depending on the instructor's familiarity with, or interest in the topic, some additional potential discussion topics include:

1. Applicability of Section 1031 to defer gains on cryptocurrency trades.

2. Strategic execution of trades near year-end to minimize taxes.
3. How cryptocurrencies could impact the banking industry and/or fiat currencies.
4. Why cryptocurrency has value without expected dividends or underlying assets.
5. Why cryptocurrencies values are so volatile.
6. Cryptocurrency mining, mining pools, and resource utilization.
7. Potential consequences of a single mining pool achieving 51%.
8. Transaction validation on the blockchain ("Proof of Work" vs "Proof of Stake").
9. Cryptocurrency exchange hacks and the consideration for, or risks of, "reversals."
10. How cryptocurrencies could reduce the risk of hyperinflation.
11. How blockchain relates to supply chain and global trade.
12. How cryptocurrencies relate to the Bank Securities Act and risk of money laundering.
13. Discussion of the SEC concerns with cryptocurrency-based EFTs.

G. Evidence of Efficacy

This case has been used in three tax courses at a university in the Midwestern United States with an enrollment of roughly 25,000 students. The tax courses include two undergraduate individual income tax courses with the same professor, and one Masters level tax research course with an adjunct professor. All students from all classes were requested to respond to both a pre-case assessment survey and a post-case assessment survey, regardless of whether or not they completed the case. Each survey was anonymous and included the same four questions asked of all students, with one additional question asked in the post-case survey. The statements provided to the students both before and after the case were as follows:

1. I have a solid understanding of cryptocurrencies.
2. I have a solid understanding of the tax consequences of cryptocurrency transactions.
3. I am confident in my ability to research IRS guidance and come to conclusions relating to taxes.
4. I have a solid understanding of what blockchain is.

Students were given five response options for each question, reflecting a Likert-type scale. In order to quantify the feedback, the responses are scored as follows: Strongly Agree = 4, Agree = 3, Neither Agree or Disagree = 2, Disagree = 1, and Strongly Disagree = 0. The count of each response, average response, and the results of the difference in means analysis are presented for each group, by statement in Table 1: Evidence of Efficacy from Student Feedback.

The case was required for students of the Masters course, allowing us to compare responses before and after performing the case. The results of these responses are presented in the right columns of Table 1. We notice an improvement in the average response of all four statements, and this improvement is statistically significant at the 1% level.[29] Student performing the case at the Masters level showed an improvement in their understanding of cryptocurrencies, blockchain, and tax implications of cryptocurrency transactions. Further, they felt more confident in their ability to research IRS guidance. However, a potential limitation to the generalizability of these results is due to the fact that all students in this class were required

---

[29] Tabulated results for statistical significance are determined from the t-statistic of the difference in means analysis, assuming unequal variances. Results are consistent with untabulated results of running the same analyses assuming equal variances.

to work through the case. With the lack of a control group, we cannot identify the marginal impact of the case relative to what students learned in the class. This limitation is mitigated with the results of the undergraduate courses.

The case was not required of all students in the undergraduate courses, instead it was an optional extra assignment. Due to the case being optional, our responses from the post-case survey were broken into two groups, participants (those who did the case) and non-participants (those who did not complete the case). This separation provides a pseudo-control group of students who learned about property transactions and tax research during the regular class, but did not apply these concepts with the case. This allows our efficacy results to compare responses between those who worked their way through the case against those who elected not to. In the undergraduate column of Table 1, the responses are presented in three columns: pre-case responses (all students), participant (treatment group), and non-participant (pseudo-control group). We also present the results of the difference in means t-test comparing pre-case average score against the participant average score (Participants vs. Pre-case), and the difference in means from comparing the participant average score against the non-participant average score (Participants vs. Non-Participants).

Across all four statements, the responses from post-case: participants showed statistically significant improvements relative to the responses from pre-case responses and relative to the post-case: non-participants.

In the post-case survey, we included one additional statement, "I would recommend that this case be assigned to students in future classes." The results of student responses are tabulated by group at the bottom of Table 1. Not a single student across all three groups Disagreed or Strongly Disagreed with this statement. Further, of those who participated in the project, the average response was between Strongly Agree and Agree. Interestingly, even those undergrads who elected not to do the case indicated that they agreed with this statement, although 13 of the 30 non-participants did not provide a response to this final statement.

Table 1: Evidence of Efficacy from Student Feedback

Statement 1: "I have a solid understanding of cryptocurrencies."					
	Undergraduate Classes			**Masters Class**	
Count of *(numeric score)*:	Pre-Case	Post: Participants	Post: Non-Participants	Pre-Case	Post-Case
Strongly Agree (*4*)	0	8	4	0	0
Agree (*3*)	24	17	12	5	19
Neither Agree nor Disagree (*2*)	19	0	5	5	3
Disagree (*1*)	13	0	9	6	0
Strongly Disagree (*0*)	9	0	0	6	0
Mean	1.892	3.320	2.367	1.409	2.864
Variance	1.13	0.23	1.14	1.3	0.12
Responses (*n*)	65	25	30	22	22

Difference in Means (T-test):

Participants vs. Pre-case	1.43***	1.45***
Participants vs. Non-Participants	0.95***	n/a

Statement 2: "I have a solid understanding of the tax consequences of cryptocurrency transactions."					
	Undergraduate Classes			**Masters Class**	
Count of *(numeric score)*:	Pre-Case	Post: Participants	Post: Non-Participants	Pre-Case	Post-Case
Strongly Agree (*4*)	0	6	0	0	7
Agree (*3*)	3	15	6	0	13
Neither Agree nor Disagree (*2*)	5	4	12	2	2
Disagree (*1*)	38	0	11	5	0
Strongly Disagree (*0*)	19	0	1	15	0
Mean	0.815	3.120	1.767	0.410	3.227
Variance	0.59	0.43	0.88	0.44	0.37
Responses (*n*)	65	25	30	22	22

Difference in Means (T-test):

Participants vs. Pre-case	2.30***	2.818***
Participants vs. Non-Participants	1.35***	n/a

***Indicates significance at 1 percent, **at 5 percent, and *at 10 percent of the t-statistic from the difference in means (T-test) analysis. Statement 5 was only included in the Post-case survey. Undergraduate Classes — Pre-case includes all students, Post: Participants reflects responses from students who elected to complete the case, while Post: Non-Participants reflects responses from the students who did not complete the case.

(continued)

Table 1 (*continued*)

Statement 3: "I am confident in my ability to research IRS guidance and come to conclusions relating to taxes."

Count of (*numeric score*):	Undergraduate Classes			Masters Class	
	Pre-Case	Post: Participants	Post: Non-Participants	Pre-Case	Post-Case
Strongly Agree (*4*)	4	6	4	0	2
Agree (*3*)	32	15	16	8	18
Neither Agree nor Disagree (*2*)	19	4	9	13	2
Disagree (*1*)	9	0	1	1	0
Strongly Disagree (*0*)	19	0	0	0	0
Mean	2.446	3.080	2.767	2.318	3.0
Variance	0.75	0.41	0.53	0.32	0.19
Responses (*n*)	65	25	30	22	22

Difference in Means (T-test):

Participants vs. Pre-case	0.63***	0.682***
Participants vs. Non-Participants	0.31*	n/a

Statement 4: "I have a solid understanding of what blockchain is."

Count of (*numeric score*):	Undergraduate Classes			Masters Class	
	Pre-Case	Post: Participants	Post: Non-Participants	Pre-Case	Post-Case
Strongly Agree (*4*)	0	4	0	0	0
Agree (*3*)	7	21	10	3	14
Neither Agree nor Disagree (*2*)	10	0	10	3	5
Disagree (*1*)	26	0	8	11	3
Strongly Disagree (*0*)	22	0	2	5	0
Mean	1.031	3.160	1.933	1.182	2.5
Variance	0.94	0.14	0.89	0.91	0.55
Responses (*n*)	65	25	30	22	22

Difference in Means (T-test):

Participants vs. Pre-case	2.30***	1.32***
Participants vs. Non-Participants	1.35***	n/a

Statement 5: "I would recommend that this case be assigned to students in future classes."

Count of (*numeric score*):	Undergraduate: Participants	Undergraduate: Non-Participants	Masters Class: Participants
Strongly Agree (*4*)	5	1	7
Agree (*3*)	18	10	10
Neither Agree nor Disagree (*2*)	2	6	5
Disagree (*1*)	0	0	0
Strongly Disagree (*0*)	0	0	0
Mean	3.120	2.706	3.091
Responses (*n*)	25	17	22

H. Recommended Solutions

Guidance on how to research the issues and complete the case are provided to the students in the case itself. The case requires the students to obtain the opening market value of 1 Bitcoin on a certain date as determined on CoinMarketCap.[30] In each of the following scenarios, the students must answer how the transaction will be taxed.

A. *Scenario 1:* In 2018 there is no taxable transaction because is no sale or exchange. However, in 2019 the taxpayer has a realized and recognized gain upon the sale of his Bitcoin. According to CoinMarketCap, the opening value of 1 Bitcoin on July 1st, 2015. was $258.62; the closing value of 1 Bitcoin on November 25th, 2019 was $7,146.13. Therefore, the taxpayer has a recognizable gain of $6,887.51 which will be reported on Form 8949, Sales and Other Dispositions of Capital Assets, then summarize capital gains and deductible capital losses on Form 1040, Schedule D, Capital Gains and Losses.

IRS Notice 2014-21, states that if Bitcoin is held as an investment, it is treated as a capital gain.[31] IRC § 1222(3) states that if a capital asset that was sold was held for over a year, any gain or loss is considered a long-term capital gain or loss.[32] Because the taxpayer held the Bitcoin for over a year, the gain will be a long-term capital gain. As such, the gain is taxed preferentially. Because the taxpayer's

[30] "Bitcoin (BTC) Historical Data," CoinMarketCap, current through March 24, 2019,
https://coinmarketcap.com/currencies/bitcoin/historical-data/.
[31] IRS Notice 2014-21, issued on March 25, 2014,
https://www.irs.gov/pub/irs-drop/n-14-21.pdf
[32] *Internal Revenue Code (IRC),* 26 U.S. Code § 1222 (2018).

other taxable income is $75,000, the gain on the sale of the Bitcoin will be taxed at 15%.[33]

B. *Scenario 2*: In 2017 there is no taxable transaction. However, in 2019 there is a long-term capital loss. Again, the Bitcoin was held for investment so it is a capital asset. It was held for over a year, so it is long-term. On December 15th, 2017, 1 Bitcoin was valued at $17,706.90; on December 20th, 2019, 1 Bitcoin was worth $7,218.82; therefore, the taxpayer has a long-term capital loss of $10,488.08. This loss will be reported on Form 8949 and Schedule D (Form 1040). However, according to the facts, there are no capital gains to net these losses against and the value of the loss exceeds the individual capital-loss limitation of $3,000[34]. This means that the taxpayer can recognize a capital loss of $3,000 in 2018, reducing his ordinary income, and will have a capital-loss carryforward of $7,488.08 that can benefit him in future years.[35]

C. *Scenario 3*: In 2018, there is not a taxable transaction. However, in 2019 there is a capital loss. On January 15st, 2018, one Bitcoin was valued at $13,819.80; while the same Bitcoin was valued at $3,843.52 when disposed of on January 1st, 2019. Therefore, the loss of $9,976.28 will be treated as short-term capital loss. This loss will be reported on Form 8949 and Schedule D (Form 1040). However, according to the facts, there are no capital gains to net these capital losses against, and the value of the loss exceeds the individual capital-loss limitation of $3,000[36]. This means that the taxpayer can recognize

---

[33] 26 U.S.C. § 1 (h) (2018).
[34] 26 U.S.C. § 1211 (b)(1) (2018).
[35] 26 U.S.C § 1212 (b)(1)(B) (2018).

a capital loss of $3,000 in 2019, reducing his ordinary income, and will have a capital-loss carryforward of $6,976.28 that can benefit him in future years.[37]

D. **Scenario 4**: On December 16th, 2018, the value of 1 Bitcoin was $3,252.84. Because the taxpayer received the Bitcoin as a bonus, it will be included in wages on the Form 1040 and will be taxed as ordinary income at the taxpayer's marginal tax rate of 22%.[38] On December 12th, 2019, one Bitcoin was valued at $7,243.13. The taxpayer sold the Bitcoin before holding for it for 1 year, therefore, there is a capital gain of $3,990.29. The gain is short-term because the investment was held for less than a year. Short-term capital gains are taxed at ordinary rates. The capital gain will be reported on Form 8949 and Schedule D (Form 1040) but the gain will be at the taxpayer's ordinary rate (22%).[39]

Students may also reference IRS Publication 525, noting the employer's noncompliance due to the exclusion of the balance from the employee's W-2. Because the virtual currency was issued as compensation for services rendered, it is subject to Federal Income Tax Withholding, Federal Insurance Contribution Act ("FICA") tax, and Federal Unemployment Tax Act ("FUTA") tax.[40]

E. **Scenario 5**: Taxpayer #1 (who won the bet): In 2018 there is no taxable transaction because there is no sale or exchange, and as a cash-basis taxpayer, he had not constructively received his gambling winnings until 2019. During 2019, he has numerous

---

[37] *Id.*

[38] *Id.*

[39] See generally 26 U.S. Code §§1(h)(3) & 1222(11) (2018).

[40] United States. Dept. of the Treasury. Internal Revenue Service, *Supra* Note 30

taxable transactions. On the Bitcoin he purchased, he has a loss on disposal of $4,863.24 proceeds =$3,413.77, basis = $8,277.01). However, on the day he purchased the Bitcoin, it was identified as a hedging transaction, thus the Bitcoin is not considered a capital asset according to IRC 1221.[41] Additionally, the taxpayer must recognize gambling income in the amount of the fair market value[42] of property received = $3,464.01 as the value of 1 bitcoin on 2/3/19. And a short-term capital loss = $50.24, resulting from the decrease in value for that 1 bitcoin he 'won' during his holding period (between 2/3/19 & 2/6/19).

Taxpayer #2 (who lost the bet): In 2018 there is no taxable transaction because there is no sale or exchange, and as a cash-basis taxpayer, he did not distribute his gambling losses until 2019. During 2019, he should recognize a capital loss of $4,863.24, from the increase in value of his purchased bitcoin until transferring to taxpayer 1 market value on 2/6/19 of $3,413.77 and a basis of $8,277.01). The Taxpayer also has wagering losses of $3,413.77, which are only allowed to the extent of wagering gains.[43] As a result, the taxpayer will have $1,586.23 of taxable wagering income.

F. Scenario 6: In 2015 and 2016, there are no taxable transaction because there was no sale or exchange.

---

[41] 26 U.S.C. § 1221 (a) 'capital asset' means property held by the taxpayer, but does not include—(7) any hedging transaction…
26 U.S.C. § 1221 (b)(2)(ii) Hedging transactions: to manage the risk of interest or price changes or currency fluctuations with respect to borrowings made, or ordinary obligations incurred, or to be incurred by the taxpayer.
[42] 26 U.S.C. § 3402 (q)(4)(B) proceeds which are not money shall be taken into account at their fair market value.
[43] 26 U.S.C. § 165 (d)

However, in 2017, the taxpayer received property which the IRS would consider a part of gross income[44] and we believe would classify the fair market value of this $380.01 of ordinary income.[45] This should be reported on line 21 of Form 1040, and this $380.01 will also be the basis of the taxpayer's Bitcoin Cash. The capital gains from the sale of the Bitcoin in 2018 are identical to the results of scenario 1 (long-term capital gains of $3,751.35), however this is reduced by the long-term capital loss of $195.43 from the sale of the Bitcoin Cash. Together, the net effect is a long-term capital gain of $3,555.92. These disposal transactions should be reported on Form 8949, and Form 1040, Schedule D.

---

[44] 26 U.S.C. § 61 (a)(c)
[45] 26 U.S.C. § 1.61-14 (a); *See also Cesarini v. U.S.* 296 F.Supp. at 5 (N.D. Ohio 1969); Rev. Rul. 61, 1953-1, Cum. Bull. 17.

www.ingramcontent.com/pod-product-compliance
Lightning Source LLC
Chambersburg PA
CBHW071159210326
41597CB00016B/1608